SERVICES MARKETING

SERVICES MARKETING

Pallavi Bahuguna

CENTRUM PRESS
NEW DELHI-110002 (INDIA)

CENTRUM PRESS
H.O.: 4360/4, Ansari Road, Daryaganj,
New Delhi-110002 (India)
Tel: 23278000, 23261597, 23255577, 23286875

B.O.: No. 1015, Ist Main Road, BSK IIIrd Stage,
IIIrd Phase, IIIrd Block, Bangalore-560085 (INDIA)
Tel: 080-41723429

Email: centrumpress@gmail.com
Visit us at: www.centrumpress.com

Services Marketing

First Edition, 2011

ISBN 978-93-80921-20-4

PRINTED IN INDIA

Printed at Mehra Offset Press, Delhi.

Contents

Preface

Prior to the time of the Industrial Revolution, virtually all trade and exchange processes involved some personal contact between suppliers and their customers. This meant that individual producers could cater to the needs of their customers, and most trade was very local in nature. The increase in overseas trading and the advent of the industrial revolution heralded the start of new types of trading practice, and the introduction of some of the processes which are part of marketing today. Initially, producers and manufacturers were concerned mainly with logistical issues—transporting and selling goods to widespread markets, often located far away from the point of production.

The focus here was on production, with consumption and consumers being seen as the end result of a production and distribution chain. For as long as demand outstripped supply, which was generally the case as western countries started to go through periods of dramatic growth in economic activity and technological change, producers could all exist profitably simply by producing more efficiently and cutting costs. Little attention was given to the role of the consumer in exchange processes. In the early—twentieth century, the realisation that marketing was, in itself, an important part of the business process led to the founding of the American Marketing Association and the development of the earliest aspects of marketing theory and practice. It was much later, however, that the need for a marketing orientation was recognised, with a clear focus on the needs of the consumer. This book charts the progress of key developments in marketing from these early stages to the present, providing the basis for understanding marketing within a services context.

Author

1

Growth of Service Sector Economy

Since the early 1990s, the world has witnessed the spectacular growth of the economies of China and India (averaging 10.2 and 6.2 per cent annually from 1992 to 2005, respectively). Associated with this growth has been the dramatic development of the service sectors in the two Asian giants. However, a comparison of China's and India's economic structures demonstrates that the role of the service sector (or, the tertiary sector as it is known in China) is very different. In India, the service sector has become the dominant contributor to the Indian economy, accounting for 54.2 per cent of GDP in 2004. The success in this sector is regarded as"India's services revolution". In China, however, the service sector has lagged well behind the manufacturing sector (or the secondary sector, according to Chinese terminology), though its role in the economy improved slightly in the last 15 years. From 1990 to 2004, the service sector as a proportion of China's GDP increased modestly from 34.3 per cent in 1990 to 40.7 per cent in 2004. Why have the two countries taken very different trajectories in developing their service economies? What are the implications foı future development in the two Asian giants? Which factors affect demand for services in China and India? These are some of the questions which are investigated in this chapter.

To date there have hardly been any comparative studies of services in China and India. However, several studies have focused on the service sector in the individual countries. For example, Gupta and Mohan both examine productivity in the Indian service sector in comparison with other Asian economies. Chanda discusses service trade in the world, particularly in India, and its implications for the World Trade Organisation (WTO) negotiations in services, while Gordon and Gupta present a detailed study explaining India's service growth in the past decade. Examples of studies on China include Li and Hou who produced an edited volume on China's WTO entry and the implications for the service sector, Jiang who edited a book focusing on growth and structural changes in services with some marginal coverage of international comparison, and Li who conducted a comprehensive investigation of China's service sector. Thus, it is the goal of this study to extend the existing literature by comparing the growth in and demand for services in China and India.

First there is a brief review of developments in the service sector in China and India. This is followed by a discussion of the determinants of the demand for services. Three empirical models are employed to examine the factors affecting demand for services internationally, as well as in China and India. Subsequently, the chapter discusses the growth outlook for services in the two countries. The final section summarises the findings.

SERVICE SECTOR DEVELOPMENT

Following the conventional classification, an economy is divided into three sectors, that is, agricultural (or primary), manufacturing (or secondary) and service (or tertiary). The agricultural sector consists of farming, forestry, animal husbandry and fisheries. The manufacturing sector is composed of mining, construction and manufacturing. All other economic activities which are not covered by the agricultural or manufacturing sectors are broadly defined as services and hence belong to the service sector.

They include services provided for the agricultural sector, activities associated with the supply of water, electricity and gas, transport and communications, wholesale and retail trade, finance and insurance, business and personal services, and community and social services. Services can be broadly distinguished between two types, that is, old and new. The old or traditional services include petty trading, domestic services, catering and hotel services. The new services are generally associated with communications, business and legal practices, culture, research and education. The latter are tradable internationally and hence are also called tradable services.

SERVICE SECTOR GROWTH

From 1978 to 2004, the service sectors of China and India achieved high annual growth averaging 10.8 per cent in China and 7.0 per cent in India. The difference in these growth rates matches the difference in the rates of GDP growth in the two countries. During the same period, an average annual growth rate of 9.7 per cent was recorded for the Chinese economy compared to 5.4 per cent for India. At the disaggregate level, the structures of the service sector in China and India are very similar.

In both countries, the service sector is still dominated by the traditional or old services, followed by business services (finance, insurance and real estate) and transport and communications. However, the new service sectors are catching up rapidly. From 1999 to 2003, communication services showed the strongest growth in both countries (with an average annual rate of 16.8 per cent in China and 23.9 per cent in India), followed by education (8.6 per cent) and research (11.9 per cent) in India, and real estate (8.8 per cent) and research (8.9 per cent) in China. Though growing rapidly in recent years, research-related services are still relatively small in both countries.

OUTPUT AND EMPLOYMENT SHARES

The development of the service sectors can also be examined by analysing the sectoral shares of output and employment over the national totals in the two countries. Output shares of the service sector in China and India have grown steadily since 1978. The role of services in the Indian economy is clearly more significant than that in the Chinese economy. Accordingly, since 1990, India's service sector has grown faster (annual growth rate of 7.5 per cent) than the manufacturing sector (6.0 per cent) while the opposite is true in China where the manufacturing sector grew at 12.1 per cent and the service sector, at only 8.4 per cent.

In contrast, the employment share of India's service sector has grown very slowly according to available statistics covering the period from 1983 to 1999, though the absolute figure was much higher than that in China in the 1980s. The employment share of China's service sector has, however, been growing steadily since 1978, in particular since the early 1990s. As a result, China's service sector has absorbed relatively much more labour than India's since the mid-1990s. In terms of creating new jobs, services have played a vital role in both economies. For example, during the decade of 1995 to 2004, more than 62 per cent of the new jobs created in China were in the service sector while India's services provided about 54 per cent of new jobs in the country from 1994 to 1999. As both countries must relocate a large pool of rural surplus labour, further employment growth in the service sector will be indispensable.

REGIONAL VARIATIONS

In terms of the level of development of the service sector, there is considerable variation across the regions of both countries. "Regions" here are defined according to the official administrative units, that is, they mean China's provinces, autonomous districts and municipalities and India's union states and territories. Several observations about service development among the regions can be made. First, regional development in services follows the national trend. In general, the service sectors at the regional level in India are on an average more developed than those in China. For example, Beijing has China's most advanced service sector, accounting for 61 per cent of GDP in 2001, while Delhi has India's most advanced service sector with a share of 77 per cent in the same year. Second, the service sector tends to be more important among relatively more developed regions in both countries.

There is clearly a positive relationship between the level of service sector development and GDP per capita in both Chinese and Indian regions. Finally, the service sector plays a more important role in regions where the level of urbanisation is high, such as in Delhi and Chandigarh in India, and Beijing and Shanghai in China.

GROWTH IN INTERNATIONAL PERSPECTIVE

The experience of economic development shows that when a country expands its manufacturing capacity, its agricultural sector declines, and that over time the service sector grows and eventually overtakes the manufacturing sector to become dominant. For example, the share of services in total GDP in 2003 amounted to 71 per cent in Australia, 72 per cent in the United Kingdom and 75 per cent in the United States. This process of change follows the stages of economic development.

However, in comparison with countries at a similar stage of development, China's service sector development is slightly below the average while India's is slightly above it. These are clearly demonstrated which illustrates service sector GDP shares against per capita income among nations with per capita GDP less than USD2000 in 2003. Information at the disaggregate level also implies that services in China and India are still at the early stage of development which is represented by the dominance of the old services, as well as weakness in real estate, education and research services.

The relative backwardness of services in China is also reflected in the role of service trade. In 2003, China was the world's fourth largest merchandise exporter but its service exports ranked only tenth. The share of service exports over total exports in China (9.6 per cent in 2003) was much smaller than the 28.4 per cent in the United States, 32.4 per cent in the United Kingdom, 22.4 per cent in Australia, 13.9 per cent in Japan and 18.6 per cent in the world as a whole during the same period. Not surprisingly, China is currently a net importer of services.

In contrast, India's service exports accounted for 30.9 per cent of total exports in 2003 making the country a net exporter of services according to the World Bank. This is largely due to India's success in information technology (IT) service exports and India's relatively small value of merchandise exports (equivalent to only 12 per cent of China's in 2003). In 2003, India's total merchandise exports ranked 31st in the world but its service exports ranked 20th.

In addition, among the service exports in 2003, the share of finance and insurance amounted to only 1.0 and 1.5 per cent in China and India, respectively, while this share was 7.8 per cent in the United States and 22.6 per cent in the United Kingdom in the same year according to the World Bank.

To sum up, the service sector as part of the national economies of China and India achieved substantial growth in recent decades. However, from an international perspective, China and India are outliers, i.e., India's service sector over-performed while China's under-performed. In addition, new services are still weak in both China and India with the exception of India's IT export sector. At the regional level in each country, the pattern of service development is similar to the national trend. In particular, service development seems to be closely related to the level of urbanisation. These features are further explored in the following sections.

It is argued that service sector growth is determined by several factors such as production specialisation, income level and urbanisation. These factors are interrelated. As an economy grows, productive activities become more specialised and urbanisation accelerates due to the rising level of income. In the meantime, as a result of the increasing specialisation of production, firms tend to outsource many service activities such as legal, accounting and security services. Some authors call this process "specialisation splintering". The main source of demand for services comes from producers.

At the household level, Engel's law shows that, as income rises, consumption of food and durable goods becomes saturated over time and demand for services such as healthcare, travel, communications and finance increases.

Growth in income also boosts demand for away-from-home consumption of food and services. Furthermore, urbanisation contributes to the growth of the service sector in two ways. Unlike farmers who, to some extent, are self-sufficient in service provision, urban consumers rely on commercial suppliers to provide most services. They are also more likely to enter the urban informal sector for employment if there are no job opportunities in the formal sector.

Services account for the lion's share of the informal sector. Thus, urban residents are both consumers and suppliers of services. It is expected that the service sector grows as the level of urbanisation increases. This is confirmed by preliminary analysis of both China's and India's regional data in the preceding section. In addition, the participation of women in the workforce has an impact on service demand as well. More women in the workforce can lead to an increase in demand for services, ranging from babysitting and catering to tuition and beauty treatments. Furthermore, regulatory policies also affect the development of the service sector. A good example is the rapid growth of telecommunications services after deregulation in many countries.

This phenomenon can also occur in other areas such as insurance, banking, health care, etc. Regulatory environments can also affect international trade and foreign investment in services. Finally, apart from the factors discussed above, service sector growth in China and India may also be affected by development strategy and historical experience. Divergence in the latter may contribute to the different role of services in the two countries. For example, India's service industry may have benefitted from the country's early and prolonged linkage with the West, in particular the UK. In the meantime, when the communist government took office in China in 1949, it adopted a biased policy towards the development of heavy industry initially, and labour-intensive manufacturing more recently, while the movement of rural-urban labour was restricted for some four decades and hence entry into the service sector (mainly old services) was very limited. Thus, China's historical development policy was anti-services and this partly explains the underdevelopment of the country's service industry. In the empirical analysis presented in the following section, the factors just discussed are taken into consideration to the extent that quantification is possible.

THE EMPIRICS

To examine the determinants of growth in services in China and India, three models are applied to Chinese provincial, Indian state and cross country databases, respectively. For panel data models, several optional models are considered, e.g., without group dummy (the same intercept for all groups), fixed effect (different intercept for each group) and random effect models (intercepts vary by a random error).

SER in equation (1) is measured as the GDP share of services in a country or region. The choice of the variables (X) in the models is dictated by the availability of data. In the three optional models considered here, X includes per capita income (I), urbanisation (U), service export shares in total exports (EX) and the proportion of women in the total non-farming workforce (W). EX and W are not available for the regions of China and India, and are therefore incorporated in the cross-country model only. The Chinese data cover 31 regions and the period 1993 to 2003. The Indian statistics are available for 31 union states and territories out of 35 for nine years. The cross-country database has one year (2003) data for 93 countries.

The estimated coefficients of both per capita income and urbanisation are positive and statistically significant, implying that both variables are important factors affecting the development of the service sector, especially in China and India. In addition, it is found that external demand also has a positive impact on service development among the countries. This partly explains the phenomenal growth of IT service exports in India. The cost of services is shown to have a negative effect but the estimated coefficient is statistically insignificant. Thus, further investigation is needed. The findings here are of course subject to qualifications due to data limitations.

GROWTH OUTLOOK

Both the Chinese and Indian economies have entered a phase of rapid growth. It is commonly agreed that this growth will last for decades. It is also anticipated that per capita income in both countries will rise over time and that urbanisation will subsequently accelerate. These factors imply that the Chinese and Indian service sectors will expand further. This growth will also be boosted by globalisation. From 2006, China's WTO commitments will allow greater foreign participation in the service sector including telecommunications, banking, insurance, etc.

Economic openness will also create more jobs for accountants, lawyers and other financial specialists. Further economic liberalisation and deregulation in India will ensure sustained growth, including growth in services. Both China and India will also benefit from the WTO's General Agreement on Trade in Services (GATS). Therefore, the growth prospect for services in both countries is bright and will be associated with the following features.

Service sector growth in China will continue while the manufacturing sector remains dominant. Both sectors will show some gain in terms of both GDP and employment shares at the expense of agriculture. According to one set of forecasts, the GDP shares of the agricultural, manufacturing and service sectors in 2020 will be 5.0, 45.8 and 49.2 per cent, respectively, while the employment shares will be 34.2, 22.4 and 43.4 per cent, respectively. By then, China's service sector will be larger than the manufacturing sector. However, China will still have a long way to catch up with the advanced economies in the world. For instance, the service sector in 1997 accounted for 58 per cent of total GDP in Japan, 64 per cent in the US, 53 per cent in Germany and 60 per cent in the UK, while the employment shares were, respectively, 62 per cent in Japan, 74 per cent in the US, 62 per cent in Germany and 72 per cent in the UK. In China, the service sector contributes to national economic growth largely through the shift of labour from agriculture into services. This shift of labour will eventually be replaced by the shift from manufacturing to services.

The current growth momentum in India's service sector will continue in the near future. However, growth in the manufacturing sector will be accelerated. This trend is already clearly demonstrated in the latest statistics. From 1994 to 2003, the manufacturing sector grew at an average annual rate of 6.6 per cent, though the growth rate increased to 8.1 and 9.0 per cent during the financial years of 2004-5 and 2005-6, respectively.

The consequence of such growth is that the GDP shares of both the manufacturing and service sectors will expand at the cost of agriculture. For example, the GDP share of services was estimated to be 57.6 per cent by the end of the 2004-5 financial year.

The dilemma for India at present is that services account for more than a half of GDP but employ less than 30 per cent of the total work force. According to the experience of developed economies as cited in the preceding section, these shares should match. A study of the Pacific Basin countries also shows that without concomitant progress in industrialisation, growth in services in terms of both output and employment is not sustainable. The same argument can be applied to India as well.

In addition, recent expansion of India's service sector, to some extent, is boosted by the IT service exports but, the IT sector employs mainly educated, urban youth, potentially leaving most of India's population further behind. Furthermore, the numbers employed in India's IT sector are relatively small (under one million) and Konana et al. argue that its rapid growth has not generated sufficient linkages with the rest of the economy. Thus, India will need growth in both services and manufacturing.

It is found that the role of services in both China and India has been rising, with China starting from a lower base. Growth has been driven in both societies mainly by increasing specialisation of production, rising living standards and accelerated urbanisation. There are also some non-economic factors which are difficult to quantify in empirical analysis but have played important roles in service development, including biased development strategies in China, India's early linkage with the West and the recent boom in Indian IT exports.

India's service sector is now the dominant contributor to GDP growth but employment absorption is not very high. India's service sector will continue to grow, but the country needs industrialisation even more as millions of rural workers have to be employed. The IT sector is not large enough to significantly affect the growth of the national economy. In comparison with India, China's service sector is lagging behind. Even by international standards, China's service sector is below average and it can be anticipated that services will expand further as Chinese companies outsource their communications, legal and accounting services and as urbanisation accelerates in the coming decades. In addition, the service sector has been the main provider of new jobs in China where there still exists a sizable pool of surplus rural labour.

The first draft was completed while the author was visiting the East Asian Institute, National University of Singapore. The author is grateful to its Director Professor Wang Gungwu, and Research Director Professor John Wong for the generous support provided. He also thanks three anonymous referees, as well as Elspeth Thomson and participants at an EAI seminar for helpful comments and suggestions.

QUALITY GAPS MODEL

Since the end of World War II, jobs in the service sector have steadily increased from a little less than half of all jobs in the U.S. economy to nearly 80%. One of the most important industries found within the service sector is transportation, which in recent years has accounted for over 20% of the nation's gross national product (GNP).

The importance of service quality in any service industry cannot be disputed. Recent political, economic, and technological changes affecting the transportation industry have made service quality a major concern for carriers and shippers alike. Shippers have increased expectations concerning the quality of service they receive and carriers are struggling to meet these expectations. This struggle between shippers and carriers would suggest that there is room for improvement in carrier managements'understanding of how shippers define service quality. This study is an attempt to analyse service quality within the industry and to determine potential areas of improvement within the carrier/shipper relationship.

Defining Service Quality

A recent Gallup survey indicated that executives ranked the improvement of service and tangible product quality as the single most critical issue facing U.S. managers. But how do we define service quality Zeithaml, Parasuraman, and Berry tried to answer this question as early as 1983. Their research showed that service quality can be defined as the extent of discrepancy between customers' expectations or desires of service and their perceptions of the service they actually receive. These same researchers have developed a model of service quality that focuses on possible communication and control gaps within the "consumer-marketer" system, which can lead to a breakdown in service quality. These gaps have been tested and supported in earlier research using several types of service organizations. Since transportation is such a vital segment of the U.S. service economy, it would seem fruitful to examine the industry to discover whether it suffers from a breakdown in service quality. This study will assess these service gaps and offer solutions to any service quality problems.

Service Quality Model

The service quality model, as adapted to the transportation industry. The first gap represents differences in expectations between shippers and carriers. This gap indicates the amount of discrepancy between what service shippers actually expect and the service carriers think shippers expect. Shippers may be saying to carriers, "We want on-time delivery" and carriers may be hearing "We don't want any late deliveries." In this case, there could be a significant difference between what the shippers are saying and what the carriers are saying. If carriers really understand and communicate well with their customers, misunderstandings should seldom occur, and gap one should be quite small.

The second gap illustrated in the model is found only on the carrier side. This gap occurs when management incorrectly translates shipper expectations into service quality specifications. For instance, management may define on-time delivery as any shipment arriving within four hours of the scheduled arrival, while the shipper may expect delivery as scheduled plus or minus two hours.

The third gap is caused when service delivery does not meet service quality specifications. This gap is also found only on the carrier side of the model and represents a breakdown in customer service implementation within the organization. According to Zeithaml, Parasuraman, and Berry, this can be caused by a lack of teamwork (employees and management not working toward a common goal), or confusion surrounding control (who is accountable for quality control). Managers must communicate standards and quality specifications clearly to employees and reward those who implement them.

For ease of analysis, gaps two and three have been condensed into one gap, which will measure the difference between what the carrier believes the shipper wants and what the carrier actually delivers. Should this study reveal a significant gap 2/3, it will be necessary to examine both gaps separately in future studies.

Gap four of the service model is the difference between the service delivered and the external communications from the carrier to the shipper. For example, if the carrier sales representative promises 90% on-time delivery (external communication), and the carrier delivers only 80% on-time, this difference will appear in the fourth gap. The two main causes of this gap, according to the model's authors, are lack of horizontal communication (i.e., a breakdown in communication between sales and operations personnel), and the propensity to overpromise (i.e., the sales force making promises to shippers that they know cannot be met). Sometimes salespeople misunderstand the fact that unless operations can deliver on their promises, the entire organization suffers.

Gap five says there is a significant difference between the customers'expectations of the service quality and the quality of service the customer receives. This gap is the direct and indirect result of adverse effects in the four prior gaps in the model. It measures the cumulative impact of the differences in any or all of the first four gaps.

Based on this service quality model, the following hypotheses will be tested in this study:

- *H sub 1*: The service that shippers expect is significantly different from the service carriers believe shippers expect. (Gap 1)
- *H sub 2*: The service that carriers actually deliver is significantly different from the service carriers believe shippers expect. (Gaps 2/3)
- *H sub 3*: The service that carriers actually deliver is significantly different from the service promised to shippers. (Gap 4)
- *H sub 4*: The service perceived by the shippers is significantly different from the service shippers expect from carriers. (Gap 5)

According to the service quality model, if hypothesis one, two, or three is supported by the study, indicating gaps in the shipper/carrier system, hypothesis four will also be supported. If there are no gaps in the system, then shippers are receiving the service quality that they expect.

Servqual, a multiple-item scale for measuring perceptions of service quality, was the survey instrument used in this study. This scale, which was developed and tested by Parasuraman, Xeithaml, and Berry, was found to have Total-Scale Reliability coefficients ranging between.87 and.90 for the various dimensions of service quality. Details about how the survey instrument was developed and tested can be found in the article cited in the reference section of this chapter.

Questions from the survey were used to test the four hypotheses formulated for this study. Each question uses a seven-point, Likert-type scale, ranging from strongly agrees to strongly disagree. The survey was mailed to attendees of a national transportation educational seminar, and members of a national transportation professional organization.

The sample could be considered a"quasi"random sample. It represents a"cluster sample"or cross-section of the industry, and includes representatives of most modal classes, as well as shippers who use various modes within the industry. This method of sampling was used due to the prohibitive cost of obtaining a listing of all carriers in the industry and a comparable listing of all the shippers who utilize the services of these carriers. Of the 950 surveys mailed, 148 usable responses were returned. The 66 respondents employed by carriers and 82 respondents employed by shippers represent a response rate of nearly 16%.

The respondents are representative and knowledgeable about the industry. The carrier respondents have been involved in transportation for an average of 17 years (modal response 10 years) and the shippers have been involved an average of 15 years (modal response 20 years). Job titles reflected in this sample include president/vice president, director, manager, supervisor, and a general category called other.

Transportation modes represented by both carrier and shipper include air cargo, motor carrier (general commodities and household), rail, and sea cargo. The questionnaire was based on the reactions of shippers and carriers to various statements reflecting features of service quality. These statements are based on a survey developed by Zeithaml, Parasuraman, and Berry. The authors describe twenty-two statements that were designed to measure service-provider gaps and their causes. Statements applicable to transportation were selected and adapted to specifically analyse possible gaps in the transportation industry. Data from the questionnaires provided information on what the service shippers expect, carriers perceptions of their shippers'service expectations, the actual service delivered, external communications to shippers, and the service shippers actually perceived that they received.

Dependent and independent t-tests were performed to test the hypothesized differences and to examine the gaps as explained in the service quality model. The results of these tests and their conclusions will be discussed in the remaining portions of this chapter. To measure the existence of the first gap of the model, shippers were asked to rate what they believe to be important features of an excellent carrier (expected service quality) and carriers were asked to rate the features the carriers were actually providing the shippers (perceptions of expected service). Respondents were asked to assign a number from one (strongly disagree) to seven (strongly agree) for each statement, representing the degree of importance they attach to each feature of service quality.

It might seem logical that, initially, one would expect differences to exist between what the shipper expects and how the carrier understands these expectations. However, the service model dictates that if the carrier is to provide excellent service, it must clearly understand the customer's (shipper's) expectations and then provide service consistent with these expectations. Therefore, we would not expect significant differences between shipper expectations and how the carrier understands these expectations when excellent service is being provided.

It is interesting to note that only six statements showed the expected and perceived results to be significantly different (alpha <.05). Modern equipment, personal and individual attention given to shippers, error-free records, and convenient operating hours were all judged to be more important by carriers than by the shippers. Carriers' delivery on promises was the only statement judged significantly higher by shippers than carriers. This finding emphasizes how important promises are to shippers.

These results may indicate that the first gap in the model is a function of carriers no understanding the importance shippers place on promises. If true, this should be reflected in the remaining four gaps in the model.

The data supports the first hypothesis—that there is a significant difference in expected and perceived service quality. However, this difference is only apparent in six of the nineteen statements, and in only one is the carrier underestimating the importance of a feature of service quality.

Gap Two/Three

Gap 2/3 is measured as the difference between what the carriers believe they are actually providing (perceptions of carriers), and what the shippers believe they are actually receiving in service quality (service delivery). However, the shippers are asked not what they want, but what they are actually receiving from their primary carriers. The differences between shipper and carrier responses appear much greater in gap 2/3 than they appeared to be in gap 1.

Not only are responses to all but three of the statements significantly different, the difference favours carriers with the higher mean score in all cases, in all of the statements, the carriers overestimate the quality of service they are providing to the shippers as compared to the shippers' estimate of that same service. It is interesting to note that while the carriers were much closer to the perceptions of what the shippers expect, what the carriers provide is much further from the target. This may be explained in terms of the service quality model as the size of gap 2/3 being much larger than that of gap 1. If this is true, it would indicate that improvement should focus on translating perceptions into quality specifications and standards, then making sure these quality specifications and standards are met.

These data strongly support the second hypothesis of this study: The service quality carriers actually provide is not the same as the service quality carriers believe that shippers expect from them.

Gap Four

Gap four of the service quality model is the difference between service delivery and external communications. One of the major components of external communications is the making of promises; carrier sales representatives me promises to their shipper customers. Therefore, this gap is measured as the difference between how both the carriers and the shippers judge how well the carriers keep those promises.

There is a significant difference in both comparisons, particularly the comparison of shippers' expectations versus their actual experiences.

It would appear that the data supports the third hypothesis of this study: The service carriers actually deliver is not the same as the service promised.

Gap Five

Since all four hypotheses have been supported by the analysed data, it would follow that Gap 5 should also be confirmed by the data.

The last gap reflects the cumulative effect of the first four gaps, and represents the difference between the service quality the shippers expect and the service quality the shippers actually receive from the carriers. The size of this gap is critical because it is this Fifth gap that forms the basis of customer dissatisfaction. It is in this fifth gap that the effects of all of the previous gaps are revealed to the shipper in the form of unfulfilled expectations.

To measure the size of Gap 5, the same statements were again given to the shippers. This time the respondents were asked to assess each statement in terms of the service they would expect from an excellent carrier and then in terms of the actual service they receive from their primary carrier.

All but one of the statements show significant differences between what the shippers want and what they believe they are receiving. Convenient operating hours is the only feature of service quality in which expectation and perception are approximately equivalent. Modern equipment shows a significant difference. However, the negative mean difference implies that the perceived service is actually superior to the expectation. Results of the remaining seventeen of nineteen statements indicate that shippers' expectations of service quality are higher than the perceived service they are getting from their carriers. This would imply a large gap between service expectation and service receipt, and could arguably be the basis for customer service problems within the transportation industry.

The fourth and final hypothesis of this study was also strongly supported by the data; the service perceived by the shippers is not the same as the service quality expected by the shippers. As the previous three hypotheses were all supported, it follows that support for the final hypothesis would also be found. The statement with the largest mean difference expectation and perception is "carrier delivers on promises." This may suggest that carrier sales representatives who make promises to shippers that cannot be kept are the major source of shipper dissatisfaction.

Based on the results of the analyses, support was found for all of the four hypotheses proposed in this study. In terms of the service quality model, the data also confirmed the existence of all five theorized gaps in the carrier/shipper system within the transportation industry.

Identifying and understanding the gaps in the carrier-shipper relationship will be a firs step in allowing individual carriers to focus their attention on areas specifically needing attention. Results of this study suggest that carriers understand what shippers expect from a carrier. This implies good communication between the shippers and carriers, a definite strength for the industry. However, there seems to be a breakdown somewhere on the carrier side. The carriers know what service quality the shippers expect, and yet it would seem that the carriers are not providing that quality of service to the shippers. Why is his happening? Do the carriers feel it is too costly, or are they failing to translate what they know of shippers'expectations into measurable quality standards and specifications that their employees can follow? Or are carriers no communicating standards and specifications clearly to their employees? These questions remain to be answered by the individual carrier. The next step in this stream of research is to examine the three gaps to determine more precisely where and why the breakdowns ate occurring.

The size of Gap 5 is consistent with the literature that states that shipper expectations of service quality are not being met. This research suggests that the gap includes many features of service quality that appear not to meet expectations and points to many areas in need of improvement. The most conspicuous offender is in the area of promises and lack of delivery on those promises. By concentrating on keeping their promises, carriers may be able to improve the service quality they offer their shippers. Because the keeping of promises is important in shaping shipper expectations, a small improvement in this area could make a significant difference in the shippers'perception of service quality. Focusing on this one area may afford carriers dramatic results in their effort to improve service quality. This in turn may translate into a significant positive impact on profits.

Several other features of service quality bear investigation. The data indicate that modern equipment is overrated by the carriers, and is of less interest to the shipper. To better meet shipper expectations, carriers should emphasize other service features in lieu of modern equipment. Other areas in need of improvement appear to be performing service on time, being more interested in shipper's problems, and error reduction in records. Again, future studies should focus on each of these areas to discover the fastest and most efficient methods for improvement.

It is important to note that this study assumes that the respondents are characteristic of the industry as whole, individual shippers and carriers may vary in how well they conform to these results. Nonetheless, it is useful for all carriers to address these issues within their organizations to ensure that the service quality they provide is the best that they can possibly provide, given their individual constraints.

The results are useful to individual carriers in several ways. First, it is hoped that the results will prompt individual carriers to constantly monitor their customers'(shippers') expectations and make sure they know how well they are being met. One way to do this would be to administer the SERVQUAL instrument regularly or develop a questionnaire.

The results from the questionnaire could be used in conjunction with customer comments and other sources of information to tell the carrier how well it is doing.

Second, the results of this study should motivate the individual carrier to determine how well its representatives keep the promises they make to shippers. This may entail developing new performance measures to evaluate carrier representative effectiveness. The literature emphasizes how critical keeping promises are to customer satisfaction.

Lastly, the results of this study indicate that from an industry vantage point, carriers can always try to improve the service they provide. As we currently find ourselves in the midst of a significant downturn, excellent service can make the difference in a carrier's survival. Whether the carrier is a trucking company or air freight company or any model, the principles embodied in the service quality model apply to each and every mode. Although the results are combined to reflect the state of service quality in the industry, it must be remembered that individual carriers and modes make up the industry.

By concentrating on the problems disclosed in this study, and evaluating their performance relative to the findings, individual carriers should be able to discover ways to improve their service quality. Findings of future research should help to pinpoint problem areas better and to offer definitive solutions to the improvement of service quality in the transportation industry. This in turn will enhance the profitability of the industry as a whole.

Quality may be the most critical component in satisfying an organization's customer. The elevation of quality as a component of customer satisfaction started with the teachings of Juran, Crosby, Deming and Feigenbaum and continued with the development of programmes such as Total Quality, Continuous Quality Improvement and Total Quality Management. Total Quality Management positioned quality as the"meeting or exceeding of a customer's expectations". Further, Garvin and Parasuraman, Zeithaml and Berry put forth the proposition that while quality was multidimensional in nature, it could be enhanced or lost unidimensionally. While this continued focus on quality contributed to a general improvement in products and services, it did not encompass all phases of a business's competitive position. Quality programmes helped define which dimensions contributed to a customer's initial perception of quality, however, they did not identify how and whether t he importance of those dimensions could vary; from the customer's initial interest in the provider's product through the product's useful life, i.e. the transaction cycle.

In order to successfully compete in the unending race for a customer's business, in an economic manner, an organization and its management must develop a competitive edge. This edge may come in the form of understanding how a company's customers value a given quality dimension (relative to the other quality dimensions) and when and if that quality dimension can increase (or decrease) in importance over time. Therefore, to clarify understanding of these quality dimensions and their interrelationships, a comprehensive model would provide operational guidelines in these competitive struggles.

In 1987, Garvin proposed a framework to describe overall product quality that consisted of eight separate dimensions. In 1988, Parasuraman, Zeithaml and Berry identified five generalizable factors (dimensions of quality) for service industries.

These quality dimensions became the foundation on which much current quality dimensional research has been founded. A review of current literature identifies a continued separation of product and service quality dimension research, an interest in service quality gaps, the relevance of these dimensions in various industries and industry-specific interpretations of these dimensions. Unfortunately, very little research has been conducted to incorporate these two sets of quality dimensions and, most importantly, no work has been done to determine the effect timing would have on the relative importance of these quality dimensions.

If timing does affect the desirability of these dimensions, then the current quality models are incomplete. This chapter is an attempt to highlight the importance of managing this comprehensive set of quality dimensions over time.

This chapter will integrate the generally accepted dimensions of quality into a general model, which can guide future research related to the interrelationships attributable to a typical transaction cycle. A general model encompassing quality dimensions and their relative importance within the transaction cycle would offer value to both academicians and practitioners. As a last step, a quantitative methodology is offered to operationalize and/or assist in the management of quality.

DIMENSIONS OF QUALITY

Quality has traditionally been viewed as:

- Conformance to requirements;
- Fitness for use; and
- Innate excellence.

In 1987, Garvin suggested that product quality is not a single recognizable characteristic; rather, it is a multifaceted characteristic that appears in many forms. He observed eight dimensions of product quality: performance, features, reliability, conformance, durability, serviceability, aesthetics and perceived quality. He also maintained that different users would require different mixes (combinations of varied amounts) of the quality dimensions. In other words, quality is in the eye of the beholder.

In 1988, Parasuraman, Zeithaml and Berry identified five quality dimensions for service industries: tangibles, reliability, responsiveness, assurance, and empathy. These dimensions and the SERVQUAL instrument, from which they were derived, have received considerable support from Carman and Fick and Ritchie and some criticism from Crosby and LeMay. Crosby and LeMay argued that price should have been added to the quality dimensions derived from the SERVQUAL instrument, thereby forcing choice and stability.

Few transactions can be identified as purely product (no service involved) or purely service (no physical product involved). Rather, most transactions provide a combination of product with accompanying service or service with some product. Goods composed of a combination of both product and service require an evaluation of both product and service quality dimensions. It, therefore, seems reasonable to merge the lists of quality dimensions from product- and service-based research.

To assist in operationalizing this dual list of quality dimensions we are suggesting a time- based approach. We, therefore, are grouping the dimensions by stages in the transaction cycle; i.e., distinguishing between those established at the time of exchange (E) and those added throughout the relationship. The transaction cycle for a product and/or service traditionally starts with the perception of demand (customer needs), moves through product/service design, manufacture and/or provision, transaction and/or sales, use of product (including support services) over its useful life and, finally, through the thought processes that may or may not lead to a repeat purchase from the same source.

The first group of quality dimensions would be established upon delivery (embedded, as it were), while the second group supports the package of delivered product/ services over the usage period in the transaction cycle (supporting). Finally, price, an estimation of the value of all attributes, will cause the customer to choose a level of each quality attribute they need or want, but not more than they want. By including price into the model, a major problem encountered during previous uses of the SERVQUAL questionnaire would be eliminated. The instability introduced into the SERYQUAL factors, due to their desirability and non-cost, would be reduced by forcing choice. Price causes the buyer to make tradeoffs between the various quality attributes and money.

The General Model

As put forward in this configuration, three components - those embedded, those supporting and their price -- contribute to customer satisfaction. The provider builds the embedded dimensions into the product before the exchange. This component is divided into two subsets of dimensions. The first subset -- performance, features, conformance, serviceability, aesthetics and perceived quality -- can be determined at the time of exchange and cannot be augmented after the exchange. The second subset -- reliability and durability -- can only be fully established (measured) after waiting long enough to allow the purchaser to evaluate the product's performance.

The second component, supporting dimensions, is explicitly or implicitly part of the transaction.

It consists of the package of dimensions that:

- Supports the exchange process itself.
- Supports the customer's use of the goods over their life, as covered by the initial transaction.

This set of dimensions may include the appearance of any facilities where the sale and any support services take place (tangibles), willingness to help customers (responsiveness), knowledge and courtesy (assurance), and apparent degree of caring about the customers (empathy). This set of dimensions can and probably will change over the usage portion of the transaction cycle. The value of this set of dimensions can be increased, held the same, or decreased according to the seller's desires and capabilities.

Price, the third component in this model, is established at or before the transaction, representing the product/service's expected value. Whether the price fairly represents the value received by the buyer cannot be ascertained until much later in the transaction cycle, when value received is compared to value expected. The buyer cannot easily modify price after the exchange, so it is established at the time of the transaction, but value is not.

DIMENSIONS OF QUALITY

At the time of exchange information concerning features, aesthetics, perceived quality and tangibles are observable while performance, conformance and serviceability are available with additional effort on the part of the customer. However, reliability and durability are largely unknown for the specific product, but can be identified for the category of product. Experience with the product or service is required to establish the extent of those latter dimensions. Further, responsiveness, assurance and empathy are generally available but are still under the on-going control of the seller, and therefore are subject to change over time.

The"Customer's Perception of Quality Dimensions over Time"was compiled by a focus group of several academics/ consultants to industry. The level of each dimension's importance and the information available to the customer were determined based on the focus group members'many years of experience. A series of empirical research projects are necessary to determine if these findings are generally held to be true by companies in one or more industrial SEC codes.

Further evaluations of these patterns and their availability would afford insight into the customer's level of satisfaction with its product or service purchases over the expected period of usage. A service provider may be chosen based on evident embedded dimensions, promised supporting dimensions and the price charged. However, repeat business comes from satisfaction

Satisfaction: A Model of Quality Dimension's Desirability Over Time

The desirability/importance of quality dimensions could be depicted from the time of exchange to the end of the product/service usability.

Each of the three groups of quality dimensions can be classified respectively by:

Dimensions embedded in the product/service, support dimensions for the product/service, and price. The correct combination and/or level of these three groups of quality dimensions would contribute vastly to any particular customer's degree of satisfaction derived from the transaction.

Certain EB1 dimensions (performance, features, conformance, serviceability and aesthetics) will be prime contributors to customer satisfaction at the time of the transaction due to the immediacy of sight, feel, sound, smell and taste of the product/service itself. These will diminish as the product loses its feel of newness. EB2 will become more important to the customer's satisfaction as the positive or negative value of the product's reliability and durability play out. The second component (support), depicted by (SP), can increase or decrease in importance due to the continuing presence or absence of the supporting quality dimensions.

Quantitative Methodology for the General Model

Traditionally, managers of the selling firm tend to view quality as inherent (embedded) in the product and/or service being sold. This leads to the mind-set that quality has been established when the product and/or service has been delivered to the buyer. Therefore, if the product did not live up to the advertised, expected levels of quality, the buyer was stuck with it and the seller's reputation"takes the hit".

This chapter takes the position that some of the dimensions of quality are still under the control of the seller and therefore can still be augmented after the point of sale or delivery. If some of these embedded dimensions do not live up to their billing, then other dimensions can be modified or enhanced to preserve the perception of overall quality of the product and the provider.

For example, if an auto manufacturer found that an unusually large percentage (i.e., 5% versus 1%) of their transmissions developed a significant problem that required those transmissions to be replaced within 75,000 miles of use, the auto manufacturer could do one of four things:

- Do nothing;
- Test all transmissions currently in stock before installing (if possible);
- Remove all the transmissions in stock from the assembly process; or
- Enhance the warranty on all transmissions.

The first option would create a frustrated, angry customer that most likely would not become a repeat customer for the auto manufacturer. The second and third options would be very expensive, and while the cost of these actions could be passed along to the customer, it may place the auto manufacturer at a price disadvantage. The fourth option would be the best for the auto manufacturer as it would require action only on those transmissions that failed and would preserve their quality reputation while the problem was researched, resolved and incorporated into the transmission's design.

This quick, no-questions-asked service, would create a customer that is confident in the auto manufacturer's ability to handle future problems (they would be WOWED!). The enhanced warranty would represent a modification of a controllable dimension of quality that would allow the auto manufacturer to preserve the customer's perception of the overall quality of the purchased product (automobile) and the provider (auto manufacturer).

2

Consumer Behaviour in Services

CONSUMER BEHAVIOUR

Consumers go through a decision-making process that can include up to five steps.

We will use an adapted version of these steps to organize the information in this chapter:

- Need recognition the customer has a need to fulfill or a problem to solve.
- Information search the customer seeks out information to help satisfy the need.
- Evaluation of alternatives The customer selects a subset of the alternatives and "evaluates them.
- Purchase The customer chooses a particular brand and then buys it.
- Purchase outcomes The customer evaluates the choice made and "decides whether it lives up to expectations.

Using an adaptation of the basic consumer decision-making process shown in we have organized this chapter into four main categories:

- Information search,
- Evaluation- of alternatives,
- Purchase and—consumption, and
- Post purchase evaluation . In purchase of services, these categories do not occur in a lin-ear sequence the way they most often do in the purchase of goods.

As you will see in this chapter, once of the major

differences between goods and services is that a greater portion of the evaluation of services succeeds purchase and consumption than is the case with oods. Therefore, while our categorization here follows the sequence consumer's use with goods, we will show how these stages in services depart from evalu-ation of goods.

INFORMATION SEARCH

Use of Personal Sources Consumers obtain information about products and services from personal sources (e.g., friends or experts) and from no personal sources (e.g., mass or selective media). When purchasing goods, consumers make generous use of both personal and non personal sources because both effectively - convey infor-mation about search qualities. Then purchasing services, on the other hand, consumers seek and rely to a greater extent on personal sources for several reasons. First, mass and selective media can convey information bout search qualities but can communicate little about experience qualities. By asking friends or experts about services, however, the consumers can obtain information vicariously about experience qualities. Second, non personal sources of information may not be available because (d) many service providers are local, independent merchants with neither the experience nor the funds for advertising;' (b) "co-operative" advertising, or advertising funded jointly by the retailer and the manufacturer, is used in frequently with services because most local providers are both producer and retailer of the service and (c) professional associations banned advertising for so many years that both professionals and consumers tend to resist its use even though it is now permitted. Third, because consumers

can discover few attributes before purchase of a service, they may feel greater risk in selecting a little-known alternative. Personal influence becomes pivotal as product complexity increases and when ob-jective standards by which to evaluate a product decrease (i.e., when experience qualities are high). Most managers in service industries recognize the strong influence of word of mouth in services. Next, consumers may find post purchase information seeking more essential with services than with goods because services possess experience qualities that cannot be adequately assessed before purchase. One model of audience response to communication describes the situation that occurs -frequently when

Consumers select services:

- The consumer selects from among virtually indistinguishable alternatives.
- Through experience the consumer develops an attitude toward the service.
- After the development of an attitude, the consumer learns more about the service by paying attention to messages supporting his or her choice.

In contrast to the conventional view of audience response to communication, where consumers seek information and evaluate products before purchase, with services most evaluation follows purchase. Perceived Risk While some degree of perceived risk probably accompanies all purchase transactions, more risk would appear to be involved in the purchase of 'services than in the purchase of goods 'because services are intangible;, non standard-ized, and usually sold without guarantees or warranties. First, the intangible nature of services and their high level of

experience qualities imply that services generally must be selected on the basis of less pre purchase infor-mation than is the case for products. Second, because services are non standardized, there will always be uncertainty about the outcome and consequences each time a service is purchased. Third, service purchases may involve more perceived risk than product purchases because, with few exceptions, services are not accompanied by warranties or guarantees. The dissatisfied service purchaser can rarely "return" a service; he or she has

already consumed it by the time he or she realises his or her dissatisfaction. Finally, many services (e.g., medical diagnosis, pestcontrol) are so tech-nical or specialized that consumers possess neither the knowledge nor the experience to evaluate whether they are satisfied, even after they have consumed the service. The increase in perceived risk involved in purchasing services suggests the use of strategies to reduce risk. Where appropriate, guarantees of satisfaction may be offered. To the extent possible, service providers should emphasize employee training and other procedures to standardize their offerings, so that consumers learn to expect a given level of quality and satisfaction.

EVALUATION OF SERVICE ALTERNATIVES

Evoked Set. The evoked set. of "alternatives-that group of products a consumer considers acceptable options in given product category-is likely to be smaller with services than with goods. One reason involves differences in retailing between goods and services.

To purchase goods, consumer generally shop in retail stores that display competing products in close proximity, clearly demonetizing the possible alterna-tives. To purchase services, on the other hand, the consumer visits an stablishment (e.g., a bank, a dry cleaner, or a hair salon) that almost always offers only a single "brand" for sale. A second reason for the smaller evoked set is that consumers are un-likely to find more than one or two businesses providing the same services in a given geographic area whereas they may find number Us retail stores carrying the identical manufacturer's product.

A third reason for a smaller evoked set is the difficulty of ob-taining adequate' pre purchase information about services. Faced with the task of collecting and 'evaluating experience qualities, consumers may simply select the first acceptable alternative rather than searching many alterna-tives. In consumer behaviour terms, the consumer's evoked set of alternatives is smaller with services than with goods. The Internet has the potential to widen the set of alter-natives.

For nonprofessional services, consumers' decisions often entail the choice between performing the services for themselves or hiring someone to perform them. Working people may choose between cleaning their own homes or hiring housekeepers, between altering their families' cloth's or taking them to a tailor, even between staying home to take care of their children-or engaging a day care centre to provide child care. Consumers may consider themselves as sources of supply for many. services, inducing lawn care, tax preparation, and preparing meals. This means that the customer's- evoked frequently includes selfprovision of the service. Nonprofessional service providers, must recognize that they often replace or compete with the consumer, which may imply more exacting standards from the consumer and may require more individualized, personal attention from the service provider.

Consumers know what they expect from providers of housecleaning or lawn care or day care because they know what they are accustomed to providing for themselves. The alert service marketer will be certain to research consumers' expectations and demands in such situations. So far, not every consumer is convinced that the cyber mall will replace the local mall. World Research found that consumers who do not buy online have these reasons for continuing to buy the traditional way: fear of hackers (21 per cent), lack of products (16 per cent), inability to see the products (15 per cent), need to reveal personal information (13 per cent) poorly designed site (8 per cent) companies' reputations (6 per cent) and fear of money or merchandise getting lost (6 per cent) Emotion and Mood Emotion and mood are feeling states that influence people's (and therefore customers') perceptions and evaluations of their experiences. Moods are distinguished from emotions in that moods refer t6 transient feeling states that occur at specific times and in specific situations, whereas emotions are more intense, stable, and pervasive.

Because services are experiences, moods and emotions, are critical factors that shape the perceived effectiveness of service encounters. If a service customer is in a "bad mood" when he enters a service establishment, service provision will likely be interpreted more negatively than if he were in a buoyant, positive mood. Similarly, if a service provider is irritable or sullen her interaction with customers will likely be colored by that mood. Furthermore, when another customer in a service establishment is cranky or fast rated, whether from problems with the service or from existing emo-tions unrelated to the service, his or her mood affects the provision of service for all customers who sense the negative mood. In sum, any service characterized by human interaction is strongly dependent on the moods and emotions of the service provider, the service customer, and other customers receiving the service at the same time.

In what specific ways can mood affect the behaviour of service customers? First, positive moods can make customers more obliging and willing to participate in behaviors that help service encounters succeed. 12 A customer in a good emotional state is probably more willing to follow an exercise regimen prescribed by a physical therapist, bus his own dishes at a fast-food restaurant, and overlook delays in service. A customer in a negative mood may be less likely to engage in behaviours essential to the effectiveness of the service but that seem difficult or overwhelming: abstaining from chocolates when on a diet programme with Weight Watchers, taking frequent aerobic classes from a health club, or completing homework assigned in a class.

A second way that moods and emotions influence service customers' is to bias the way they judge service encounters arid providers. Mood and emotions enhance and amplify experiences, making them either more positive or more negative than they might seem in the absence of the moods and emotions. 13 After losing a big account, a sales-woman catching an airline flight will be more incensed with delays and crowding than she might be on a day when business went well. Conversely, the positive mood of a services customer at a dance or restaurant...will heighten the experience, leading to positive evaluations of the, service establishment. The direction of the bias in evaluation is consistent with the polarity (that is, positive or negative) of the mood 'or emotion.

Finally, moods and emotions affect the way information about service-is absorbed anti retrieved. AS memories about a service are encoded by a consumer, the feelings associated with the encounter become an inseparable part of the memory.

If travellers fall in love during a vacation in the Bahamas, they may hold favourable assessments of the destination due more to their emotional state than to the destination itself. Conversely, if a customer first realises his level of fitness is poor when 'on a guest pass in a health club, the negative feelings may be encoded and retrieved every time he thinks of the health club or, for that matter, any health club. Service marketers need to be aware of the moods and emotions of customers and of service employees and should attempt to influence those moods and emotions in positive ways. They need to cultivate positive moods and emotions such as joy,' delight, and contentment and discourage negative emotions such as distress, frustration, anger, and disgust.

SERVICE PROVISION AS DRAMA. RESEARCHERS AND MANAGERS

Service businesses have compared service provision with drama, observing that both aim to create and Maintain a desirable impression before an audience, and both recognize that the way to accomplish this is by carefully managing the actors and the physical setting of their behaviour.14 In fact, the service marketer must play many drama-related roles (including director, choreographer, and writer) to be sure the performances of the actors are pleasing to the audience. The Walt Disney Company explicitly considers its service provision a "performance," even using show-business terms such as "cast member," "onstage," and "show" to - describe the operations at Disneyland and Walt Disney World.

The skill of the service "actors" in performing their routines, the way they appear, and their commitment to the "show" we all pivotal to service delivery. While service actors are present in most service performances, their importance increases when the degree of direct personal contact increases (such as in a hospital, resort, or restaurant), when the services involve repeat contact, and when the contact personnel as actors have discretion in determining the nature of the service and how it is delivered (as in education, medical services, and legal services). The physical setting of the service can be likened to the staging of a theatrical production including scenery, props, and other physical cues' to create desired impressions.

Among a setting's features that may influence that character of a service are the colors or brightness of the service's surroundings; the volume and pitch of sounds in the setting; the smells, movement, freshness, and temperature of the air; the use of space; the style arid comfort of the furnishings; and the setting's design and cleanliness The setting increases in importance when the nature of a service is distinguished by its environment, as is the case with Steak and Ale and Ponderosa Steak-houses or a "downtown" law firm.18 In essence, the delivery of service can 'be conceived as drama, where service personnel are the "actors," service customers are the "audience," physical evidence of the service is the "setting," and the process of service assembly is the "performance.

The drama metaphor offers a useful way to conceive of service performances. Among the aspects of a service that can be considered in this way are selection of personnel (auditioning the actors),'training of personnel (rehearsing), clearly defining the role (scripting the performance), creation of the service environment (setting the stage), and deciding which aspects of the service should be performed in the presence of the customer (onstage) and which should be performed in the back"roomJback-stagey.

SERVICE ROLES AND SCRIPTS: IF WE THINK OF SERVICE PERFORMANCES

We can view each player as having a role to perform. Roles have been defined as combinations of social cues that guide and direct behaviour in a given setting.

The success of any service performance depends in patron how well the "role set" or players-both service employees and customersact out their roles. Service employees need to perform their roles according to expectations of the customer; if they do not, the cus-tomer may be frustrated and disappointed.

As we discussed earlier in this chapter, the customer's role must also be performed well. If customers are informed and educated about the expectations and requirements of the service (i.e., if the customer plays the proper role) and if the customer cooperates with the service provider to deliver the best possible service (i.e., if he or she is reading from the same script), the service performance is -likely to be successful.

One of the factors that most influences the effectiveness of role performance is a script-a, "coherent sequence of events expected by the individual, involving her ei-ther as a participant or as an observer."

Service scripts consist of a set of ordered actions, actors, and objects that, through repeated involvement, define what the customer expects. Conformance to scripts is satisfying to the customer, while deviations from the script lead to confusion and dissatisfaction. Consider the script that you hold for the first day of class in a college course.

Among the actions you expect are the following:

- Enter the classroom;
- Listen to the professor describe the course;
- Get a syllabus of the class; and
- Leave class early and start the actual education on the second class day.

If a pro-fessor performs in accordance with the script you hold, you feel comfortable, familiar, and satisfied with the service encounter.

Experiencing a script that is incongruent with this expected pattern leads to confusion and dissatisfaction. What if you showed up and there were no other students in the class with you the first day?

What if the pro-fessor sent a graduate student instead of coming herself? Suppose the professor told you she hadn't had time to write a syllabus? In these and other situations, negative departures from the customer's expected script will detract from service performance.

Positive discrepancies from the script are not as easy to specifythey may also detract or could "surprise" and add -to the service encounter. Suppose the college class we just discussed was filled to capacity on the first day. Would you interpret that as positive (a sure sign that the class was popular) or negative (a signal that personal attention from the professor may be reduced)? What if the professor was unusually friendly and so engaged students that they stayed to the end of the period on the first day of class?

While some students might be delighted because the friendliness of the professor exceeded expectations, others might be disgruntled, having counted on more free time between classes. Still others may be suspicious, not trusting the friendliness because it doesn't follow the expected pattern. More personalization or attention is not always better. In summary, departures from the customer's expected script includ-ing provision. Of more of an attribute than expected, may detract from or add to the service experience.

THE COMPATIBILITY OF SERVICE CUSTOMERS: WE HAVE JUST

Discussed the roles of employees and customers receiving service. We now want to focus on the role of other customers receiving service at the same time. Consider how central the mere presence of other customers is in churches, restaurants, dances, bars, lounges, and spectator sports: If no one else shows up, customers will not get to socialize with others, one of the primary expectations in these types of services. However, if the number of customers becomes so dense that crowding occurs, customers may also be dissatisfied. The way other customers behave with many services such as airlines, education, clubs, and social organizations also exerts a major influence on a customer's experience. In general, the presence, behaviour, and similarity of other customers receiving services has a strong impact on the satisfaction and dissatisfaction of any given customer.

Customers can be incompatible for many reasons-differences in beliefs, values, experiences, abilities to pay, appear rice, age, and health, to name just a few. The service marketer must anticipate, acknowledge, and deal with heterogeneous consumers who have the potential to be incompatible. The service marketer can also bring homogeneous customers together and solidify relationships between them, which increases the cost to the customer of switching service providers. Customer compatibility is a factor that influences customer satisfaction, particularly in high-contact services.

POST PURCHASE EVALUATION

Attribution of Dissatisfaction: When Consumers are Disappointed

With purchases-because the products did not fulfill the intended needs, did not perform satisfactorily, or were not worth their price-they may attribute their dissatisfaction to a number of different sources among them the producers, the retailers, or themselves. Because consumers participate to a greater extent in the definition and production of services, they may feel more responsible for their dissatisfaction when they purchase services than when they purchase goods. As an example, consider a female consumer purchasing a haircut; receiving the cut she desires depends in part upon her clear specifications of her needs to the stylist. If disappointed, she may blame either the stylist (for lack of skill) or herself (for choosing the wrong stylist or for not communicating her own needs clearly).

The quality of many services depends on the information the customer brings to the service encounter: A doctor's accurate diagnosis requires a conscientious" case history and a clear articulation of symptoms; a dry cleaner's success in removing a spot depends on the consumer's knowledge of its cause; and a tax prepare satisfactory performance relies on the receipts saved by the consumer. Failure to obtain satisfaction with any of these services may not be blamed completely on the retailer or producer, because the consumer must adequately perform his or her part in the production process also. With products, on the other hand, a consumer's main form of participation is the act of purchase. The consumer may attribute failure to receive satisfaction to her own decision-making error, but she holds the producer responsible for product performance. Goods usually carry warranties or guarantees with purchase emphasizing that the producer believes that if something goes wrong, it is not the fault of the consumer. With services, consumers attribute some of their dissatisfaction to their own inability to specify or perform their part of the service. They also may complain less frequently about services than about goods because of their belief that they themselves are partly responsible for their dissatisfaction..

Innovation Diffusion: The rate of Diffusion of an Innovation

Depends on consumers' perceptions' of the innovation with regard to five characteristics: relative advantage, compatibility, communicability; divisibility, and complexity. An offering that has a relative advantage 'over existing or competing products; that is compatible with existing norms, values, and that is communicable; and that is divisible (i.e., that can be tried or tested on a Limited basis):diffuses more quickly than others. An offering that is complex, that is, difficult to understand or use, diffuses more slowly -than others.

Considered as a group, services are less communicable, less divisible, more complex, and probably less compatible than goods. They are less communicable because they are intangible (e.g., their features cannot be displayed, illustrated, or compared) and because they are often unique to each buyer (as in a medical diagnosis or dental care). Services are less divisible because they are usually impossible to sample or test on a limited basis (e.g., how does one "sample" a medical diagnosis? a lawyer's services in settling a divorce? even a haircut?).

Services are frequently more complex than goods because they are composed of a bundle of different attributes, not all of which will be offered to every buyer on each purchase. Finally, services may be incompatible with existing values and behaviours, especially if consumers are accustomed to providing the service for them selves. As an il-lustration, consider a novel day care centre that cooks breakfast for children so that parents can arrive at work early. Mothers accustomed to performing this service for their children may resist adopting the innovation because it requires a change in habit; in behaviour, even in values. Consumers adopt innovations in services more slowly than they adopt innovations in goods. Marketers may need to concentrate on incentives to trial when introducing new services. The awareness interest evaluation stages of the adoption process,may best be bypassed because of the difficulty and inefficiency of communicating information about intangibles. Offering free visits, dollars-off coupons, and samples may be appropriate strategies to speed diffusion of innovations in services.

Brand Loyalty: The degree - to which Consumers are Committed

To particular brands of goods or services depends on a number of factors: the cost of changing brands (switching cost), the availability of substitutes the perceived risk associated with the purchase, and the degree to which they have obtained satisfaction in the past. Because it may be more costly to change brands of services, because they may have more difficulty being aware of the availability of substitutes, and because higher risks may accompany services, consumers are more likely to remain customers of particular companies with services than with goods.

Greater search costs and monetary costs may be involved in changing brands of services than in changing brands of goods. Because of the difficulty of obtaining information about services, consumers may be unaware of alternatives or substitutes for their brands, or may be uncertain about the ability of alternatives to increase satisfaction over present brands.

Monetary fees may accompany brand switching in many services:

Physicians often require complete physicals on the initial visit; dentists sometimes demand new X rays; and health clubs frequently charge "membership fees" at the outset to obtain long-term commitments from customers. If consumers perceive greater risks with services, as is hypothesised here, they probably depend on brand loyalty to a greater extent than when they purchase products. Brand loyalty, described as a "means of economizing decision effort by substituting habit for repeated, deliberate decision," functions as a device for reducing the risks of consumer decisions.

A final reason consumers may be more -brand loyal with services is the recognition of the need for repeated patronage in order-to obtain optimum satisfaction from the seller Becoming a "regular customer" allows the seller to gain knowledge of the customer's tastes and preferences, ensures better treatment, and encourages more interest. In the consumer satisfaction. Thus, a consumer may exhibit brand loyalty to cultivate a satisfying relationship with the seller. Brand loyalty has two sides.

The fact that a service provider's own customers are brand loyal is not a problem. The fact that the customers of the provider's competition are difficult capture, however, creates special challenges.

The marketer may need to direct communications and strategy to the customers of competitors, emphasizing attributes and strengths that he or she possesses and the competitor lacks.

Marketers can also facilitate switching from competitors' services by reducing switching costs. AT&T promised MCI customers that it would handle the transfer from MCI to AT&T and also guaranteed it would pay to allow the customer to switch back if necessary, making it virtually costless for customers *to* switch long-distance carriers.

THE ROLE OF CULTURES IN SERVICES

Culture is learned, shared, and transmitted from one generation to the next, and is multidimensional. Culture is important in services marketing because of its effects on the ways customers evaluate and use services. It also influences the way companies and their service employees interact with customers.

Culture is important when we consider international services marketing taking the services from one country and offering them in others-but it is also critical within countries. More and more individual countries are becoming multicultural, making the need to understand how this factor affects evaluation, purchase, and use of services critical.

Because culture is important in every stage of the decision-making process for services-and is likely to become more so in the future. Unfortunately, human nature" dictates that we tend to view other cultures through the often cluttered lens of our"own.

One expert on culture, Edward T. Hall, observed that in the United States people tend to view foreigners as underdeveloped Americans." Another, Geert Hofstede, sums up the message of one of his books as follows: Everybody looks at the world from behind the windows of a cultural-home, and everybody prefers to act as if people from other countries have something special about them (a national character) but home, is normal. Unfortunately, there is no normal position in cultural matters.

Definitions of the elements "of culture vary, but a simple list of the major areas would include:

- Language (both verbal and nonverbal),
- Values and attitudes,
- Manners and customs,
- Material culture,
- Aesthetics, and
- Education and social institu-tions.

These cultural universals are manifestations of the way of life of any group of people. Services marketers must be particularly sensitive to culture because of customer contact and interaction with employees.

VALUES AND ATTITUDES DIFFER ACROSS CULTURES

Values and attitudes help to determine what members of a culture think is right, important, and/or desirable. Because behaviours, including consumer behaviours, flow from values and attitudes, services marketers who want their services adopted across, cultures must understand these differences While American brands often have an "exotic" appeal to other cultures, U.S. firms should not count on this as a long-term strategy.

In the late 1990s, Wal-Mart found that the cachet of U.S. brands was falling in Mexico. The Mexican news media alerted consumers to shoddy foreign goods and some Wal- Mart customers turned to a spirit of nationalism. The retailer responded with an "Hecho en Mexico" programme similar to the "Made in the U.S.A." programme that was successful in the United States. In some situations it is more than a case of nationalism: Brand attitudes are negatively influenced by specific prejudices toward "dominating" cultures. The Korean ban on Japanese movies and the French phobia about Euro Disney are good examples of the latter.

MANNERS AND CUSTOMS

Manners and customs represent a culture's views of appropriate ways of behaving. It is important to monitor differences in manners and customs, because they can have a direct effect on the service encounter. Central and Eastern Europeans are perplexed by Western expectations that unhappy workers put on a "happy face" when dealing with customers. As an example, McDonald's requires Polish employees to smile whenever they interact with customers. Such a requirement strikes many employees as artificial and insincere.

The fast-food giant has learned to encourage managers in Poland to probe employee problems and to assign troubled workers to the kitchen rather to the food counter. Habits are similar to customs, and these tend to vary by culture. Japanese take very few vacations, and when they do they like to spend 7"to 10 days. Their vacations are unusually crammed with activities-Rome, Geneva, Paris, and London in 10 days is representative. The travel industry has been responsive to the special preferences of these big-spending Japanese tourists. The Four Seasons Hotel chain provides special pillows, kimonos, slippers, and teas for Japanese guests. Virgin Atlantic Airways and other long-haul carriers,have interactive screens available for each passenger, allowing viewing of Japanese (or Am rican, French, etc.) movies, TV, and even gambling,if regulators approve. Differences across cultures influence how consumers evaluate service, as explained in the Global Feature.

MATERIAL CULTURE

Material culture consists of the tangible products of culture, or as comedian George Carlin puts it, "the stuff we own." What people own and how they use and display material possessions varies around the world. Cars, houses, clothes, and furniture are examples of material culture. The majority of Mexicans do not own cars, limiting retail's' geographic reach. Further, most Mexicans own small refrigerators and have limited incomes that restrict the amount of groceries they can purchase at one time.

Instead of the once-perweek shopping trip typical in the United States, Mexicans make frequent smaller trips. Promotional programmes in Mexico are also constrained by the availability of media. Ownership of televisions and radios affects the ability of services marketers to reach target audiences. Zoos as entertainment represent an interesting reflection of culture's influence. Any American visiting the Tokyo Zoo is impressed by two things: the fine collection of animals and the small cages in which the animals are kept. To the Japanese who live in one of the most crowded countries in the world an own relatively small houses, the small cages seem appropriate, whereas to the American eye the small cages may be perceived as mistreatment.

3

Customer Perception of Service

Online shopping is developing rapidly on the internet today, but the amount of money involved remains very low. According to the Market Intelligence Centre of the Information Industry Institute, the number of web users who shopped through the Internet in 46 per cent in 2004 (including service category products such as investment and finance management, on-line games and on-line education).

In a recent report of the Institute for Information Industry's ACI group, domestic online purchases in Taiwan in 2005 totaled NT$51.073 billion, with forecasts for 2006, to be as much as NT$73.146 billion. However, over 70% of consumers are satisfied with their online shopping experience, while over 50% said they might shop online again in the coming half year. In consumer-to-consumer e-commerce, Taiwan's leading auction site Yahoo! Kimo had a total of NT$15 billion in transactions in 2004. Yahoo! expects 50% growth in domestic online auction sales in 2005, and for the total to reach approximately NT$25-26 billion. Those figures give some indication of the extent to which the internet's freedom from space and time constraints facilitates web users shopping for merchandise and placing orders online.

The application of the internet to commercial activities does not increase costs, but allows the producer to contact customers directly; this enables the producer to see market variations and consumer trends immediately. It enables managers to rapidly differentiate markets and to dynamically adjust their marketing to meet consumer demand to 'customise' their marketing efforts. For the producer, understanding the nature of online consumers is critical for selecting a target market to determine the appropriate marketing model to employ or use. As for research on web consumers, little has been done apart from that offered by research organizations such as the well-known GVU Centre/ Hermes WWW User Survey and the Commerce Net/Nielson Internet Demographic Surveys. Most research is based on consumers' descriptions. However, to model consumers' web shopping actions through such data is inadequate. Critical to understanding consumer behaviour in Cyberspace is to understand how the individual consumer makes purchase choice decisions.

Most current research on web-shopping examines consumer characteristics or products, or uses the uncertainty of transaction cost model and merchandise properties alone to explain consumers' shopping actions. This study uses the Theory of Reasoned Action to explore the influence or effect of consumer evaluations, consumer cognitions and reference groups en the web-shopping intentions of college students. The result of the study should enable web retailers to understand consumer evaluations better and to grasp the significance of various broadcasting channels, as well as to offer guidance for improved website layout and design so that they can attract more consumers.

The main research issues are to understand how web shoppers evaluate products and to determine the important differences between the products or merchandise shopping they select, and what influences their relevant cognitions. It is also to understand the relationship between the preferences and attitudes of internet users toward internet shopping and their actual shopping behaviour intentions. Also to analyse different population statistics in such a way as to suggest how target consumers more accurately. Finally, it is to test or examine whether the Theory of Reasoned Action is an appropriate theory to use in research into internet shopping intentions.

After an appropriate introduction, the second section of this chapter examines the main topics to be covered in this chapter, namely consumer behaviour, internet shopping, and the Theory of Reasoned Action, the latter chosen as a theory that should help or assist researchers to explain how and why consumers engage in different forms of internet shopping behaviour. In the third section, internet shopping behaviour is examined from the point of view of university students, the subjects of this study using the Theory of Reasoned Action. In the fourth section an integrative model and a factor model-of this behaviour are developed and tested to see whether a single discriminating model can be established to explain the online shopping behaviour of such a group of subjects. Finally, the fifth section offers a conclusion, summarizing the significant findings and making a number of recommendations.

In the present context, consumer attitudes refer to the integrated set of feelings, beliefs and action-tendencies of persons to various aspects of shopping, including products and services. In terms of multi-attributive models, what is important about such attitudes is the attitude target and its connection with various attributes of the consumer and the desired products or services. Such models can, in our opinion, be used by researcher to diagnosis what is going on and to identify the factors that determine consumer choice as well as to inform researchers what they should measure in order to test the model and to investigate the online shopping intentions of consumers empirically supply. To measure the online shopping attitudes of the present sample of college students the present research developed and tested an appropriate multi-attributive model based on the Theory of Reasoned Action.

Internet shopping is a way of purchasing merchandise through the internet. It provides consumers with another choice besides traditional store shopping and has been shown to provide more satisfaction to modern consumers seeking convenience and speed. Graziol and Jarvenpaa applied a Random Effective Model for analyzing the decisive factors in choosing electronic shopping to substantial consumer behaviour. Gefen and Struab used the concept of perceived risk in an individual purchase behaviour model, and concluded that shopping behaviour can be regarded as a form of information gaining behaviour. They looked at the selective shopping process in four areas: shopping outdoors, shopping in regional shopping malls, electronic shopping, and mail order shopping.

Consumer choice of type of shopping is mainly affected by three factors: merchandise features, shopping device attributes and consumer characteristics. In his research Richmond developed five teams, each of 15 persons, and used a computer software simulation of an internet shopping mall to study the relationship between different kinds of behaviours of web users (deciding whether to shop, length of time online, consumptive amount) and website features (payment mechanism, price discount, interactive effectiveness, merchandise on the web page and virtual reality) and to analyse the shopping behaviour of browsers and substantial shoppers.

Mokhtarian and Salomon surveyed 628 people in San Diego for their preferences, perceived restraints and facility requests with regard to internet shopping, using a Binary Logit Model. Assuming that population features (socio-economic position, work, family) will always affect whether or not consumers choose to shop on the internet, Butler and Peppard used the EKB model to investigate how the decision-making process of consumers with respect to internet shopping affects or influence firms or businesses in their decisions about advanced informational technology The relevant information is mostly a review of previous empirical research.

In Taiwan, the characteristics of sales outlets, the design of producers' distribution and consumer habits are quite different from those researches. As internet shopping matures, the analysis of internet shopping behaviour has become for firms or businesses wishing to develop their electronic aspects of their operations

THEORY OF REASONED ACTION

Based on social psychology research, Fishbein and Ajzen and Ajzen and Fishbein developed the Theory of Reasoned

Action (TRA) to predict and understand individual behaviour in a social context. TRA is a well-established general theory of social psychology which asserts that specific beliefs influence behavioural perceptions and actual behaviour.

According to TRA, behaviour intention (BI) is the immediate antecedent of an individual's execution or carrying-out of a piece of behaviour. TRA specifies that behavioural intention is a function of two determinants: a personal factor termed 'attitude toward the behaviour" (A) and a person's perception of social pressures, termed 'subjective norm" (SN).

Behavioural intention is not equally influenced by these two factors (i.e., attitude and subject norm) all the time. There are often conflicts between attitude and subjective norm. TRA states that the relative weights of the two determinants of intention should be considered as measures of behavioural intention because the relative importance of attitudinal and normative factors may vary from person to person and across situations.

TRA has been successfully applied to consumer behaviour. The basic theory is that behaviour is influenced by behavioural intentions, while behavioural intentions are affected by attitudes toward the behaviour and subjective norms about such behaviour. From the initial territory of marketing, it was applied to electronic non-store retailing, and to the utilization of information systems.

TRA can be used to explain why people want (or don't want) to be engaged in some specific behaviour. However, it has not been used to try to explain the purchase behaviours and intentions of internet shoppers

In this study, the research process was to first search out and to gather together information related to TRA; then to decide on the variables to be measured and how they should constitute an appropriate questionnaire, based on an integration of existing literature. From this literature review, a list was made of the important factors likely to affect internet shopping and these combined into an initial questionnaire of 47 items. This questionnaire was then pre-tested with 100 students from the Transworld Technology College (in Taiwan) to determine whether the questionnaire is suitable for the student population of this study and to decide which items should be modified for a factor analysis.

In the questionnaire, item eight was about the security of internet transactions. Internet security is an obstacle for internet consumers, but from the analysis of Strader and Shaw and Kueter and Fisher, it seems that middle scale corporations or ordinary internet stores feel they can do little about the security of integrative internet transactions, and can only join transaction accreditation organizations or comply with juridical provisions. Most transaction accreditation organizations are international institutes or government institutes. Electronic payment mechanisms for diverse transaction platforms have been developed by different experts and governmental organizations as result of which there can be problems of compatibility.

Transaction security is beyond the control of most non-retailers and consumers who do not have the knowledge to identify what kind of payment mechanism is the safest. In this study, questions relating to internet transaction security were all removed, but for the assessment criteria thirteen variable items, such as merchandise discount, product quality and merchandise were presented to find the attitude of the subjects toward online shopping behaviour, especially individuals who have shifted their shopping from traditional stores to internet stores.

Ajzen and Fishbein suggested that when applying the Theory of Reasoned Action, the relevant reference groups need to be identified before doing the questionnaire, the subjects first should list their reference groups. In this study, we identified the most important reference groups for our sample from the results of the pre-test of the questionnaire with 100 of the pre-test students, each of whom selected the most important reference group who influenced them in their internet shopping. These included media/commercials, friends, family/relatives, government or experts' opinions and internet commercials, whose influence-on the subjective norms of the subjects toward online shopping-was assessed by five items in the final questionnaire. The higher the subjects score on this five-item measure, the more the reference group supports their internet shopping behaviour. The external variables are derived from population statistic variables, including age, sex, educational degree, monthly disposable income, etc. These external variables will indirectly influence the attitude toward the behaviour and subjective norms, and also affect the behaviour intention.

The Internet Group Survey by the Institute for Information Industry shows that the average internet user is 26.8 years old; 50.16% of users have more than a college level education and 39% are students. Thus, college students are appropriate subjects for this study fundamental group for the survey. This research aims to produce results which can help stores develop appropriate strategies for when they have to deal with consumers after the change to internet shopping. The important variables and their operational definitions for this research are shown below:

In this research 'behaviour intention" is the subjective probability which the individual identifies with his own behaviour, the probability that he or she thinks they will engage in or do this action. The more positive the individual's toward the behaviour, the higher the behaviour intention. On the contrary, the more negative the attitude towards the behaviour, the lower the behaviour intention. The following studies all examine consumers attitudes towards their own target behaviour and the effect on these attitudes on their behaviour intentions. The more positive consumers' attitude toward their intended behaviour is, the higher their behaviour intention will be; the more negative the attitude toward the behaviour, the lower the behaviour intention. From this we can develop our first hypothesis (H1). The more positive the attitude toward the 'behaviour' of internet shopping, the stronger the intention to shop on the internet, suggesting that behaviour intentions can be used to distinguish between customers who intend and who do not intend to shop online.

In this study 'subjective norms' refers to recognition and acceptance by individuals that other persons expect the individual to act or behave in certain ways, in this case with regard to online or internet shopping, it refers to the strength of social pressure on the individual to act in a particular way. The higher the subjective norm 'score' is, the stronger the perceived pressure on an individual to comply or act in accordance with relevant social norms. Hartwick and Barki studied the adoption of information technology under institutional circumstance and found a direct effect for social norms on behaviour intentions. From this we can develop the second hypothesis (H2) that the more positive or stronger are the relevant subjective norms' in favour of internet shopping, the higher the intention to shop online, suggesting that subjective norms can be used to distinguish between customers who intend and who do not intend to shop online. Hansen, Jensen and Solgaard (2004) investigated the relations between consumers' behaviour toward renovated products, attitudes toward this behaviour on their part and subjective norms. They found that both attitude towards the behaviour and subjective norms were made up or constituted by a number of factors, rather than just by a single factor. When this is taken into account in research, better predictions can be made than by using or relying just on the Theory of Reasoned Action, on TRA alone. This suggests the third hypothesis (H3) that combining attitudes toward the intended behaviour with relevant subjective norms discriminates more strongly or better than either factor alone between consumers who intend and who do not intend to shop online.

The subjects of the study were individual online consumers. Previous research on internet shopping has either used convenience samples or samples that were targeted to match the demographic of the current Web population. This study follows the recommendations of Jarvenppa and Todd and uses a similar sampling strategy to them.

The study distributed the specially-developed questionnaire to a sample used a questionnaire on a student internet population in three technology colleges in Taiwan. The survey lasted for four weeks, with the researchers giving the questionnaires individually and directly to respondents to fill out. In all, 900 questionnaires were issued, with 745 being were returned, a percentage of 82.77%. Of these, 52 were invalid, leaving 693.

From the returned questionnaires it was found that the age of 82.2% of the interviewees was 19-24 years, with approximately an equal male-female ratio. The average disposable income rate of the subjects was low since all the respondents were students, making comparison with national income figures difficult; 75.6% were educated to either two-year junior college level or two-year technical college level or to four-year technical college level. Since population statistics or demographic variables influence consumer attitudes and behaviours toward internet shopping as does the amount of their experience of online shopping, one must be cautious about applying the results from this study to groups who are very different in respect of the same population statistics or demographic variables, especially that of age.

In the present study the measured variable "behaviour intention" was transformed and analysed as a dummy variable by giving it a value of either 1 or 0. To examine the validity of the model the subjects were divided randomly into two subsamples. One, the analysis sample (N1=217), was used in the factor analysis and to estimate the discriminant function, and the other, the holdout sample (N2=112), was used to produce or form the classification matrix. Using factor analysis we extracted the common factors that 'underlie' the 13 behaviourial attitudes and five subjective norms measured in the questionnaire completed by all the subjects. This was doe to identify the basic dimensions according to which these attitudes can be compared, and to help reduce the variation among the items that measured these attitudes. The primary activity conducted during this phase was exploratory analysis to test the applicability of the item development. Exploratory factor analysis using principal components extraction was performed to test the data. Using the scree test and calculated eigenvalues following the greater-than-one rule, we extracted three behavioural attitude factors (shop service image, shopping reliability/facility, basic merchandise nature) and two factors of subjective norm factors (major reference group, minor reference group) that could account for most of the variation among the relevant items in the questionnaire. A reliability analysis was calculated for each of these common or basic factors, with results that produced 'reasonable' alpha values for each measure of reliability of between 0.5880-0.8285. To assess the convergent validity of the subscales-that measured each of these factors, we calculated the item-to-total correlations, the correlation of each item to the sum of the remaining items, for each subscale. Items which had item-to-total correlations lower than 0.4 were dropped from further analysis. As regards consumers attitudes toward their own intended behaviours, items measuring the 'pleasure of shopping with others' was eliminated due its relatively low factor loading of 0.469, and because it had loadings of greater than 0.3 on more than one factor.

Consumer attitudes toward the criteria used in this study were measured by a subscale consisting of 12 items, the first five of which measured shopping facility (0.972), merchandise information integrity (0.904), merchandise category variety (0.757), merchandise discount (0.614) and payment tool versatility (0.588), all of which were 'highly regarded' by the student subjects of the present study. As regards the variable of subjective norms, the attributes measured by the five items in the subscale were about: media/commercials (3.142), family/ relatives (2.917), friends (2.531), internet commercials (2.284) and government or expert opinions (1.91), each of which are reference groups that felt by the student subjects to affect online shopping intentions. SAs can be seen from these results the students felt they were most affected in this respect by media/commercials.

This study used discriminant function analysis with regard to both the integrative model and factor model. The technique estimates the degree to which (how well, in fact) the various independent variables identified by means of the factor analysis and measured by the various subscales can collectively predict membership the two groups formed by dividing subjects on the basis of their'scores'on the measure of the dependent variable. The Wilks'Lambda index was used to calculate the efficiency with which the independent variables considered together was able to predict membership of the two groups on the dependent variable, the extent to which the independent variables could successfully predict which subjects would be in the one group or the other.

Their P-values, that give the levels of significance of these Lambda indices, were all above 0.0001, suggesting that the two models-combining these independent variables-are able to discriminate the internet shopping behaviour intentions of the subjects, who intended to shop online and who did not. The canonical correlation coefficients for the two models were 0.4766 and 0.5348 respectively. The squared canonical correlation values that indicate how much (as a percentage) variation in the dependent variable can be ascribed to the model in question were 22.72% and 28.59% respectively. Both these multivariate discriminant functions were significant at P <0.001, confirming the ability of the independent variables to collectively discriminate the internet shopping behaviour of the subjects. In this respect, it was'less effective'to try to discriminate between the two groups of subjects by means of canonical correlation analysis from the integrative models than from the factor models.

There are'discrepancies'between each variable under the different configurations or models. The'discriminating power'of a given variable is not the same when the variable forms part of the one model than when it forms part of the other. However, all variables were supported at a 0.01 significance level. Attitude toward the subjects own intended behaviour and subjective norms were both able to discriminate effectively between different behaviour intentions according to the chart of the relevant model, with the accuracy or accurate hit ratio of the model being 73.73%.

The variables of shop service image and minor reference group were both able to discriminate significantly between the two subgroups formed from the dependent variable of behaviour intentions. The variables of nature of merchandise, of reliability of shopping facility and of major reference were also able to discriminate significantly between the two subgroups, subjects willing, and not willing to shop online. The extent to which the model was able to accurately predict or classify the subgroup of the individual subjects, expressed as a percentage, was 75.12%, with the proportional minimal chance criterion of 56.3% and a maximum chance criterion of 67.7%, results which, when taken together, support both H1 and H2.

The classification accuracy (hit ratio) is the percentage of cases correctly classified. It can be determined by summing the'diagonal elements'and dividing by the total number of cases. As an additional test of the predictive power of the model, the analysis sample's and the holdout sample's Press's Q values were calculated as 8.0 and 20.6, both considerably higher than the 6.6 value required for statistical significance at the 0.01 level. For both the analysis and holdout samples, the factor model had a'hit ratio'exceeding the threshold of 70.36%. We can confidently conclude thus that the factor is accurate, with adequate levels of statistical and practical significance, in line with H3.

These number findings have a number of practical implications for internet shopping behaviour, especially among college students. In this respect, the specific items (with their relative discriminating power in brackets) that were able to accurately predict which subjects intend to shop online and which do not were: shopping facilities (0.972), integrity of merchandise information (0.904), variety of merchandise (0.757), merchandise discounts (0.614) and versatility of payment tools (0.588). These findings suggest that main operation strategies of most internet shops should be about improving internet facilities, making more relevant information available and having more flexible prices and promotions. However, if there is an increase in internet users and in their demand for a greater variety of merchandise, then such shops should'integrate'their operations and try to offer customers a one-stop shopping service that will sell merchandise in different ways from digitalized merchandise. Information about which are most convenient transportation methods to get the merchandise to the customers and be directly transmitted through the internet. Internet shops should form strategic alliances with specialist distributors to improve the movement of merchandise to customers-from warehouses or shops to where customers want the merchandise, thereby increasing their competitive position. As regards the variable of subjective norms, the most important influences, as given by the discrimination power of the relevant items in the questionnaire were: media/commercials (3.142), family/relatives (2.917), friends (2.531), internet commercials (2.284), and the opinions of government or experts (1.91).

Due to the problems of having less'practical channels'and of sometimes having a poor reputation, pure internet stores can only improve consumers'awareness through marketing commercials. As regards advertising strategy, it may be a good idea to concentrate on media commercials, with the goals of shifting consumers'habits, setting up customer feedback channels on the internet, establishing direct interactions the customers, increasing their loyalty, helping to build the profits from internet shopping and, where possible, shifting the costs of websites to the customers and reducing the costs to customers of searching on the net. As regards, the integrative model findings 1, the variables of attitude toward the customer's own intended behaviour and of subjective norms were significant whereas in the factor model the best or most significant discriminators were shop service image, minor reference group, nature of merchandise, reliability of shopping facilities and major reference group.

On the whole, the present findings suggest that the most important and perhaps urgent task for internet shops is to strengthen their service image and make their advertisements more effective. Perhaps they should make improving their image, as a brand, a priority, possibly forming online groups among customers in such a way that online behaviour does not just consist of browsing for information content, but also of actually purchasing goods and products online.

This study has a number of limitations, the overcoming of which can suggest guidelines for future research aimed at improving our understanding of online shopping behaviour. First, this study was not concerned, in detail, with safety issues for internet shopping consumers, despite this being a big problem. Despite over 70% of internet shops having safety features built into their online ordering functions providing methods of payment, at present only 39% of customers use credit card SSLs with passwords, only 12% fax credit card numbers for safety, a mere 15% pay cash on delivery, 8% pay remittances telegraphically and 7% make payments through postal accounts. Most customers still make payments traditionally.

The present study must be seen in perspective though with prior studies having shown that non-electronic shopping still dominates. The second limitation comes from the limited nature of the sample, consisting of Taiwanese students. This is an impoıtant drawback because internet shopping behaviour is likely to vary according to the amount of personal experience and the age of the consumers, among other things. This limitation makes it difficult to generalize the findings of this study. Thus, it is hoped that future research will use different groups of consumers to examine the present findings and hopefully to improve our understanding of online shopping behaviour. The third limitation derives from the statistical methods employed here. Perhaps future research can employ different methods to examine the relative accuracy of the factor and integrative models developed in this study.

CUSTOMER EXPECTATION OF SERVICE

As the consumer market segment of the Internet economy continues to grow, the role of customer service in the emerging logistics supply chain systems will continue to change. Therefore, the need to improve logistics customer service (LCS) to consumers is greater than ever before. Finding meaningful ways to meet consumer service expectations requires LCS programmes that strategically blend website service activities (e.g., online ordering procedures) with offline logistics supply chain activities (e.g., order delivery). This balance may be a key strategy in satisfying and maintaining loyalty relationships with online consumers. Yet very little is understood about the nature of website-enabled LCS and the impact on online customer loyalty, although the level of e-logistics service expectations is often thought to be higher than that demanded by customers in brick-and-mortar environments.

The purpose of this study is to examine:

- The factors that determine the level of perceived LCS quality in the Internet-enabled logistics supply chain, and
- The impact of LCS quality on customer loyalty towards online retailers'websites.

Internet-enabled logistics supply chain refers to the total logistics system of transportation, warehousing, inventory, order processing, information flow, and website-enabled order processing procedures that drive the level of perceived quality of LCS in this system. Perceived LCS quality is defined as the level of expectation-minus performance gap and customer intended loyalty is defined as the tendency of online consumers to repurchase from the same website, as reflected in repurchase intentions or intention to recommend a website to peers. Following conventional practice, LCS was defined as the total output of the logistics system, but with emphasis on cognitive impact: perceived service speed and consistency of service speed, perceived availability of merchandise on the retailer's website and in the supply chain, and perceived responsiveness of the retailer.

This study contributes to the literature on two levels. At the conceptual level, the study provides an empirical validation of the logistics customer service-customer loyalty linkage in the online environment. While this linkage has been widely established in traditional business-to-business markets, it remains to be established in the online environment where the impersonal and self-service nature of customer service may raise doubts about the validity of the LCS-customer linkage.

At the managerial level, the study suggests ways to create a consumer-oriented online logistics customer service strategy by identifying the relevant web-based and traditional supply chain logistics activities that are important in creating and maintaining loyalty relationships with online consumers. As with all service activities, not all website features are likely to be relevant to consumer perception of online LCS quality. Moreover, different website features are likely to play different roles in consumer perception of LCS quality. Thus, this study provides insight into which website features should be emphasized in the different phases of the Internet-enabled logistics supply chain.

The following discussion presents an overview of the influence of website design strategy on LCS quality assessment among online consumers. Using the consumer disconfirmation theory as a theoretical foundation, a conceptual framework is proposed including the hypotheses isolating influences of key website design features on LCS quality, followed by the field study that was conducted to specifically examine the service encounter evaluation of 373 online transactions. Finally, analysis and findings are discussed followed by a discussion of the managerial implications and suggestions for future research.

WEBSITE DESIGN FEATURES AND LOGISTICS CUSTOMER SERVICE

As defined earlier, LCS refers to those customer service activities that are direct outputs of the total logistics supply chain of warehousing, transportation, inventory management, order processing, and related information flow.

The construct has been variously defined to include three common performance dimensions:

- In-stock availability,
- Cycle time, and
- Customer responsiveness.

In-stock availability generally refers to availability of merchandise to fill customer orders when needed. Cycle time refers to the elapsed time from when a customer places an order until it is delivered. When this elapsed time is measured for two or more transactions, it refers to average cycle time and consistency of cycle time. Responsiveness refers to customer service elements other than in-stock availability and cycle time, including error correction, follow up on customer complaints, after sales services, and effectiveness in the handling of information.

Consistent with findings of a positive relationship between LCS and customer loyalty in the brick-and-mortar business-to-business markets, a positive influence of web-based LCS on online customer intended loyalty is proposed.

However, this loyalty effect depends on the ability of online firms to transition their physical world business models to online business models to take advantage of the customer service capabilities of web design features.

Three such pertinent website design features include:

- Website ease of use,
- Website product information content, and
- Website content vividness.

Website ease of use refers to website features that allow online customers to conveniently navigate online so that the site is perceived to be user friendly, simple, and intuitive. Website product information content refers to availability and relevance of information about the firm's product offerings including what is offered, how it is offered, and where it is offered. It includes price, product quality, product availability, and order status information on a virtual basis. Website content vividness refers to the "representational richness of a mediated environment as defined by its formal features", such as color scheme, icons, and other visuals of the site's content.

While research suggests that all three dimensions of website design features have customer service capabilities, the relative importance of each feature on LCS quality assessment remains to be established empirically for Internet enabled logistics supply chain systems.

Such research is important in identifying those website features that are relevant to online consumers' expectations of LCS and in understanding their impact on the determinants of LCS expectation-performance gaps.

The impact of website design features on LCS quality assessment in the Internet-enabled logistics supply chain was examined using consumer expectancy disconfirmation theory.

DISCONFIRMATION THEORY

Consumer disconfirmation theory consists of two processes used by consumers to determine their satisfaction with an exchange: formation of expectations and the disconfirmation of those expectations.

The theory posits that consumers form expectations of product performance or hold attribute norms for product performance prior to an exchange.

Upon using or experiencing the product or service, consumers compare actual performance levels with the prior expectations to determine satisfaction with the exchange process.

These evaluations can result in better than expected (positive disconfirmation), worse than expected (negative disconfirmation), and as expected (confirmation) judgments. Positive disconfirmation judgments increase satisfaction, while negative disconfirmation judgments decrease satisfaction. These posited linkages are generally affirmed by subsequent satisfaction research for consumers, although mixed results have been obtained for business-to-business firms.

In general, consumer research assumes that disconfirmation has a stronger effect on behaviour than expectancy because expectancy effects decay over the purchase interval.

More recent satisfaction research links the different levels of confirmation with behaviours other than satisfaction, including approach behaviours (e.g., positive word of mouth) and avoidance behaviours (e.g., switching behaviours or behaviours that are the opposite of approach behaviours).

Following disconfirmation theory, the relationships between website characteristics, disconfirmation judgments of LCS quality, and customer intended loyalty. In essence, it is argued that online customers' assessment of LCS quality is a function of their LCS expectations and perceived performance of the overall Internet-enabled logistics supply chain. Online consumers' LCS expectations are shaped primarily by their experiences with website design features when shopping at a website. Barring any serious LCS failures, such as encountering an out-of-stock merchandise situation, shoppers proceed with the shopping transaction and assess the quality of LCS experience after taking delivery of the order.

This quality assessment involves a comparison of the LCS expectations with overall performance (e.g., on time delivery, completeness of order filled, and action on complaints). Comparisons that are judged to be better than expected (i.e., positive disconfirmation outcomes) lead to customer delight, satisfaction and a higher level of customer intended loyalty (e.g., intention to repurchase or recommend retailer's site to peers). Comparisons that are judged to be worse than expected (i.e., negative disconfirmation outcomes) lead to customer dissatisfaction and lower levels of customer intended loyalty (e.g., switch to a different website or discourage peers from buying from this website).

INFLUENCE OF WEBSITE DESIGN FEATURES ON ONLINE LCS QUALITY

The application of consumer expectancy-disconfirmation theory to service research has a long and rich tradition. Environmental psychology research indicates that customers in a service or retail setting respond to various dimensions of their physical surroundings on cognitive, emotional, and physiological levels.

Many services, including the LCS, are intangible in nature. Moreover, they tend to be characterized by experience and credence attributes that the customer can assess only after the service has been delivered, rather than search attributes that can be examined prior to purchase as is the case with most goods.

In such situations, consumers tend to use extrinsic cues, such as those related to the physical surroundings, to form expectations about the quality of the service they will receive.

Although the available research information is based on the brick-and-mortar environment, such information is relevant to the online environment because both environments share a number of similarities. First, they are both artificial, that is, man-made, as opposed to natural settings. second, many of the service dimensions advanced by Bitner have correspondence in the web environment.

For example, the functionality dimension, which refers to the ability of the physical setting elements to facilitate performance and accomplishment of goals, is similar to the ease of use dimension of the website. The signs and the various artifacts present in a physical surrounding have an important communication role that corresponds to the information content of the website. Finally, the ambient conditions affecting the customers'senses in a physical setting parallel the concept of website vividness. These features are now elaborated upon with emphasis on their different roles in shaping online consumers'expectations of LCS.

Ease of Use

Online retailing is widely promoted for its shopping conveniences. Many of these conveniences are direct outputs of the Internet-enabled logistics supply chain system, such as fast order placement time (cycle time) and ability to locate a myriad of merchandise with ease (in-stock availability). From the perspective of a retail atmospheric impact, positive perceptions of website ease of use increase cycle time expectations. That is, a website that is easy to use enables online shoppers to order items quickly and with little effort. Hence, as the level of ease of use increases, consumers'on time delivery expectations also increase relative to perceived level of cycle time performance. Consequently, the likelihood of cycle time expectations exceeding performance (negative disconfirmation judgment) also increases.

A similar atmospheric effect argument may be made for in-stock availability assessment. Website ease of use increases consumers'ability to locate merchandise easily with just a click of the mouse (i.e., in-stock availability). Therefore, it is conceivable that online consumers have higher expectations of in-stock availability as they are able to locate items with ease. However, most offline logistics systems cannot respond to unpredictable demand. For example, firms like Amazon.com and other users of dedicated distribution centre supply chain systems often experience low order fill rates because of unpredictable demand. Moreover, considerations of optimal cost constraints suggest that online firms cannot respond to all levels of in-stock availability expectations. Hence, as expectations of merchandise availability increase following the ease of use, the likelihood of perceived in-stock availability expectations exceeding performance (negative disconfirmation outcomes) increases.

Finally, website ease of use is also likely to have a positive influence on online consumers'expectations of retailer customer responsiveness. As the level of ease of use increases, it becomes easier for online consumers to interact more freely with retailers during all phases of the online transaction process.

For example, customers'complaint and return purchase activities are more effectively handled when the website is easy to use. However, given prior knowledge of the impersonal nature of online LCS (i.e., the customer cannot feel or touch the item, or even speak with salespersons), any increase in website ease of use is likely to generate the same customer delight effects as would be seen with salespersons.

As a consequence, online consumers'expectations of retailer responsiveness would increase as the level of ease of use increases. The likelihood of perceived customer responsiveness expectation exceeding performance will therefore increase.

Based on the preceding discussions, a negative influence of website ease of use on all LCS quality assessment is hypothesized below:

- *H1a*: The higher the perceived ease of use of a site, the higher the level of negative disconfirmation of cycle time performance of the retailer.
- *H1b*: The higher the perceived ease of use of the site, the higher the level of negative disconfirmation of in-stock availability performance of the retailer.
- *H1c*: The higher the perceived ease of use of the site, the higher the level of negative disconfirmation of customer service responsiveness of the retailer.

Product Information Content

The second set of website design features posited in the e-commerce literature to influence customer service is product information content on a website. Research suggests that online customers are more interested in product information, including the firm's product offering or in-stock availability and location of the product or service, than in any other type of online information.

Furthermore, research shows that easy access to abundant information increases the efficiency of online buying decisions. With the ability to compare merchandise availability, prices, locations, delivery policies, etc., online shoppers can avoid time-consuming errors that often result in wrong orders, late deliveries, and return goods.

Consequently, cycle time expectations will be more realistic (i.e., expectations will be lower than performance) under high product information content websites than under low product information content websites. For similar reasons, perceived in-stock availability and retailer customer responsiveness performance should be higher than expected when online shoppers make use of online product information.

Based on the above argument, a positive influence of site product information content on the level of positive disconfirmation of LCS activities is predicted:

- *H2a*: The higher the perceived product information content of the site, the higher the level of positive disconfirmation of cycle time performance.
- *H2a*: The higher the perceived product information content of the site, the higher the level of positive disconfirmation of cycle time performance.
- *H2b*: The higher the perceived product information content of the site, the higher the level of positive disconfirmation of in-stock availability performance.
- *H2c*: The higher the perceived product information content of the site, the higher the level of positive disconfirmation of customer responsiveness performance.

Vividness of Site Content

The third and final set of website design features posited to serve as cues for LCS quality assessment involves vividness of the site's content. As in the case of website ease of use, a positive influence of website vividness on LCS expectations is posited following Bitner's atmospheric effect argument. One argument is that, online firms stressing the vividness of the sites content, through such features as color schemes, icons, and other visuals, enhance the purchasing decision because online customers can see the product before they make the purchase decision. Hence, they are less likely to place the wrong order or are likely to use less time in placing the order.

Expectations of the order placement time and total cycle time would, therefore, be higher for sites perceived to have high content vividness than for sites lacking content vividness. As cycle time expectations increase relative to performance, the likelihood of perceived cycle time being judged to be worse than expected (i.e., negative disconfirmation outcomes) also increases. Similarly, the more vivid the content of the site, the better the perceived product availability and, hence, the higher the level of expectations of product availability. As product availability expectations increase relative to perceived performance, the likelihood of in-stock availability being judged to be worse than expected also increases.

Various web storefronts may reflect varying emphases on aesthetics and/or functional attributes. Functional emphasis includes the accessibility and ease of use of the site as well as provision of such information as product, price, and order status (information content). On the other hand, aesthetics emphasize the look and feel of the site (vividness).

Positive customer perceptions regarding functional attributes of the site, such as ease of use and information content, reflect the online retailer's technological sophistication. As indicated above, a positive impression of the customer about the retailer's technological acumen shapes customers' expectations of technology-related aspects of LCS, such as good inventory management (as manifested in product availability) or speed of delivery (timeliness). The same functional attributes of the site, namely ease of use and information content, also reflect the online retailer's preoccupation with the well being of the customer, by keeping the customer informed and by ensuring a smooth navigational experience with as little frustration as possible. Accordingly, as indicated in the above hypotheses, functional attributes will also affect the customers' expectations of online retailer responsiveness.

In contrast, vividness represents an aesthetic attribute of the site and reflects the online retailer's technical sophistication in terms of managing the display of icons and other visual symbols, as well as the online retailer's artistic sense. The customer can use these cues to make expectation shaping inferences about the technical side of the logistics process (in terms of product availability and timeliness).

However, technological sophistication and artistic sense cannot communicate anything about the online retailer's capacity for empathy and customer care.

Consequently, higher perceptions of aesthetic attributes of the website, such as vividness, will drive up customers' expectations (and subsequently, lower the perception of service quality) only for product availability and timeliness, but not for responsiveness. For example, expectations that a retailer will follow up on customer complaints or will accept return purchases will not be affected by the vividness of the site's content.

Based on this discussion, a positive influence of site content vividness on cycle time and in-stock availability expectations, leading to worse than expected (negative disconfirmation) judgments is predicted:

- *H3a*: The higher the level of positive perceptions of site content vividness, the higher the level of negative disconfirmation of cycle time performance of the retailer.
- *H3b*: The higher the level of positive perception of site content vividness, the higher the level of negative disconfirmation of in-stock availability performance of the retailer.

Influence of LCS Quality on Customer Loyalty Intentions

As proposed under consumer disconfirmation theory, customer service evaluation outcomes affect approach behaviours and avoidance behaviours. Approaches behaviours include making a purchase, positive word-of-mouth, repurchase intentions, etc.

Avoidance behaviours are the opposite of approach behaviours (negative word-of-mouth, no repurchase intentions, switching, etc.). This assertion is also supported by the extant service quality research.

Accordingly, the following relationships are proposed:

- *H4a*: As perceived cycle time quality increases, the level of customer intended loyalty towards the online retailer will increase.
- *H4b*: As perceived in-stock availability quality increases, the level of customer intended loyalty toward the online retailer will increase.
- *H4c*: As perceived customer responsiveness quality increases, the level of customer intended loyalty toward the online retailer will increase.

The influence of website design features on LCS quality assessment and its impact on customer intended loyalty were examined with data from actual online shopping transactions of 373 employees at two Southeastern universities. Respondents were asked to complete a questionnaire at the time of their next online shopping visit. Some parts of the questionnaire were completed before the transaction and other parts after receipt of the order.

This approach was considered more likely to produce an accurate measure of online customer service experience than one that would simply ask respondents to recall their latest shopping experience.

As an incentive to participate in the study, respondents were promised a chance to participate in a lottery to win $100. Of the 470 employees who volunteered to participate in the survey, 373 usable questionnaires were returned, for a net return rate of 79.4%.

Characteristics of Respondents

The age profile reflects a representation of most age groups, with the majority (59%) being in the 24-30 age range. Sixty per cent of the respondents were women. Thus, the sample is more gender-balanced than that of similar online studies that report over 70% men. Forty per cent of respondents had shopped online at least four times in the last four months before the study. Typical purchases were clothing and shoes (35.05%), personal entertainment products (19.76%), travel (15.9%), and books (10.75%). This product profile is consistent with the types of product/or services purchased most frequently online. Approximately 28% of the respondents reported an annual income of $50,000 or higher, followed by another 39% who reported an annual income between $30,000 and $50,000; the remainder (33%) reported annual income under $30,000. Thus, the age and income distribution profiles suggest considerable heterogeneity of respondents.

Online customer intended loyalty was measured with items capturing repurchase intentions and intention to recommend retailer to peers, while LCS quality was measured with three commonly used measures of logistics customer service. These include cycle time length and consistency, perceived in-stock availability, and customer responsiveness. Separate measures were developed for LCS expectations and perceived performance by following the service gap model. Measures of website features were developed by first collecting items from various sources and matching them with items contained in the most widely used online shopping data, Bitz-Rate. Because of the limitations of the Bitz-Rate measures, other questions were developed based on the e-commerce literature using two student samples.

The scale development process followed conventional procedures for scale development. The initial pool of 60 items was administered to a student sample (N = 115) for face validity and subsequently reduced to 48 items. The reduced list was further refined and pre-tested on a second student sample (N = 125). An exploratory factor analysis was then performed as part of the process of selecting the final list of items for the study. This analysis resulted in a final list of 20 items.

Analysis Approach

To provide preliminary analysis of the relationships between website design features, LCS and customer intended loyalty. When the correlations for the study variables are examined, customer intended loyalty is found to be positively related to all three LCS quality assessments and all three website design features. Also, LCS quality assessment is positively related to all three website design features. Specifically, site ease of use is positively related to perceived quality of in-stock availability and responsiveness. Site information content is positively related to perceived quality of in-stock availability and cycle time, while site vividness is also positively related to perceived quality of cycle time and customer responsiveness. These findings suggest that website information content has the most pervasive influence on LCS quality assessment by virtue of its positive correlation with all three LCS activities.

When the means for LCS quality are examined, the level of LCS performance is found to be very close to expectations. The mean disconfirmation (expectancy-performance) judgments approach zero for all three LCS activities, especially for in-stock availability (–.15), followed by cycle time (–.37) and responsiveness (–.45). Thus, customer responsiveness offers the most abundant opportunities for improvement in website-enabled LCS quality. Additionally, such improvements are likely to enhance customer loyalty relationships. However, these preliminary results do not indicate the relative importance of each construct, nor the direct and indirect influences (nomological relationships) among these constructs and the main criterion variable, customer intended loyalty. Below, results of a structural equation model designed to offer a more rigorous test of the website-LCS-loyalty linkage are presented.

The two stage approach involves the estimation of a measurement model, essentially confirmatory factor analysis

(CFA), followed by a structural model that tests the hypotheses. The measurement model assesses how well the observed indicators represent a measurement instrument for the latent variables. As the result of the confirmatory factor analysis indicates, the factor loadings of the observed variables on each latent variable were all statistically significant at $p < .05$ level. Moreover, the measurement model presents a relatively good fit, as indicated by various fit indices, including chi-square, GFI, CFI, NNFI, or RMSEA.

When compared with the chi-square value of the measurement model, a chi-square difference of 13.13 for 7 degrees of freedom was obtained. This difference was not statistically significant, as the corresponding tabled chi-square value was 12.59. This result indicates that there are no additional unspecified paths in the structural model tested. In addition, other goodness of fit indicators, including a GFI of.90, a CFI of.91, a RMR of.052, and a RMSEA of.062, were all at a satisfactory level.

Website Antecedents Of Lcs Quality Assessment (H1-H3b)

The results of the structural equation analysis indicate that all paths linking customers'perceptions of website features to LCS quality assessment were statistically significant. The signs are in the predicted direction as shown below:

The data demonstrate, as predicted in H Ia, HIb, and HIc, that perceptions of website ease of use are associated with negative disconfirmation judgments for all LCS activities. Thus, there is support for the hypotheses that, as the level of ease of use increases, expectations of logistics-related shopping conveniences (faster and reliable shopping times, ability to locate merchandise, and retailer customer responsiveness) also increase. As a result, all LCS quality assessment outcomes were judged to be worse than expected (i.e., negative disconfirmation judgments).

The explanation that information content decreases the level of unrealistic expectations of LCS activity is thus supported. On the effect of site content vividness, the relationships are also in the predicted direction in that site content vividness is associated with negative disconfirmation of in-stock availability and cycle time activities. Again, as in the case of ease of use, positive perceptions of site content vividness seem to have a positive influence on customers'expectations of in-stock availability and cycle time, resulting in negative disconfirmations of both LCS assessments.

LCS Quality-Customer Intended Loyalty Linkages (H_4) only one of the three paths from LCS quality disconfirmation outcomes was significantly linked to customer intended loyalty. Specifically, responsiveness disconfirmation judgment was significantly and positively related to customer intended loyalty, as predicted in H4c. The paths from cycle time disconfirmation judgment and in-stock availability disconfirmation judgments were not significantly related to online customer intended loyalty. These findings suggest that of the three LCS activities, only retailer customer responsiveness disconfirmation, H4c, is linked to customer intended loyalty, and this link is positive.

This study examines the logistics customer service-loyalty relationships in the business-to consumer segment of the Internet-enabled supply chains. A key contribution of the research is the theoretical approach. By organizing LCS quality as a disconfirmation of expectancy-performance judgments of online consumers, the study provides insight into how website features influence the extent to which consumers'expectations of LCS are met, and the loyalty impact of meeting such expectations.

The first research objective was to investigate the antecedents of online customer service in the Internet-enabled supply chain. The analysis shows that all three website design features - ease of use, information content, and site content vividness - have significant influences on consumers' assessment of LCS quality. The most pervasive website influence is information availability, followed by site ease of use and site content vividness. Also, a comparison of the means showed that LCS service is very close to expectations, especially in the area of in-stock availability (-.15), followed by cycle time activities (-.37) and moderately close for customer responsiveness activities (-.47). This finding suggests that the provision of abundant and accurate product information on the website is the most meaningful design strategy for meeting online consumers'expectations of LCS quality.

Moreover, improvements in website design features other than information content would seem to increase the LCS disconfirmation gap among online consumers. Hence, ease of use and content vividness play a different role than product information content. It is conceivable that website ease of use and content vividness may be more relevant to the pre-transaction phase of LCS and, thus, may play a positive role in attracting online consumers to a site. However, these features are likely to increase transaction expectations related to cycle time and in-stock availability, hence, their negative disconfirmation impact on LCS quality assessment.

These findings parallel those in the brick-and-mortar studies that suggest that pre-transaction customer service activities (customer service policies, etc.) are primarily important for customer attraction, while inventory availability, cycle time, and related information are more relevant to customer retention because they affect customers'gross margin and other efficiency measures. Likewise, research indicates that the online consumer buying decision is very efficient because consumers have access to abundant information and can switch to a different website if such information is lacking. Consequently, website product information availability content is perhaps more relevant to the efficiency of the online buying decision than are website ease of use and content vividness.

The second research objective was to investigate the impact of LCS quality on customer loyalty towards a retailer's website. The LISREL analysis reveals that website design features have no direct influence on customer intended loyalty. Of the three LCS activities, only customer responsiveness quality assessment shows significant and positive influence on customer intended loyalty.

This finding may be attributed to the impersonal and self-service nature of online customer service. Given the impersonal nature of e-logistics customer service, it is understandable that online customer responsiveness exhibited the biggest disconfirmation gap in the study. The implication of this finding is that any website feature that supplements or reduces the impersonal nature of online customer service offers greater satisfaction than improvements in operational and technical efficiency.

From a managerial perspective, the results offer several meaningful ways that logistics managers can improve website-enabled LCS strategy and foster loyalty relationships with online consumers. First, managers should be cognizant of the pervasive but different influences of all three website design features on LCS quality assessment of online consumer. Website ease of use and content vividness may be strategically more relevant in attracting customer to a website but less relevant in meeting consumers'expectations of LCS expectations, and may in fact increase such expectations. By contrast, product information availability may directly increase perceived quality of all LCS activities.

By recognizing these different roles of website features, logistics managers can encourage the design of websites that take full advantage of the LCS capabilities of website and still avoid the cost of website improvements that do not significantly improve consumers'perceptions of LCS quality. Additionally, given the potentially negative impact of technological sophistication of the site (ease of use and content vividness) on LCS expectations, online LCS must be constantly monitored to ensure that any level of improvements to attract consumers is matched simultaneously with a corresponding level of improvements in product information availability to avoid further increases in LCS expectations-performance gaps.

The second LCS strategy element suggested pertains to the customer loyalty impact of various LCS elements. Given that perceived quality of customer responsiveness is the only LCS element that has significant influence on customer intended loyalty in this study, this suggests that managers should constantly monitor websites to ensure that adequate emphasis is given to relevant customer responsiveness activities.

Unlike the brick-and-mortar retail environments, monitoring of customer responsiveness activities can be done effectively through the provision of abundant and low cost product information.

This is because product information not only increases perceived responsiveness of the site, but also increases perceived performance of all LCS activities, including cycle time, and in-stock availability. By implication, retailers can not successfully increase customer loyalty intentions if the information on their website is first and foremost perceived to be inaccurate or inadequate for product availability and cycle tune (delivery date).

Given the variety of logistics supply chain systems in the Internet economy (distributed centres, dedicated centres, customised distribution systems, virtual warehouses) with different emphasis on customer responsiveness and operation efficiencies, managers should be cognizant that inducing and sustaining any level customer intended loyalty behaviour would be nearly impossible in some Internet-enabled logistics supply chain systems.

Several limitations to this study should be considered in interpreting the results and conclusions. First, to keep the study focus manageable, other situational factors, such as the attributions relating to LCS quality evaluations and other website design features, could not be included in this study. The loyalty effects of these evaluations may differ upon direct examination of related attributions and other website design features. Future studies should consider the effects of attributions on the LCS disconfirmation and loyalty linkage. Other website features that might be interesting to examine include site customization and website interactivity. Moreover, the current chapter only examined direct effects of website characteristics. Future research might be able to also analyse potential interacting effects among these website characteristics.

Second, because the pretest results indicated that respondents were unable to track the entire order cycle effectively for two or more transactions, the strategic decision was made to limit the study to one transaction in order to capture the complete Internet-enabled supply chain. Consequently, actual loyalty behaviour could not be captured as manifested in repeat buying, but only in loyalty intentions. Future research should examine more than one online transaction.

Third, the effect of explicit delivery dates on LCS expectations is a topic that may offer additional insight into consumer expectations of LCS. Only website conditions that shape delivery date expectations were examined. However, it may be argued that such expectations are fundamentally shaped by the retailer's delivery date and may also be moderated by the method of shipment chosen by the consumer (e.g., express delivery, regular delivery time of 3-5 days, etc.). Thus, future research should explore the effect of explicit delivery on expectations with an appropriate research design, preferably experimental design.

Fourth, the study was based on a correlation and cross-sectional design. Therefore, causal inferences could not be drawn and the findings are suggestive only. A longitudinal design would bring greater insight into the LCS-loyalty linkages by examining whether this relationship changes over time, and if so, how the antecedents prevail over time as well as over different Internet-enabled logistics supply chain systems.

4

Understanding Customer Expectations

Franchising, as a form of market organization, has experienced rapid growth over the last several decades. Both the franchisor and the franchisee can improve performance from a marketing perspective and a profitability context when there is an effective franchising arrangement. Market advantage can be achieved when the franchise system successfully develops an identifiable product or service which assures customers of a uniform and predictable level of product quality and service.

The strength of a franchise operation is focused around the dual roles of:

- Excellent management and operations and
- Outstanding quality and reliability of the product and service.

A franchisor must therefore be concerned with both the quality of its franchisees and its products.

The franchisor faces a dichotomous problem of marketing to both:

- Perspective franchisees and
- End consumers or customers.

In order to grow, the franchisor must recruit additional franchisees. Effective recruitment calls for a market programme targeting perspective franchisees. In addition, the franchisor often has the responsibility of promoting the product or service to the end consumer.

The advantages inherent in franchising systems are often recognized by scholars and practitioners alike. The success that franchising has achieved during the past several decades attests to the merits of franchising. Nevertheless, there still exist within franchise relationships classic problems of control and self-interest. The conflict that arises between franchisors and franchisees may be one of the most difficult and frustrating challenges in franchising. There are often several sources of conflict within franchise channels.

Franchisees may not provide an expected level of managerial talent and energy to properly handle the business. The franchisee may be buying a vision of the American dream with unrealistic expectations of the work necessary to make the business succeed. The franchisee may not desire the hard work or long hours that are expected at the beginning of a franchising operation.

The franchisee may be motivated to purchase a franchise to escape from either unemployment or poor job prospects but may not have the skills to manage his or her own business. The franchisee may not have thoroughly investigated the franchisor nor may he or she have sufficient operating capital to start up or run the business. When problems arise, the franchisee's disenchantment may seriously impair the relationship with the franchisor and cause serious harm to the business operation.

Conflict arises when one party believes that its goal attainment is being impeded by another. In a franchising relationship, the franchisor and franchisee usually have different objectives. The franchisor generally will be considering performance of the entire system while the franchisees are focusing on their individual outlets. Both franchisor and franchisee will attempt to maximize profits for themselves. As each organization within the franchise system strives to meet its own goals, the problem of self-interest can create serious difficulties for the harmonious operation of the franchise relationship. One problem which must be addressed is the responsibility of the franchisor to properly select those franchisees whose goals complement their franchising system. Training can also be provided on an ongoing basis to ensure that the franchisees' goals remain consistent with those of the franchisor. In both cases, market research can prove to be a valuable tool to understanding franchisees' goals and aspirations.

When a suitable franchisee is enlisted, the franchisor must continue to monitor and analyse the sales and profits of each unit. Such research can provide insight into the customers' buying habits and the demand for the product or service being offered. Of course, franchisors need to adequately understand the end consumers and their desire for the franchisors' products in order to ensure their own survival. But even more important, the franchisor can collect information which can identify and define the marketing opportunities and problems for a particular business. The ability of the franchisor to understand demand from a total systems perspective yields greater coordination of franchisor/franchisee effort, greater capacity to take advantage of economic efficiencies in the research process, and more openness and adaptiveness to change on the part of franchisees.

The decision by franchisors to conduct marketing research is generally centred around a recognized need for specific information and the desire to manage and maintain proper organizational functions. It is generally not thought of as a tool to enhance franchisor/franchisee relationships. It is in this area that marketing research shows great promise. To be effective, however, marketing research should address marketing issues in both target markets. First, it should help the franchisor choose franchisees whose goals will enhance franchise system performance, and second, it should help the franchisee better serve its end consumer.

THE MARKETING RESEARCH PROCESS

There are basically four steps in the marketing research process that franchisors must follow:

- Define the problem and research objectives.
- Develop a research plan for collecting information.
- Implement the research plan by collecting and analyzing the data.
- Interpret and report the findings.

When defining the problem and research objectives, it is important that the franchisors doing the research work closely with the decision makers to determine what research is needed and how it will be used.

If this step is skipped, the results generally will not address the major problem. In a franchise setting, the research people must work closely with those people in the franchise who handle recruitment of potential franchisees. They must also work with the franchisees themselves to understand the needs of the market.

Marketing research is designed to reduce uncertainty and provide knowledge for the franchisor. Thus, marketing research will help determine what is going right and what went wrong. Research can help the franchisor understand consumers' buying motivations and determine the strengths and weaknesses of the products or services.

When developing a research plan, there are three objectives of market research to remember:

- *Exploratory*: To gather primary information that will better define problems and suggest improvements.
- *Descriptive*: To describe the market potential for a product or the demographics and attitudes of consumers who buy the products.
- *Causal*: To understand the cause and effect relationships in market practices.

The three major functional roles in marketing research are descriptive, diagnostic, and predictive. The descriptive role focuses on gathering and presenting statements of fact. For example, what has been the sales trend for the franchise outlet during the last five years? What are the consumers' attitudes toward the product or service? The second role of research goes beyond description and is diagnostic.

A researcher attempts to explain the data. What was the impact on sales when we introduced the new product? Have sales increased as a result of the new product line introduced? The final function of research would be predictive. Will this individual operate a franchise in a manner consistent with franchise philosophy? Can we predict how a new advertising campaign will affect sales? If we replace the manager, will we improve on employee morale and performance?

The third stage of a marketing research project is implementing the research plan by collecting and analyzing the data. The franchisor must determine the best instrument to use to collect data for the project. Interviews, focus groups, and surveys can all be used to collect data, but the costs, ease, and depth of information vary from one method to another. For example, when conducting research about a franchisee's goals, more in-depth information will probably be required than can be provided by a simple questionnaire.

The fourth step in marketing research is interpreting and reporting the findings where conclusions are drawn to the franchisors. The purpose of this research is not to overwhelm management but provide information which will be useful for making decisions.

The Franchise Dilemma

The franchise dilemma is that franchisors have two distinct and different target markets, including:

- The prospective franchisee and
- The end consumer.

Unlike most major retail or service outlets, the franchisor does not sell directly to an end consumer but through a franchising organization. The franchises are generally owned and operated by franchisees who actually run, manage, or supervise the outlet stores. It is, therefore, important for the franchisor to first develop a success profile for prospective franchisees.

Using Research to Create a Franchisee Profile

The successful franchisee profile is best developed by devising a preference research model. Such an approach involves research using both personal interviews and a general survey instrument. The personal interview is generally completed with existing successful franchisees. The purpose of the interview is to measure franchisees' attitudes toward their managing experience, as well as general demographic information. The franchisees selected for the study are generally among the top quartile or top third in sales or other success criteria as determined by the franchisors.

In addition to the personal interview, a general survey is made of all franchisees concerning what they believe would be a success profile for franchisees. This general survey is often developed by first using focus groups. The focus group generally includes 6-10 people gathered together for a few hours with a trained interviewer to talk about franchisees, managers, and successful management techniques.

These individuals may be the franchisor's franchisees, but they may also include other managers and owners of different types of businesses, as long as they have some understanding of management and ownership responsibilities. The trained interviewer generally begins with broad questions before moving to specific issues. The interviewer encourages open discussion, hoping that the interactions between the participants bring out actual experiences and recommendations for successful franchisees. These discussions are generally taped for future playback and study.

Once a focus group has determined critical factors that lead to successful franchisees, a survey of franchisees can begin. The purpose of the survey is to obtain primary data concerning attitudes toward the franchisor and the franchise system, and goals of the franchisee, as well as demographics. It is with this information that the franchisor can begin to understand where problems with relationships with their franchisees are occurring.

Using Market Research To Create A Customer Profile

One of the most typical functions of a marketing research programme is to understand the habits and attitudes of customers. This information, when provided to franchisees by the franchisor, can build stronger channel relationships. The customer profile is often conducted through exit interviews as well as a general survey.

The exit interview generally is conducted as customers leave a store. At this time, their attitudes about the product or service are measured.

In addition, perception indicators can indicate how individuals felt about the quality of the product or service being sold compared to competitors'offerings. Also, demographic information will provide valuable information about the customer segment currently visiting the franchisee's outlet. With the customer profile for each outlet, franchisors may be able to tailor their franchise programme to better meet the unique needs of each franchisee, hence reducing conflict within the relationship.

Additionally, marketing research may be conducted with focus groups which will allow for greater insights into the end consumer. Focus groups may indicate the strengths or weaknesses of a particular company, product, or service. The focus groups may easily be divided up into heavy users, moderate users, light users, or non-users of a particular franchise outlet.

Marketing research can play an integral part in proper decision making in a franchising organization. More and more franchisors are recognizing the benefits of implementing a marketing research programme. Along with the commonly recognized benefits of marketing research, franchisors should also recognize that marketing research can be an effective tool in building strong relationships with its franchisees. First, marketing research can help franchisors select franchisees whose goals are consistent with system-wide growth. Second, franchisors can conduct customer research and share the findings with franchisees.

Marketing research provides information which franchisors can use to properly determine the profile for both the successful franchisee and the target customer. When both the franchisee and customer profiles have been developed, the franchisor will be better able to select franchisees who can manage the franchising outlet and serve the customer. Marketing research becomes one tool to reducing unnecessary conflict within franchise channels.

The increasing efforts by marketers to target diverse groups of consumers call for a closer examination of the ethical implications of market segmentation and differentiated marketing. Previous research suggests that marketers and consumers often differ in their perceptions of marketing ethics. Based on contingency theory, this research proposes an integrated framework-which includes the nature of the product, consumer characteristics, and market selection-to analyse the ethical complexities of the marketing exchange. Interactions among these factors lead to various contingencies with different ethical implications for marketing managers and public policy makers. Marketers should assess consumer interests and the ethics of marketing programmes before their implementation

In the last several decades, targeting distinctive consumer segments with differentiated marketing has been a popular strategy among many marketers. The distinctive nature of various consumer groups such as children, the elderly, women, and ethnic minorities has made them attractive market segments. However, market segmentation and targeted marketing have, from time to time, met with tremendous difficulties. Targeting potentially harmful products at vulnerable and disadvantaged consumers such as children, the elderly, and inner-city residents has received negative publicity and been subjected to damaging litigation. The increasing willingness of some large corporations to exploit vulnerable consumers indicates unfair treatment of these consumers and a lack of justice in the marketplace.

On the other hand, cases of discrimination and redlining still occur in certain product and market areas, such as the discrimination directed at minority consumers by insurance and mortgage companies. Disenchanted consumers are increasingly rallying consumer interest groups to put pressure on firms that they consider to be predatory or discriminatory in their marketing practices. Companies such as R. J. Reynolds, Prudential Insurance, and Texaco Oil Company have suffered from tarnished images, consumer boycotts, and court penalties of hundreds of millions of dollars.

Although the modern marketing concept emphasizes its mission to satisfy consumer needs and wants, that promise, in reality, is sometimes lost or misplaced, resulting in outcomes that are not in the best interests of either the customers or society. A lack of understanding of the ethical issues associated with market segmentation and selection has contributed to these problems, which have tremendous social and economic costs. While targeting harmful products at vulnerable consumers has received harsh criticism, restricting the marketing of certain products and labeling some consumers as vulnerable are considered equally troublesome, suggesting that the ethical implications of marketing practices are complicated. Although researchers have examined the ethics of market segmentation and selection, effort is lacking in synthesizing various issues to provide a holistic understanding of the ethical implications of the marketing exchange.

Based on contingency theory, we integrate previous research and propose a three-dimensional framework--which includes the nature of the product, consumer characteristics, and market selection--to analyse the ethics of market segmentation and related marketing strategies. Interactions among these variables lead to various scenarios with different ethical implications for marketing management and public policy making. Particular attention is given to areas in which marketers and consumers differ in their perceptions of ethical propriety with respect to the nature of the product and market selection. To avoid ethical conflicts in marketing, we suggest that companies consider consumers'interest and assess the ethical implications of their marketing plans before implementation.

In the marketing field, market segmentation and the differentiation of the marketing mix have become so prevalent that they are almost synonymous with competitive strategies. While targeted marketing has largely been beneficial to both consumers and marketers, cases of consumer discontent from time to time raise questions about the ethical implications of market segmentation and targeted marketing, most notably the targeting of harmful products at vulnerable consumers, such as targeting alcohol and cigarettes at inner-city consumers and churning insurance policies to the elderly. Meanwhile, the opposite of targeting--the exclusion of certain consumers from a company's offerings--is just as controversial.

These problems are not unique to marketers of consumer goods. Business service providers and public and nonprofit organizations are not immune to such challenges. Organizations, including educational institutions and government agencies, that cater to certain segments of society have also become the targets of public scrutiny and face the prominent possibility of consumer discontent and legal actions. While consumers and marketers continue to struggle with these complicated issues and seek viable solutions, researchers have studied the ethics of market segmentation and market selection. Recent studies have focused on the ethical implications of targeted marketing of harmful products at vulnerable consumers.

Targeted Marketing

Targeted marketing, as a popular marketing strategy, refers to the concentrated marketing of a product to a segment of consumers due to the attractiveness of the group, in terms of such factors as its size and growth rate. Theoretically speaking, there is nothing inherently wrong with targeted marketing. When marketers promote a product beneficial to a group of consumers, targeted marketing is largely ethical and welcome by consumers. For instance, some restaurants and hotels have special promotion programmes aimed at children, and indirectly at their parents, with inexpensive toys and special vacation packages. In recent years, however, many cases of targeting potentially harmful products at vulnerable consumers have raised ethical concerns in terms of justice and fairness, such as targeting sweepstakes at the elderly and handguns at women. Even indirect and subtle targeting of potentially harmful products at vulnerable consumers has received criticism, such as targeting children with R-rated movies and using animal characters to promote cigarettes and alcohol.

Product Harm

Many products in the marketplace, such as wholesome food and medicine, are beneficial or at least beneficial to the target group.

However, products that are intended to be beneficial have from time to time been found harmful to some consumers, resulting in "market failures". For instance, unless a pharmaceutical company tests a new product on everyone (instead of limited clinical trials), it is difficult to determine whether the product will cause any harm. The key issue here is the marketer's knowledge of the product's potential harm, even to a small group of people.

If a company discovers that a small percentage of people may suffer negative reactions from its products and it immediately takes corrective measures, the company may be deemed as acting ethically, believing that it should take responsibility for the incident as part of its business liability.

If the company had prior knowledge of the side effect and it took no remedial measures upon such discovery, it would be considered as intentionally harming the consumers. Having prior knowledge of the harmfulness of a product and withholding that information have been used as evidence against companies, such as in the Dow Corning case of silicone breast implants and the legal battle against tobacco companies.

However, the evaluation of a product's harmfulness is not always clear-cut. Even the marketing of seemingly beneficial and harmless products can sometimes take an unexpected turn, because such products can be harmful to consumers who have known characteristics.

Some products, even though not inherently harmful, can be potentially harmful to consumers due to abuse or misuse. For instance, targeting alcoholic beverages at poor inner-city consumers is particularly problematic, as this segment already suffers from a greater number of alcohol-related health and social problems than the general population.

Thus, ethical evaluations of many products depend on their interaction with consumer characteristics and marketing practices.

Vulnerable Consumers

Recently, consumer vulnerability has drawn much attention in studies of marketing ethics. In numerous legal cases, the court system in the U.S. has defined vulnerable consumers as a group of people who, due to various idiosyncrasies, are sensitive and susceptible to the potential negative effects associated with using a particular product. For instance, a small group of people, due to their body biology, may suffer side effects from using certain medications. Moreover, children do not have the same level of knowledge, experience, or maturity as adults to process commercial information.

Many elderly people, due to their physical and/or mental conditions, also face challenges as consumers. In addition, some consumers may be prone to addiction or compulsion while others may be disadvantaged due to their social and economic conditions. Such examples of targeting vulnerable consumers include the targeting of high interest loans of credit cards to consumers with poor credit histories and less financial sophistication. Thus, product harmfulness is heightened for consumers at a risk or disadvantage, and poses ethical concerns.

Discrimination

While much recent research has examined the ethics of targeting harmful products to vulnerable consumers, some researchers continue to investigate the opposite case: the exclusion of certain consumers in marketing. Discrimination in marketing refers to the practice of denying access to products to a group of consumers due to their racial or ethnic background, age, gender, or other characteristics. Discrimination may also have to do with discrepancies in product quality and variety, and the terms of exchange such as pricing and payment method. Since the 1960s, many studies have investigated pricing discrimination against the poor and minority consumers. Despite the tremendous progress in the last few decades, discrimination and redlining have persisted in areas such as housing, mortgage lending, and financial services. Here, the important gauge points are the equivalence or proportionality in marketing intensity and the disparate treatment of consumers.

Existing studies have made significant progress in conceptualizing the ethics of market segmentation and differentiated marketing. In several important respects, their findings have elevated our understanding of the ethical implications of the marketing exchange. First, these studies emphasize that the concern with the ethical consequences of marketing practices in the United States is well grounded in the fundamental beliefs in social and moral equity, fairness, and justice for all people.

Second, researchers have emphasized the ethical risks inherent in market segmentation and differentiated marketing. Dunfee, Smith and Ross suggest that due to the boundary-expanding nature of marketing, ethical concerns may arise in certain situations when marketers cross such boundaries. For instance, marketing products to youth that are intended for mature consumers, such as alcoholic beverages, leads to different ethical evaluations.

According to Star, the social discontent and ethical concerns associated with marketing stem from the functional limitations of the marketing concept. Contemporary marketing practices often rely on market segmentation, which divides consumers into submarkets based on characteristics such as age, gender, race, and nationality.

To provide unique values to consumers and to avoid head-on competition, each market segment may require a unique marketing mix. Thus, segmentation and subsequent marketing practices often imply differential albeit unequal treatment of various consumer groups, and raise ethical concerns.

Third, extant studies have found that ethical concerns or dilemmas often arise when a marketer's perception is in conflict with that of consumers or the public. In fact, the customer interface represents the area of marketing in which conflicts in the perception of the ethical propriety of marketing practices frequently occur. Thus, marketers must study the perception of the public when formulating marketing strategies in order to avoid potential misunderstandings.

NEED FOR INTEGRATION

The review of literature reveals several deficiencies in the existing research. First, previous studies have focused on one or another issue of the marketing exchange and lack the integration of disparate perspectives. While much recent research has concentrated on targeting harmful products at vulnerable consumers, the practice of excluding some consumer groups is equally controversial. However, discussion of these two topics has largely been separate in the existing literature. Theoretically speaking, these two issues are closely related to each other because discrimination and redlining have as much to do with market segmentation and selection as targeted marketing, but in opposite directions. Moreover, insufficient effort has been expended to examine the many positive marketing activities that target disadvantaged groups, such as charity, corporate sponsorship, and public service programmes.

Although the existing literature condemns unethical marketing practices, it has not offered consistent guidelines to determine exactly when the marketing of certain products to some consumers becomes ethically problematic. There are also questions as to whether some consumer characteristics are the causes of vulnerability or simply its correlates. For instance, when controlling for education and income, the effect of vulnerability among ethnic groups may be less pronounced. Thus, several authors have cautioned against the use of race- or ethnicity-based vulnerability. Government intervention to restrict marketing may have some merit, and at the same time finds strong opponents among those who support the free market and free speech. Often, consumer advocates and industry spokespeople find themselves in deadlocks in the heated debate about the ethics of market segmentation and selection.

Recent studies have revealed complex interactions among products, consumer characteristics, and marketing practices in ethical evaluations of marketers, and have recommended that marketers should tread carefully when venturing into certain market segments. Despite these research efforts and the many theories of marketing ethics that have emerged, a framework for comprehensive analysis of the ethical implications of market selection and related marketing strategies remains elusive. Noting the manifold issues and perspectives, several researchers stress the need for a normative theory of ethics about market selection and marketing strategies. A more integrated approach to analyzing the ethical implications of the marketing exchange can help chart a coherent discourse on these critical issues and a better understanding of marketing ethics for managers and public policy makers.

A CONTINGENCY APPROACH

Since the early 1980s, businesses and researchers have devoted much attention to the ethical implications of business practices, which has signaled the arrival of the "ethics era" in which consumer sovereignty is given more emphasis than marketers' interests, and there has been a decline of the caveat emptor assumption. A creative variety of frameworks and theories has been developed within the marketing ethics literature, such as the general theory of marketing ethics, moral decision-making theory, and social contracts theory. These theories typically rely on one or more of the classical theories, such as Kantian ethics and perspectives of rights, duties, and justice.

Existing theories of marketing ethics have developed various "tests" to examine the ethicality of marketing practices. Some of these ethical tenets are related to product harm, consumer characteristics, and market selection. For instance, Laczniak and Murphy's framework of ethical reasoning elaborates several such tests. The motive test asks whether the intent of the contemplated action is harmful. The consequence test establishes whether any major damage to people or organizations will result from the contemplated action. The justice test asks whether the proposed action leaves another person or group less well off, and whether this person or group is already a member of a relatively underprivileged class. Although these tests have pragmatic appeals, there may be conflicting responses to their questions due to multiple stakeholders in the marketing exchange.

Despite the frequent ethical problems that involve consumers, few theories have considered the role of consumer perceptions in marketing ethics. The exceptions include the consumer sovereignty test and distributive justice. The consumer sovereignty test (comprising three dimensions) requires marketers to examine whether consumers are vulnerable or disadvantaged, perhaps due to age, education, of income. Marketers need to establish whether a target market has the capability to understand the benefits and risks associated with a product, has sufficient information to judge whether their expectations for purchases will be fulfilled, and has the choice of going elsewhere. The theory of distributive justice suggests that the unequal and differential treatment of consumers, when it leads to detrimental effects on their well-being, particularly of those who are disadvantaged, may result in a perceived lack of fairness and justice.

However, most normative theories of marketing ethics that have emerged in the last two decades have focused on either defining the fundamental principles of ethics to develop guidelines, or on the moral development and ethical reasoning of managers. Although this approach undoubtedly has merit in assisting marketers to reflect on the ethics of their decisions, it is less satisfactory in providing definitive ethical evaluations of specific practices. Meanwhile, others have proposed universal codes of marketing ethics, such as those of the American Marketing Association, that deal with various ethical issues in different marketing areas such as advertising, sales management, and marketing research. However, they do not specifically address the complex interplay among consumer characteristics, product types, and marketing strategies.

CONTINGENCY THEORY

Dunfee, Smith, and Ross contend that the pluralistic

approaches in current marketing ethics research reflect the inadequacy of general normative theories of marketing ethics to handle the rich and complex context of the marketing function. Thompson argues that making decisions on the basis of the context-independent general principles while disregarding the contextual details can result in socially irresponsible, and even detrimental, consequences. Although most marketing ethics theories, particularly the classic utilitarian (teleological) theories of ethics, consider the interests of various parties and complex situations, they have been criticized as too abstract and general to provide adequate guidance for managers. Due to the great number of ethical issues inherent in customer relationships and marketing functions, one set of universal rules or principles of ethics may be too simplistic to apply to all marketing situations.

To provide clear guidelines for ethical decision-making in marketing, several researchers have emphasized the role of various cultural, organizational and environmental factors in ethical evaluations of marketing activities, including the contextualist approach and the social contracts theory. The contextualist approach stresses that the sources of ethical concerns for marketers come from the interests of different stakeholders and affect the evaluation of the ethical justifiability of a particular marketing activity. According to the social contracts theory, ethical concerns arise when one community's legitimate norms (e.g., those of marketers) conflict with those of another community (e.g., consumers or the larger society). Therefore, a theory that considers different stakeholder interests and distinguishes various marketing scenarios and their ethical evaluations would be the most fruitful.

One of the theoretical approaches well suited to analyzing complex interactions among various dimensions of a phenomenon is contingency theory. Rooted in organizational behaviour research by Herbert Simon, contingency theory deals with the effect of interactions among various organizational and environmental factors on performance outcomes. According to Zeithaml, Varadarajan, and Zeithaml, contingency theory emphasizes the importance of situational influences on the management of organizations and questions the existence of a single best way to manage.

Contingency theory contributes to practical management by encouraging managers to:

- Identify important contingency variables that distinguish between contexts,
- Group similar contexts based on the variables, and
- Determine the most effective solution for each group.

The contingency approach is particularly helpful in analyzing the ethics of marketing activities. Based on contingency theory, we reject the possibility that a single set of criteria can determine marketing ethics in all circumstances. Instead, we examine the interactions between the contextual variables and emphasize the analysis of the ethical implications of specific scenarios.

As the most frequent ethical conflict that faces marketing managers involves attempting to balance corporate interests against those of consumers, a useful framework should first examine how a marketer's perception of marketing ethics interacts with that of the consumer, who is as an integral and indispensable party to and a key stakeholder of the marketing exchange process.

Marketing is often considered as an exchange between marketers and consumers that aims to satisfy consumer needs and maximize the return on investment for shareholders. Thus, there is an inevitable and omnipresent tension between marketers' interests and those of consumers. This conflict forms the basis for different positions on the ethics continuum of marketing practices. However, placing consumers' interests against those of marketers on the ethics continuum may bc too simplistic, because it may imply that marketing is a zero-sum game and reject the possibility of a win-win outcome. Both marketers and consumers may form their perceptions of the ethics of specific marketing scenarios according to ethical principles such as rights, justice, fairness, and equity. In many cases, marketers and consumers agree on the ethical evaluations of certain marketing scenarios and raise no ethical concerns. For instance, both groups agree in principle that providing beneficial products to consumers is ethical as well as desirable and responsible.

However, existing research has documented significant gaps between marketers and consumers in their ethical philosophies as well as ethical evaluations of specific marketing practices. From time to time, a marketer's perception may conflict with that of the public, which results in ethical concerns and, perhaps, disapproving behaviour by the public such as protests and boycotts.

For instance, consumers may believe that reduced pricing for medications such as AZT for the critically ill is ethical and laudable, but manufacturers may consider it unacceptable and unethical based on their obligations to shareholders. In other cases, while consumers perceive targeting harmful products at vulnerable consumers as unethical and exploitative, some marketers consider any restriction of marketing as an infringement of their legal right to free speech under the First Amendment. Thus, consumers' ethical evaluations of a particular marketing situation may be negative, while the marketer's perceptions are based on different moral priorities.

Given such complexities, this research integrates previous studies, applies contingency theory to analyse the ethical implications of the marketing exchange, and explains how ethical concerns arise in various marketing situations based on the agreement of lack thereof in the perceptions of ethics between marketers and consumers. Several recent studies have used two-dimensional frameworks and focused on the targeting of harmful products at vulnerable consumers.

In our three-dimensional model, we include three concepts as the contextual variables, i.e., the nature of the product, consumer characteristics, and market selection. Furthermore, we examine three categories in each variable. In the following sections, we define each of the three contingency variables and discuss how interactions among these dimensions distinguish between various contexts, and how ethical conflicts or dilemmas may arise under certain circumstances.

NATURE OF THE PRODUCT

The nature of a product is an important contingency variable that affects the ethical impacts of marketing practices. Although there is a continuum of product benefits and harms, products can generally be classified as beneficial, harmful due to abuse/misuse, of inherently harmful. Many products, such as wholesome food and medications, provide a variety of benefits to consumers, including physical, functional, emotional, and social benefits.

On the other hand, products such as cigarettes and other tobacco products are inherently harmful, and it is unethical to market such products. Moreover, some products are benign to sophisticated consumers but may be harmful to others due to abuse of misuse. Alcoholic beverages, for instance, may be beneficial or benign for mature adults who use them responsibly, but are harmful to under-aged youths. The greater the harm of a product, the harsher will be the criticism of marketing practices promoting the product.

Although a physical product itself may be beneficial, the nature of a product's marketing correlates may be unethical. Besides bodily harm, consumers may suffer from economic harm such as the loss of benefits due to deceptive pricing, and psychological harm such as disrespect, humiliation, and a sense of powerlessness that is caused by fraudulent and irresponsible marketing practices such as product defects and deceptive investment schemes.

In addition to consumer discontent and social censure, awareness of the economic impact and psychological effects of unethical marketing practices on consumers has become more important, given the penalties for both economic and psychological damages under the current corporate sentencing guidelines.

Consumer Characteristics

Existing studies suggest that consumer capability is the most salient factor in ethical evaluations of marketing practices. Clearly, consumer capability/vulnerability is multifaceted. Consumers need mental, physical, and economic abilities to effectively execute a marketing exchange. At times, however, some consumers may lack one or another type of ability to the extent that they can not make informed decisions about a product or benefit from it. Lack of such capabilities may lead to some degree of vulnerability.

In general, a consumer's ability falls on a continuum that runs from being sophisticated to being vulnerable. Here, we group consumers into three categories: sophisticated, at-risk, and vulnerable. Many consumers may be sophisticated due to maturity, education, prior experience, or professional background.

Some consumers are considered at-risk when they are prone to addiction or compulsion even though they may possess basic skills and capabilities. These consumers also include those who are socio-economically disadvantaged. For instance, some consumers may be at greater risk if they already suffer from a disproportionate occurrence of harmful behaviour patterns, including those who may not be able to control their own behaviour, such as alcoholics, smokers, or other drug addicts. Moreover, some consumers may be vulnerable due to personal characteristics such as age, education, and physical and mental health.

Market Selection

With respect to any consumer group, a marketer basically has the following options: to target the group with a unique marketing mix, to market to the group via integrated mass marketing, or to exclude the group from marketing programmes. While integrated mass marketing remains a popular strategy for many products, targeted marketing is considered more effective for companies to gain competitive advantages. When a product has universal benefits, market selection involves decisions about the inclusion of one group of consumers or the exclusion of another, and may be perceived as unequal or unfair. When a company's marketing programmes exclude certain consumers inadvertently or by design, consumers may have limited choice or incur higher switching costs of going elsewhere.

According to the contingency approach, each of the dimensions discussed above is important in ethical evaluations of marketing activities. However, none of the dimensions alone can determine the ethicality of a marketing situation. The degree of negative or positive ethical evaluation depends on the interaction among the three dimensions. To inform marketing practice and provide ethical guidelines, a normative framework of marketing ethics should enable decision-makers to make better moral judgments that are applicable to specific and often complex situations. Thus, analyzing the specific contingencies of a given marketing activity would be more helpful for assessing the ethical evaluations of marketing than would offering a limited set of general prescriptions.

Contingencies and Ethical Implications

They have different ethical implications due to differences in perceptions between marketers and the public based on the universal principles of equality, fairness, and justice. Each block provides a unique interaction of the three factors. The white block indicates positive or non-negative ethical evaluation. Black indicates negative ethical evaluation that marketers should avoid. These two areas often represent situations of universal agreement about ethical practice. The gray block suggests caution due to potential ethical concerns and represents the area in which there are different ethical perceptions and hence disagreement on the ethicality of marketing practices. Based on contingency theory, we describe the following seven common marketing practices and discuss their ethical implications.

Scenario 1. Mainstream Marketing

First, companies may market beneficial products to sophisticated and at-risk consumers through targeted marketing or mass marketing, as in the blocks from A1B1C1 to A2B1C2. In these cases, companies will receive positive evaluations from consumers and should proceed. Ringold suggests that marketing transactions with equal participants (i.e., capable and informed consumers) are typically regarded as fair and ethically sound. While many consumers are sophisticated and will not be considered at-risk or vulnerable under normal circumstances, this is not to say that unethical practices would not occur in these situations. Unethical practices may affect capable consumers (who do have bounded rationality and are sometimes vulnerable to unscrupulous marketing) as evidenced by numerous fraudulent investment schemes. As well, in the case of silicone breast implants, many sophisticated consumers fell victim to unethical practices.

Scenario 2. Positive Targeting and Social Marketing

Second, targeting and integrated marketing to vulnerable consumers is positive as long as the products are beneficial, and may be meaningful in some product categories (blocks A1B1C3 and A2B1C3). Children, due to their body size and stage of mental development, are often targeted with beneficial products and features such as specially formulated medications, safety caps for medication containers, and educational toys. Targeting beneficial products at vulnerable consumers mostly receives positive ethical evaluation. Based on the concept of social responsibility, many businesses provide beneficial products to vulnerable and disadvantaged consumers, such as charitable donations to those who are weak and poor. Social marketing programmes also target beneficial products at these consumers, such as free vaccinations for the children of poor families, and low interest rate mortgages for households with limited income. Marketers should receive positive evaluations from the public for these goodwill practices that contribute to consumer well being.

Scenario 3. Marketing Potentially Harmful Products

Third, the gray areas are the most challenging for marketing organizations and merit caution (blocks A1B2C1 and A2B2C2 are coded gray). Targeting products that are harmful due to abuse/misuse at any consumers is generally a questionable practice. The marketing of such products to consumers who are already at risk and disadvantaged is even more problematic. For instance, targeted marketing of malt liquor of higher alcohol content to inner-city minorities by some companies led to severe criticism and consumer boycotts due to the disproportionate consumption of such products and more frequent alcohol-related health problems among these groups. Therefore, when marketing products that are potentially harmful due to abuse or misuse, it is important that marketers examine the characteristics of their target markets and use extreme caution to avoid marketing such products to consumers at risk or a disadvantage.

Scenario 4. Predatory Marketing

Fourth, marketing of harmful products to any consumer group is unethical, as indicated by blocks from A1B3C1 to A1B3C3, which are coded black. Targeted marketing is appropriately met with intense public scrutiny and even consumer boycotts when products are detrimental to consumer well being and lead to health and social problems. For this reason, the marketing of cigarettes has been curtailed in the U.S. and many other countries. Negative ethical evaluations are even stronger when harmful or potentially harmful products are targeted at vulnerable consumers, because companies are considered to be preying on the weaknesses of such consumers (A1B2C3 and A2B2C3). Because cigarettes and other nicotine products are detrimental to consumer health, it is even more problematic when they are targeted towards the vulnerable (e.g., young children). The U.S. Food and Drug Administration recently ordered several companies to stop making lollypops that contained nicotine due to their potential to harm children.

Scenario 5. Discrimination and Redlining

Fifth, the exclusion of certain consumer groups, particularly vulnerable and disadvantaged consumers, from access to beneficial products is unethical because such actions limit consumer choices. It is also illegal to exclude any consumer groups from marketing programmes specified under U.S. laws such as the Fair Lending Act and the Fair Housing Act. However, segmentation and targeted marketing often mean the inclusion of some groups and exclusion of others, which results in inadvertent redlining. For instance, when marketers launch new products or expand into new geographical markets, they often select business locations based on criteria such as demographic statistics, the cost of doing business, and crime rates. Naturally, companies choose areas where consumers are affluent and the cost of doing business and crime rates are low, thus bypassing poor communities.

Hence, the conflict between consumer interest and corporate objectives poses an ethical dilemma. A number of banks, insurance underwriters, and mortgage companies, such as American Family Insurance and Chevy Chase Bank, faced lawsuits by minority consumers for alleged discrimination and redlining under the Fair Lending Act and the Fair Housing Act. Although the companies admitted no wrongdoing in the consent decrees, it is the effect, not the intent, of these marketing practices that causes cries of "redlining" from those experiencing the lack of equity and fairness. In such cases, marketers need to ensure that their market selection and marketing activities are based solely on valid business criteria and consumer characteristics that are not directly related to factors such as age, gender, or ethnicity.

Scenario 6. Demarketing

However, not all exclusive marketing practices are unethical. Some exclusion is not only positive but also necessary to protect consumers (blocks A3B3C1 to A3B2C3). Many social marketing programmes are designed to dissuade consumers from adopting harmful of potentially harmful products, such as alcoholic beverages, cigarettes, and other addictive drugs. In addition to efforts by government agencies and civic organizations, many corporations also sponsor and participate in these programmes. To encourage responsible consumption of alcohol products and to prevent drunk driving, Anheuser Busch Company, for instance, sponsored a consumer education programme that included advertising, designated drivers, and free taxi rides. These demarketing efforts play a critical role in educating and protecting consumers and minimizing the potential harm to them.

Scenario 7. Reverse Discrimination

Finally, targeting beneficial products at vulnerable and disadvantaged consumers is not entirely without controversies, especially when other groups are not included in these programmes. While marketers may face discontent from disadvantaged consumers—who are the traditional targets of discrimination—lawsuits also come from the non-target segments. For instance, long distance telephone carriers and airlines have designed special promotions for certain nationality groups who make more calls or travel more often to certain destinations. These and other affinity programmes give the target consumers special rates or discounted fare. Members of other ethnic groups, who are automatically disqualified, may cry discrimination for exactly the same reasons as traditional victims of discrimination.

Although most reverse discrimination cases have to do with employment-related issues, some are directly related to social marketing programmes that are designed to assist the disadvantaged. In a number of cases, white entrepreneurs have charged the U.S. Small Business Administration with reverse discrimination, in that these non-members of protected groups have been discriminated against precisely due to their ethnic background. Thus, marketers need to pay attention to the perceptions and responses of non-target groups, who may derive different meanings from such marketing efforts. Any targeted marketing programme should be fair and sensitive to non-target consumer segments.

ETHICAL IMPLICATIONS ASSESSMENT

A society has many avenues to ensure that marketing will benefit rather than harm consumers. Consumer activism, legislative activity, and government enforcement help to guard against unethical conduct by corporations. While "obey the law" and legal clearance of marketing programmes by companies may be necessary for ethical conduct, they are apparently not sufficient. Ethical decision-making for businesses requires companies to act in "enlightened self-interest" to ensure the integrity of their marketing programmes. Today, many marketing organizations have adopted the consumer-centred business philosophy, making "customer satisfaction" their number one priority. If marketers truly subscribe to that mission, then consumers' interests should be given more weight in resolving potential ethical conflicts in marketing decisions.

To fully respect consumer sovereignty and uphold the principles of fairness and justice, we recommend that marketers conduct an "ethical implications assessment" of their marketing programmes. Companies could establish a Marketing Ethics Committee, which includes consumer voices, to conduct such exercises and make the decisions about marketing practices for a given product.

Companies can take the following steps using the contingency framework that we have outlined. First, prior to the launch of products or marketing programmes, companies need to study the perceptions of consumers, including those of non-target segments, in terms of consumer capability, nature of the product, and marketing strategies.

In the second stage, the above dimensions should be examined simultaneously to determine the type of contingencies that the company may be facing and whether "ethical clearance" should be given to the proposed marketing programme. If the marketing programme lands in the black zone, the committee should recommend stopping or aborting the programme.

The committee can endorse a marketing programme only if it appears in the white zone. If the results point to the gray zone, the committee should recommend further revisions to avoid potential pitfalls. Finally, only when all negative or questionable contingencies are cleared should the committee give the final seal of approval. By so doing, marketers have a better chance of ensuring that their marketing programmes will benefit consumers, thereby creating benefits as well for the company in a win-win situation.

COMPARISONS WITH OTHER THEORIES

Normative theories of marketing ethics provide a basis for moral deliberation by practitioners and others of the many complex and often troubling ethical issues in marketing. As researchers and practitioners search for meaningful guidelines amidst complex interactions, the contingency approach provides a plausible framework for analyzing the ethics of the marketing exchange and can help sound decision-making in marketing and public policy. The contingency framework considers the parties to and objects of the exchange, and related marketing strategies. Thus, it is comprehensive and enables systematic analyses of the ethical implications of marketing across multiple dimensions and various scenarios. Analyzing the specific contingencies can help generate concrete guidelines for ethical decision-making.

Compared with the general normative theories of marketing ethics, the contingency approach is more flexible in analyzing the ethical implications of various situations based on the three contextual variables. Meanwhile, unlike ethical or moral relativism, the contingency approach stresses the universal principles of equity, justice, and fairness in analyzing specific scenarios, hence remains truthful to a normative theory. Because the framework considers different products and consumers with different levels of capability as well as the differential impact of marketing on consumers, the perspective of justice provides the most compelling basis for the ethical evaluations of marketing practices. In a sense, the contingency framework serves as a bridge between the principled approach and the utilitarian perspective of marketing ethics, which seem to be incommensurable with each other.

The framework can be expanded in greater detail and applied to other consumer characteristics such as age, income, and education. Products may range from economic models to premium models with enhanced features. The ethical implications of other components of a marketing mix, i.e., distribution, promotion, and price, should be explored. Distribution strategies, for instance, may range from exclusive to selective of intensive distribution. These marketing practices, when interacting with consumer characteristics and product categories, may lead to ethical concerns. Given the increasing efforts by marketers to target various consumer segments with unique marketing mix strategies, the ethical implications of a marketing campaign based on market segmentation and differentiated marketing warrants systematic and rigorous examination before implementation.

Several practical implications of this approach can be derived. First, to encourage ethical behaviour, companies and industry organizations have established codes of ethics of relied on self-regulation, consumer ombudsmen, or external audits. However, these efforts alone are not enough to eliminate unethical conduct. Many companies have been relatively passive in examining their positions in marketing ethics and are still operating according to traditional business models and processes that do not consider consumer interests and the ethical implications of their actions as critical issues. The ethical implications of marketing activities often remain afterthoughts, and are yet to be systematically incorporated into management decision-making. The contingency framework can facilitate this preemptive approach to ethical decision-making.

To integrate ethics into a firm's planning and strategy formulation processes, marketers should study consumers' ethical evaluation of their marketing programmes. An"ethical implications assessment"is necessary before the implementation of a marketing programme. In addition to financial, market, and competitive objectives, marketers should include consumers'interest and ethical integrity as important criteria for management decision-making. Furthermore, ethics must be coordinated throughout the marketing planning process from product development, market selection, advertising and promotion to implementation and evaluation. Given the competing priorities facing companies in their decisions, finding an ethically sound synergy among product types, consumer characteristics, and marketing strategies is as complicated as solving a crossword puzzle--it has to make sense in all dimensions.

The contingency approach can also serve as a framework for public policy makers to analyse the ethical implications of marketing activities. While public policy makers can take the initiative to protect consumers and promote good corporate citizenship, they also face tremendous challenges and complex dilemmas when making critical decisions, such as restricting certain types of advertising or the availability of some products. For instance, should the legislature make marijuana and similar drugs legal for distribution because they may benefit one group of people?

Regulators need to consider the benefit accruable to one group of consumers as well as the potential harm to another. As Laczniak and Murphy put it,"weighing the concerns of multiple stakeholder groups... becomes the essence of appropriate ethical decision-making... [and] the root of the complexity of such decision-making". While public policy makers should certainly protect the rights of marketers in a free market economy, they must also consider the interests of consumers, particularly those with various degrees of vulnerability, such as children and the elderly.

Future studies of marketers'and consumers'ethical evaluations of the various marketing contexts would help to validate the contingency approach. How consumers form their perceptions of marketers'intentions and make ethical evaluations of marketing will be a fruitful avenue for future research. Researchers may focus on specific situations that would raise ethical concerns for marketers, especially variations in consumers'ethical evaluations of marketing practices (e.g., advertising and distribution) for different market segments (e.g., children and the elderly). In addition to consumer capability, information and choice are two important criteria to determine marketing ethics under the principle of consumer sovereignty. Thus, how companies present information about their products, and how they handle potentially damaging information, may help to shed some light on the ethical decision-making of marketers.

The increasing diversity of the marketplace in the U.S. has significant and complex implications for marketing practices. As more companies are concentrating their resources on the most desirable and profitable segments of consumers, they inevitably exclude other groups.

Consumer and marketing research should use more representative samples of diverse groups to examine consumer responses to marketing programmes, including the responses of non-target markets. In the foreseeable future (around 2020-2050), the United States will be a marketplace in which all Americans are minorities, and that will pose special challenges and opportunities for both private companies and public organizations. Determining when segmentation and differentiation may lead to perceptions of discrimination or reverse discrimination will continue to be a focal issue for future research.

This research focuses on marketing and consumers in the United States. Cross-country and cross-cultural research would help to understand marketing ethics in a broader context. In the past, multinational corporations experienced difficulties with their marketing strategies in other countries, as in the case of Nestle's baby formula. Despite adverse public attitudes at times, multinationals and local companies used a variety of techniques and media to promote their products to consumers in developing countries without close scrutiny of the consumer perceptions of such practices.

In light of increasing globalization, more companies are crossing national boundaries to produce and market their products in other countries. Thus, how the local communities of the global marketplace evaluate the marketing practices of multinational corporations has become an important subject of investigation.

5

Relationship Marketing

In today's turbulent environment of global business, successful organizations must be able to provide high-quality products and services on the basis of personal knowledge of customers. Customer service needs to be constructed on the premise that consumers are increasingly demanding to be treated as individuals, not just as members of a large group. Consequently, personalization - the social content of interaction between service or retail employees and their customers - becomes an important mediator of customer satisfaction and patronage behaviour. Successful implementation of such relationship marketing, however, demands the integration of timely and accurate market, consumer, and product information.

In response to the growing demand for integrated information, organizations have expended great effort to utilize the latest information technology (IT) to build and maintain information systems. Effective use of such systems requires a high degree of data quality, defined as data that is fit for use by data consumers. Many managers, however, are unaware of the quality of the data they use and perhaps assume that IT ensures that the data is perfect. Customer data may be of poor quality if it does not reflect real world conditions or is not easily used and understood by the data user. Poor quality data can cause immediate economic harm and also have more indirect, subtle effects.

Organizations, however, have largely ignored the issue of poor data quality. The need for data quality management arises as the focus shifts from production process to customer concerns. Achieving customer satisfaction mandates quality production policies and production systems, and these, in turn, necessitate quality data policies and systems. Therefore, to successfully implement a relationship marketing strategy, corporate management should develop data quality policy, identify the critical data quality requirements, and establish quality data production systems.

This chapter discusses relationship marketing as a relatively new marketing strategy, emphasizing the importance of high-quality data to the implementation of such strategy, the problem of poor data quality, and data quality management (DQM) as an approach to dealing with such a problem.

RELATIONSHIP MARKETING

The history of marketing can be broken up into three periods in terms of buyer and seller relationships: the simple trade era, the mass production era, and the new marketing era. The simple trade era was a real relationship between the buyer and the seller. Retailers, bankers, and auto dealers knew their customers personally, understood what they wanted, and satisfied their needs through personalized service. The proprietor of a general store, a bank, a barbershop, or a town livery stable visualized business primarily in terms of share of customers. For example, a local grocer's business was built on a one-to-one relationship with individual customers and what the grocer knew about each of them.

This allowed the retailer to solve problems for customers, to give special attention to the most valuable customers, to sell them more products, and to adjust the service or product offerings to meet their evolving needs. Therefore, the pre-twentieth-century store owners were relationship marketers who nurtured customers as individuals and had to keep data about their customers in their head.

After the onset of the Industrial Revolution, most companies had moved into the mass production era. During this era, customers traded relationships for greater variety and lower prices. The advent of mass media in the early part of this century undercut the relationship between customer and companies and replaced it with mass marketing techniques. Standardized messages could be communicated to millions of people. A branded product that used a symbol took the place of a relationship, and consumers became statistics in the marketers' databases. Further, a mass production strategy could focus on market share and plan the necessary steps to increase it. For example, marketers run discount promotions for occasions like Washington's Birthday, Mother's Day, or Valentine's Day to increase traffic, sales, and market share.

The modern marketing concept, on the other hand, seeks ways to build long-term relationships with customers by treating them as specific market segments. In fact, this movement, labeled "relationship marketing," leads companies back to the nineteenth century when retailers knew each customer personally but with the global scale of the twenty-first century. The focus of relationship marketing is on attracting and retaining customers through cooperation, trust, commitment, and sharing of information.

Relationship marketing facilitates a company's effort to identify, maintain, and build a network of individual consumers and to continuously strengthen the network through interactive, individualized, and value-added contacts over a long period. Further, relationship marketing, as a retailer-customer alliance approach, refers to all marketing activities directed toward developing and maintaining successful relational exchanges with customers. It seeks to establish, maintain, enhance, and commercialize customer relationships so that the objectives of the parties involved are met, which is done by a mutual exchange and fulfillment of promises. In other words, relationship marketing is based on talking with consumers, listening to them, learning their wants and catering to them.

The term "database marketing" is sometimes used synonymously for relationship marketing. Such a misuse of the term can easily lead to an erroneous exclusion of many of the marketing activities that legitimately fall under the purview of relationship marketing. However, the foundation for effective relationship marketing lies in the development and effective use of database marketing principles. Donnelly recognizes this and uses the term "date-driven relationship marketing" to refer to retail management and a marketing approach that is based on an organization-wide database system. Such a system gathers and stores data to identify and understand customers and prospective customers as individuals or groups.

To respond to the growing demand for integrated information for relationship marketing, organizations are expected to use the latest tools. IT allows high-speed, efficient, and effective processing of data and a better interpretation of information. This will give an organization the ability to development relationships with individual customers. IT makes it possible for large corporations to be as effective in one-to-one customer relationships as the small proprietor. With a database providing a powerful memory of every customer's different needs, a company with 10 million customers can make its goal customer share, instead of market share.

Clearly, the more a company is able to engender loyalty from its customers, the more likely the relationships will be enduring and profitable. The development of customer loyalty comes from constantly refining the information available on specific customers including customer preferences, buying habits and patterns, product usage, and other data specific to individual customers. Keys to better marketing are customer focus and systems built to track customer relationships.

Finally, relationship marketing seems to be the marketing strategy of choice for corporations that have to complete in a turbulent environment of global business. According to a report by the Direct Marketing Association retailers who operate as they have for the past 30 years, employing mass media advertising, sales-driven merchandising, infrequent consumer research, and non-segmented promotions, will slowly be eclipsed by those who have augmented or replaced traditional marketing with database and relationship marketing. Successful corporations need to interact on the basis of personal knowledge of customers, and quality data is a key to such interaction. Quality data is a preconditions to creating and sustaining a measurable advantage in the competition for this specific customer's business.

RELATIONSHIP MARKETING AND DATA QUALITY

A principal impetus behind relationship marketing strategy is that getting new customers by taking them away from a competitor is usually more costly than retaining current customers. Executives in many companies such as Marriott, American Express, ATandT Electronic Data Systems, Motorola, Owens-Corning, American Airlines, Hertz, and USAA are making long-term customer relationships the main focus of their marketing strategies using quality customer data.

Relationship marketing strategy requires the market segment to be an individual customer rather than a group of customers. To target the individual, companies need to get fast and accurate data from the point of sale. Today, PCs are everywhere - from the factory floor to the sales office - so that data are fed in as soon possible. The whole process is telescoping as technology allows the fast dissemination of data. When an order is placed for a Saturn car, for example, the information is immediately sent to the factory. A car going down the assembly line is built with the exact color and features requested by a customer.

The key element of a successful relationship marketing strategy is a flexible and customised sales and marketing database created by tools that provide flexible access to marketing information. A marketing database can be classified as a major corporate asset. Such a database is also perceived as a learning tool for the tuned-in corporation, a competitive listening post as well as a strategic weapon. Further, a marketing database serves as a vital tool in companies' efforts to build strategic sustainable relationships with customers. For example, Burger King uses a database to push brand loyalty while its customers are still in diapers.

For most companies, whether product, service, or nonprofit, the objective in building quality data is the same; to keep customers coming back. An increasing number of product and service companies are establishing frequency programmes using quality and accurate data. Credit and loyalty cards are an important aspect of such programmes to move companies toward relationship marketing. When customers need to use their cards each time they shop, the companies are able to capture huge amounts of data about what and how often they buy.

Nevertheless, successful implementation of relationship marketing demands the integration of timely and accurate market, consumer, and product data. Managers need information that encourages insight and helps them make a day-to-day decisions that enhance profitability, increase value for customers, and differentiate their products and service. Marketing strategies and programmes change rapidly, and, therefore, customer data need to be modified accurately, quickly, and easily.

Customer data can also become a weapon in the information war between suppliers and retailers. Big manufacturers of fast-moving consumer goods have been attempting to cut out the middle man - at least in information terms - by building huge customer databases and promoting directly to shoppers through the mail.

A private hospital in Louisville, Kentucky, provides a good example of using quality data to relationship marketing. Patients can be tracked from the point of initial contact (e.g., Health and Information Centre, emergency-room visit, telemarketing contact, etc.) through all subsequent interactions with the hospital. The database also provides the information needed to implement the hospital's targeted direct mail programmes. All individuals in the data base receive Choices for a Healthy Lifestyle magazine and other medical information consistent with their area of concern. The database also helps the hospital's management to assess the effectiveness of its marketing programmes. Additionally, identifying the point of initial patient contact provides valuable information about which marketing activities were instrumental in creating awareness and attracting new patients.

Effective use of relationship marketing strategy requires excellent data quality. By providing high-quality data about individual customers' buying habits and preferences, information systems enable marketing managers and salespersons to improve productivity and boost customer satisfaction. Many marketing practitioners, however, are unaware of the quality of their data and perhaps assume that IT ensures good data. Customer data is never perfect, however. Errors creep in through inaccurate self-reporting by consumers or during data entry and compilation. Poor data can have substantial social and economic effects.

THE PROBLEM OF DATA QUALITY

As mentioned, data quality is critical to organizations that rely on data analyses for decisions pertinent to relationship marketing. In making such analyses, the quality of data are often assumed, which is a big mistake. There is considerable evidence that the quality of organizational data may often be quite poor and may be a major source of errors and losses.

In a survey of 50 Fortune 500 companies in 1990, two-thirds of the companies reported significant problems with the quality of their data. In a 1990 report to Senator Sam Nunn the US General Accounting Office reported that at a single agency more than $2 billion in federal loan money had been lost because of poor data quality. Also, Hardjono reports that 60% of information systems managers have poor data.

Large databases can be mined to find sales prospects among existing customers and can be analysed to divine future trends. Yet, those databases may be full of corrupted data, often caused by field-originated transaction errors. McGee argues that if data is captured in the field with a 1% error rate and then is keyed by a third party at a separate time (usually out of the context in which it was captured) for another 1% error rate, the data may be 100% defective.

In many cases, the data that are created by one group (e.g., salespersons) in one part of the world are used for decision making by another group (e.g., marketing managers) thousands of miles away. Further, data that are gathered for one business purpose and intended to be stored in a single base may actually be used for many business purposes and replicated in a number of databases accessed by multiple users. While the initial users of the data may be fully aware of the meaning of the various data items, the later users may not. Consequently, data can be easily misinterpreted.

The consequences of poor data quality can be catastrophic. Defective data represents a real hidden cost to the organization's bottom line and to customer satisfaction. Even a 1% defect rate can lead to an enormous impact on the way a company does business and makes decisions and ultimately affects customer satisfaction. In a major transportation company, 77% of the reasons for incorrect delivery and consequently customer dissatisfaction, were related to erroneous data, missing data, mistrusted data, or the inappropriate use of data. In addition, the social ramifications of data quality can be very important to individuals and organizations since errors can create huge problems and embarrassment to those affected.

It should be noticed that the problems mentioned are further complicated by the fact that ensuring data quality is difficult. In a world of multiple, ad hoc data users, much of the certainty of the data production environment disappears. Data may be of uncertain quality and their uses may be known only in part. Additionally, the effectiveness of possible inspection procedures is uncertain, since the data undergo a series of ad hoc processing procedures. Other factors include the uncertainty regarding what constitutes the data resource that should be maintained, the perceived lack of data quality importance, the multiplicity of potential problems with data, the inadequate documentation of data definitions and meaning, and the uncertainty regarding the seriousness of deficiencies.

For all these reasons, the quality of data is often problematic. Therefore, data quality management (DQM) becomes both a necessity and a challenge for organizations that are attempting to compete by implementing relationship marketing strategies.

DATA QUALITY MANAGEMENT (DQM)

As organizations move increasingly towards relationship marketing, the demand for quality data is expected to grow. Furthermore, more employees than ever are expected to work directly with computer-based data. The Department of Labour has estimated that well over 40% of those in the workforce will be in data services by the turn of the century.

In addition, since organizations are increasingly adopting total quality management (TQM) programmes, data quality management (DQM) becomes one of the critical management issues. TQM programmes call for 100% customer satisfaction but this requires data that are 100% free of errors and are available in a timely manner. Just-in-time data allows an organization to respond to its customers with a true commitment to customer satisfaction. However, this is seldom the case. A clear understanding of the meaning of"data"is critical to the planning and implementation of a DQM programme."Data"is multifaceted and complex, the word is used in many different ways. However, a life-cycle view of data is useful from a DQM perspective.

A data life-cycle includes the sequence of phases through which data pass as they progress from creation to storage and use. At different stages in their life, data change in many ways. Therefore, data must be defined in a way that counts for the fundamental operations of defining conceptual data models and views, collecting and updating values, storing, retrieving, and manipulating data, and presenting and using them for a variety of purposes. Within this framework, a datum or data item is defined as a triple where e is an entity in a conceptual model, a is an attribute of entity c, and v is a value from the domain of attribute a. In other words, a datum asserts that an entity e (e.g., customer) has a value v (e.g., $60,000) for an attribute a (e.g., annual income). Thus, data are any collection of data items.

To improve data quality, an awareness of data quality

must emerge. TQM is expected to provide managers with excellent opportunities to identify their data quality problems and become aware of their consequences. A DQM programme should involve the determination of a data policy, the identification of techniques, and the use of procedures designed to ensure that any organizational data resource possesses a level of quality commensurate with the various current and potential uses of the data.

Within the context of DQM, management should take the following steps: develop a data policy that is compatible with the other policies; define quality objectives, such as performance, costs, and losses regarding data creation and consumption; and establish a data quality system, including the organizational structure, responsibilities, procedures and resources for implementing DQM. This quality system applies to all phases of data production, from initial identification to final satisfaction of requirements.

One way to help identify and implement such policies, techniques, and procedures is to apply an analogical approach that considers information as products. Information manufacturing can be viewed as a processing system that acts on raw data to produce information products. Therefore, continuous data quality improvement is critical to ensure high-quality information products. TQM literature includes principles, guidelines, and techniques that can be applied similarly to data and information quality practice.

Deming's cycle for quality improvement consists of planning, doing, checking, and acting. By adapting Deming's cycle, Wang introduces a total data quality management (TDQM) cycle with data quality definition, measurement, analysis, and improvement as its four phases. The definition component of the TDQM cycle identifies important data quality dimensions - e.g., accessibility, timeliness, completeness, consistency, etc. The measurement component produces data quality metrics - e.g., the percentage of incorrect customer address zip codes, the percentage of customer records with missing phone numbers, the date when customer data were last updated, etc. Using techniques such as statistical process control, the analysis component identifies root causes for data quality problems and calculates the effects of poor data quality. Once the analysis phase is complete, the improvement component provides techniques for improving data quality. Also, this analogy allows, for example, the utilization of ISO 9000 as an international standard for product manufacturing, and the application of product quality management frameworks for data quality management. In this case, the quality problem could be investigated in terms of prevention, repair, and detection throughout the sequence of data-related activities from creation to consumption.

A DQM programme is expected to include articulating a vision of data quality, establishing responsibility for data quality, educating personnel regarding the importance of data quality, teaching appropriate quality skills, and institutionalizing systematic data quality enhancement procedures.

These aspects of DQM should be dealt with at the macro level since they have an impact on the organizational policies. A data quality manager could be assigned the primary responsibility for the design and implementation of tasks and activities that support organizational policies. While the exact responsibilities of a data quality manager may vary from one organization to another, ultimately they involve determining who uses the data for what purpose, identifying the data quality needs of the users, and then fixing any data quality deficiencies that may exist.

These tasks, which range from tactical to strategic, are briefly discussed below:

- *Identification of data users*: The differing needs cannot be addressed unless the data quality manager knows who the users are. There are various techniques (e.g., questionnaires, interviews, database usage analysis, etc.) that can be used to obtain information as to who uses what data for which purpose. During this phase, data quality problems should be clearly identified, especially when the same data are shared by different users. For example, one department may complain that the sales data are inaccurate when, in fact, the problem is that different definitions are being used as to what constitutes a sale.

- *Analysis of the impact of data deficiencies*: As mentioned, data errors can cause serious consequences. The assessment of the potential impact of data deficiencies is not limited to inconsistent coding schemes. When a data value is used only for one purpose, systems designers can ensure that a particular value possesses the requisite data quality. However, in the case of multiple uses, a level of data quality that is fine for one user may be inadequate for another. Unfortunately, there is no simple way to determine with certainty the seriousness of the impact of data deficiencies. However, a good starting point is to consider the perception of those who use the data on a regular basis.
- *Determination of the nature of data deficiencies*: There are many ways for data to be wrong, especially in a multi-user environment. This problem is further complicated by the multiple, and sometimes conflicting, attributes of data (e.g., accuracy, completeness, precision, consistency, timeliness, etc.). Wang, Strong, and Guarascio identify four broad groupings of data quality: intrinsic data quality (i.e., accuracy); contextural data quality (i.e., completeness, timeliness); representational data quality (i.e., consistency); and accessibility data quality (i.e., availability).

  A set of data may be completely satisfactory on some of these attributes but inadequate on the others. Therefore, there may be a data quality problem on one dimension but not on another. A data quality manager should become sufficiently acquainted with the data and their uses to be in a position to identify potential problems. Such problems are usually organization-dependent.
- *Determination of the appropriate level of data quality*: It

is essential to know whether the quality is sufficient for the particular use. Determining an appropriate level of data quality is context-dependent. It is even more difficult when differing users have differing needs. The data quality manager should not only determine the level of quality required by each use of the data set but also try to balance conflicting requirements for data quality. In doing so, cost-benefit analysis can be a useful technique.

While data accuracy seems to be the most important attribute for the successful planning and implementation of a relationship marketing strategy, a comprehensive DQM programme should consider and balance all the relevant attributes of data quality. This is particularly important since the same data (e.g., consumer, market, and product data) are used for multiple purposes.

- *Choosing procedures to ensure data quality*: Regarding the process of producing and delivering data to users, there are at least three approaches to achieving high-quality process output (Ishikawa, 1990): inspections and rework, process management, and process design. Although such approaches have been pioneered in manufacturing and service industries, they can be equally applied to data quality control and improvement:
  - *Data inspection and rework*: According to this approach, the common way for controlling and improving data accuracy is to detect and correct erroneous values. The simplest procedure is to compare the recorded data values with the real world and fix those that are wrong. For example, consider a customer database containing data on addresses. It is common to survey customer data regularly to verify and correct addresses. This can work well depending on how cooperative the customers are and whether the address verification and correction forms reach them.

A second method, called database hashing, can be used when data values are stored in two or more databases. Corresponding values of the databases are compared, and when a disagreement is detected, an investigation finds the correct value, and the databases are fixed. A third possible method, called data editing, involves computerized checking of data values against constraints. Once a record is found in error, further investigation locates and corrects the erroneous field or fields.

Inspection and rework methods are not very effective for improving data quality because they are conducted downstream of data value creation, usually either during a storage activity or during usage activities of the data life-cycle. Although they result in short-term data quality improvements, inspection and rework methods cannot provide lasting improvements because they do not attack the sources of errors.

Data process management: An alternative to inspection and rework is focusing on the processes that create data values. This approach first places such processes in statistical control. Errors are then reduced by identifying where and how they occur and changing processes to prevent them. For example, suppose a process for collecting and filling service orders is measured and found to be out of control. After study, several problems with ill-defined procedures are identified and eliminated. The process then operates in a state of statistical control with an average error rate of 0.1%. A further study of the process reveals error-prone activities that can be improved, thereby reducing its average error rate to 0.05%. The net outcomes of these activities are that they make the output of the process predictable and known, and they produce measurable improvements in process performance. The data process management approach requires more effort than the inspection and rework approach. However, the data quality improvements are sustainable and therefore are cheaper in the long run.

- *Process design for data quality*: This quality improvement approach involves reengineering or redesigning processes to minimize errors. It is usually more expensive than the other two approaches. However, when successful, this approach yields large gains in a short time and may be cheaper than the first two approaches in the long run. Typically, process redesign involves new information technologies such as the installation of point-of-sale systems to read product codes faster and more accurately than a person can.

A mature DQM programme is expected to use a combination of the foregoing three approaches. For example, an organization may have carefully designed a process to minimize errors and may be managing it actively to steadily improve and optimize its performance. Nevertheless, bad data may still find their way to a customer, where they must be replaced or fixed. Thus, a mechanism for inspection and rework may need to be used even in the most sophisticated environment.

As more and more products compete in the global marketplace, relationship marketing appears to be an effective strategy for dealing with fierce competition. The movement towards relationship marketing, however, requires organizations to manage a large amount of data, including market, consumer, and product data. Such data may take different forms, e.g., voice, data, image, audio, and video, and could be

> generated by individuals dispersed around the world. The quality of such data is an essential ingredient for facilitating a company's effort to identify, maintain, and build a network with individual consumers and to continuously strengthen it through interactive, individualized, and value-added contacts over a long period.

Organizations must harness the full potential of their data to adopt business strategies such as relationship marketing. There are many ways for data to be wrong. In a world of multiple, ad hoc data users, much of the certainty of the data production environment disappear. Data may be of uncertain quality and their uses known only in part. The effectiveness of inspection procedures is uncertain, since the data undergo ad hoc processing procedures. Data quality is also affected by uncertainty regarding the data resource, the perceived lack of data quality importance, the inadequate documentation of data definitions and meaning, and the uncertainty regarding the seriousness of deficiencies.

Data must be managed as a perishable. Capturing and managing data with a 100% commitment to zero defects will allow companies to adopt relationship marketing strategies and deliver 100% customer satisfaction. It is management's responsibility to plan and implement data quality management programmes to attain and maintain high-quality data. These programmes should help determine data policies, identify quality improvement techniques, and use procedures designed to ensure that data resources possess a level of quality commensurate with current and potential uses of the data.

Organizations should consider creating a data quality manager who must have a sound understanding of the nature of the organization's data, must identify and enforce policies that help ensure data quality, and must effectively balance conflicting requirements for data quality and make appropriate trade-offs. Successful relationship marketing strategies depend on the effective accomplishment of these data quality responsibilities and tasks.

6

Market Segmentation and Targeting

The increasing internationalization of consumers as well as the growth of technology have created important opportunities for marketers to target customers across borders. The growth in international consumer marketing along with the development of sophisticated database-driven customer relationship management (CRM) capabilities has reinforced the interest of practitioners and researchers in customer segmentation. Segmentation continues to be the focus of considerable attention in the popular business press as well as in academic journals.

In particular, the international segmentation literature has focused upon criteria to select target countries and behavioural bases to select target consumers as drivers in defining segments. Several authors have presented general conceptual models that propose specific segment/product relationships.

While researchers have been successful in identifying market segments suitable for a number of narrowly defined purposes, relatively little of the research offers any insight into the process by which managers make decisions about segmentation in the international consumer market.

As a first step in addressing this topic, this chapter examines the decision process by which finds develop international market segmentation strategy. Specifically, this chapter synthesizes a substantial body of literature to present an integrated multi-step framework of the international consumer market segmentation strategy-making process.

Further, this chapter presents qualitative case examples from fieldwork with six international organizations, with the purpose of examining the veracity of the framework in actual practice.

INTERNATIONAL SEGMENTATION DECISION PROCESS

Markets and the customers who make up those markets are not homogeneous. Wendell Smith suggested that segmentation, the division of a market into groups of customers who share certain characteristics or propensities toward a product or service, might be an effective way for an organization to manage diversity within a market. Since that time, a rich literature has developed suggesting techniques and bases upon which a single domestic market might be effectively broken into actionable customer segments.

A distinct track of the literature in international segmentation began with Wind and Douglas'pioneering treatment of international market segmentation in 1972. Prior to that, market segmentation was viewed primarily as a domestic strategy, and the occasional mention of international market segmentation in scholarly research was cursory at best. Wind and Douglas (1972) put forward the argument that segmentation is not just equally important in the international market, but in fact may be more important because international markets are more diverse than domestic markets.

The development of international segmentation strategy has been alternately conceptualized as a linear process or as a portfolio of interrelated decisions.

However, in each case at least two distinct decisions for defining international market segments are implicitly assumed. Wind and Douglas termed the first decision as the"macro"segmentation decision in which countries are classified and targeted based upon national market characteristics. The second decision is to analyse and sub-divide each qualifying target country by customer characteristics to form market segments. The two decisions are assumed to be normative.

The two decisions also are assumed to follow a clear temporal order-country selection followed by customer segmentation within the country. The argument for a temporal relationship is that the cost of examining customers and their behaviour (second decision) in a number of countries is likely to be significantly higher than determining country attractiveness (first decision).

Therefore, a firm will seek to economize by selecting among countries prior to examining customer behaviour within each country. The cost difference is driven by the assumption that the selection of target countries could likely be accomplished based upon secondary data while within-country identification of segments would likely require primary research.

Similar in intent to Wind and Douglas, the first decision presented by Kale and Sudharshan was referred to as"country screening"-selecting countries that qualify as potential markets. The second decision was termed"microsegmentation,"where consumers are classified based upon product predisposition and consumption patterns.

Once these segments are identified, it is suggested that firms look for"strategically equivalent"segments across a range of countries that may be served with a common marketing mix. Strategically equivalent segments share a similar predisposition toward at least one type of product and exist in multiple markets. Like Wind and Douglas, Kale and Sudharshan assumed a linear or hierarchical order to the decision steps.

Ter Hofstede, Steenkamp and Wedel found that a segmentation model will better form segments that share consumption patterns by integrating both country factors and consumer characteristics versus traditional models employing country factors alone. The study did not address the nature of segmentation decision-making or the steps involved in formulating segmentation strategy. However, their findings do reinforce within-country examination of market segment bases as a key step in the international segmentation strategy decision process.

Once segments have been identified, they must be appropriately grouped and managed. A number of authors have suggested that the scale of segment management may be multi-local (country by country), regional (based upon clusters of countries), intermarket (based upon a global customer segment which transcends national boundaries), or global in nature.

Some recent research suggests that a multi-local scale of segment management might enhance market performance. Arnold (2000) uncovered a long-term trend toward higher performance among firms that allowed local control of distribution.

"In the long run, multinationals come to see that it makes sense to continue working with independent local distributors who handle sales and distribution system [sic], even after the international companies have taken control of marketing strategy and major global accounts". However, in actual practice, it is possible to find examples of each scale of segment management as well as a variety of hybrid combinations.

SYNTHESIS DECISION FRAMEWORK

Relying on a synthesis of the relevant literature, this chapter adopts country selection based on the attractiveness of the country or countries as potential markets as the first step in the synthesis decision framework. Likewise, within-country consumer selection is adopted as the second step, based upon the literature.

Case Methodology

The study consists of six company case profiles developed through secondary research, site visits, and in-depth interviews with a group of qualified executive-level key informants.

A qualified key informant is: 1) responsible for marketing to consumers outside of the United States; 2) closely involved in developing marketing strategy for their firm or strategic business unit; and, 3) recently involved with either a new product introduction or expanding an existing product into one or more new countries. The case fieldwork began with each firm between 1999 and 2001 and is ongoing.

Multiple interviews have been conducted in these six companies over time on site and via telephone by the author. A standardized interview protocol is utilized; however, topics are followed as appropriate. Probes follow questions where necessary to spur further discussion. Interviews have been captured on audiotape to aid in analysis. In exchange for their participation, interview respondents were promised and have subsequently been given summary reports of the study to date. To protect confidentiality, the identities of specific participants are disguised.

Interviews opened with a warm-up discussion during which respondents were told of the tape recording, the academic nature of the research, and assured of confidentiality.

In addition, there was an informal discussion of the respondents' experience in international markets that set the stage for the following main topics:

- Description of product/service and countries of operation
- Nature of involvement in marketing to consumers internationally
- Priority of international markets to the firm
- Decision process to expand internationally
- Decision process by which your firm targets a country for entry
- Decision process by which your firm identifies targeted consumers
- Decision process for managing customer relationships
- Performance criteria by which international operations are evaluated
- Importance of specific performance criteria to the firm

Cases are meant to illustrate segmentation decisions and not to be a projectable sample. Therefore, the order of the questions remained relatively constant across the interviews although no attempt has been made to follow the protocol in a lock-step fashion.

Analysis and Findings

The following points represent the consensus of respondents. In some cases, specific organization references have been limited to protect the confidentiality of respondents.

International markets are important: Even in a heightened state of security concern, there was a clear consensus among the case organizations that international markets are an important source of growth. Therefore, the firm's international segmentation strategy receives a great deal of managerial attention. Subsequently, each case organization reported on international segmentation decisions as significantly involving the most senior levels of division and corporate management. The organizations reported international operations contributing from 9% to 73% of sales and up to 80% of revenue. In each organization, international markets are viewed as an important engine for building both brands and revenues.

Segmentation is a critical issue: There was clear consensus among the organizations that market segmentation is a critical step for success in the international market. Although there was some variation in the emphasis of country selection relative to consumer selection, all of the case organizations used segmentation techniques to drive international product development and marketing. One respondent stated "we used to design products for a market, now to make money we have to design products with a specific consumer segment in mind."

Identifying a specific customer segment is far more important than simply selecting a market. A respondent stated, "inertia in country selection was important in the past (i.e., going with new product lines where you already do business), however, our recent expansion strategies have virtually ignored existing product sales in market country selection decisions. We are going after business and we don't really care where it is located or what other business we have there."

Proposed synthesis framework reflects practice: The case organizations showed a clear consensus in validating the three-step international market segmentation strategy decision framework. Case organizations indicated that they made country selections, analysed and targeted consumers within the countries, and made decisions about the scale of segment management. It is important that respondents were not shown or told of the framework or decision steps due to concerns that exposure might cause respondents alter their answers to fit the framework. While the emphasis as well as the order of each step varied to some degree, the synthesis framework decision steps derived from the literature appeared to be universal across the case organizations.

As the international market segmentation strategy decision framework suggests, respondents are active in assessing country attractiveness. Typical among respondents, Maytag identifies and classifies countries into three target categories: primary, secondary, and emerging. A primary market is a "first entry" market. Secondary targets are specifically targeted for entry at a later time. Frequently, secondary target markets are less immediately attractive or accessible but may be geographically adjacent to primary target markets.

Emerging markets are not yet targeted for entry. A respondent noted, "there are some countries that you just can't get into—tariffs and other trade barriers, inability of retailers to get hard currency, banking systems that are suspect... other factors considered are population size, gross domestic product per capita, etc." Interestingly, segmentation-based country selection does not appear to be confounded by mode of entry decisions among the case study organizations.

In accordance with the decision framework, case organizations indicated that within-country consumer analysis is critical to the success of segmentation decisions. When selecting a target segment in a nondomestic market, one respondent described the process as seeking commonalties of "lifestyle and psychographic characteristics" to existing customers. These commonalties are the links that allow for a unified global strategy. In the words of one respondent, "if you don't find commonality among consumers, then you have to reinvent the wheel in each country—which we don't want to do—the more links you find among consumers in different countries the more possibility for error you eliminate."

In addition to country selection and within-country consumer analysis, case organizations indicated that the scale of segment management is critical to successful international marketing. "Going country specific is a huge gamble—if you develop a different strategy for each country and it fails, you have no way of knowing if the strategy was poor or if the country is just not receptive due to idiosyncrasies of the people (i.e., Germany being nationalistic). However, developing a single strategy for many countries (managed regionally) means that you can test the strategy and if it does not work somewhere but it does work in other countries then it is a better test of the strategy itself. A lot of companies have tried country specific strategies globally and have failed." One respondent summarized the scale of segment management issue as "we want to be able to have a template, if you will, and copy it and reapply it to the next place." However, the same organization might be managing customer segments at multiple levels across products.

Order of decision steps varies: The international market segmentation decisions presented in the managerial decision-making framework suggest a standard order or hierarchy to the segmentation decision steps. While there is a strong consensus among case organizations that each decision in the proposed international market segmentation decision framework is distinct, there is not a clear consensus among respondents regarding the order in which the decision steps are executed. For example, Startec and Black and Decker both have specific consumers in mind. Startec is seeking transplanted populations with some specific ethnic identity. Black and Decker is seeking the "do-it-yourself" homeowner. Therefore, Startec and Black and Decker place first priority emphasis on step two (consumer analysis) and use this information to drive country selection. In comparison, Maytag and Exxon/Mobil follow the decision process order as presented in the framework, with country selection as a first step.

Scale of segmentation, scope of globalization, and internationalization of the firm: The case organizations represent a spectrum of the degree of internationalization. On one extreme is Coca Cola, deriving 60% of sales and 80% of revenue from international business. This contrasts with Startec, deriving only 20% of sales from abroad. However, the case organizations are generally more internationalized than companies at large.

While respondents agreed that product customization is necessary in some circumstances, there was consensus that standardization is the strategy of choice when possible. However, standardization may take different forms for different firms. For example, Maytag has developed a world platform for its home appliances. Maytag's intention is that the only product changes in their appliances are the language of the owner's manual and the plug on the electrical cord. In contrast, Startec is standardizing to specific customer segments. Startec has tailored international long-distance calling programmes to ethnic Turkish communities offering customised calling and native language operators to ethnic Turks virtually anywhere in the world. The case organizations do not see a conflict between world standardization and mass customization of products or marketing campaigns, with the implication being that one-to-one marketing would not limit the applicability of segmentation as a strategy in international markets. Mass customization would simply be a feature in all markets for appropriate segments built upon a standardized product or communications platform.

The scale of segment management is related to both the scope of globalization and the internationalization of the firm. Organizations that are more internationalized are also more willing to invest in infrastructure to support a marketing presence outside of the domestic country. Once a firm's international operations contribute a significant percentage of sales, then it is easier to cost-justify a world regional or multi-local management presence. Obviously, an in-country or in-region marketing management presence must exist (or be outsourced) for segments to be managed outside of the domestic country. In addition, case organizations report a high existing or at least evolving degree of standardization of products. There is a strong consensus that the choice of the scale of segment management will be related to the degree of product standardization achieved.

Cross-industry research is critical to understanding the best practices of firms in international consumer marketing. Among the case study firms, there is substantial commonality among the criteria used to identify and select countries to enter. While the outcome of the country selection decision will vary based upon the needs and capabilities of individual organizations, the process by which the decision is made is substantially similar across industries and firms in the cases. Clearly, there is much less variation in the criteria used to evaluate the attractiveness of countries among case organizations compared with the many criteria suggested in the literature. In each case, the organizations relied heavily upon national income, financial system development, and regulatory considerations in country selection.

Selection of specific consumer segments within target countries is increasingly important to the case organizations. These firms are taking advantage of increased data handling capabilities combined with increased research into transnational lifestyles to accumulate data on specific consumer market segments in many parts of the world. This is complicated but not curtailed by the varying privacy restrictions in gathering and holding consumer level data—notably in Europe. The desirability of using behavioural criteria as a decision step in the international consumer market segmentation decision process has spurred growth in behavioural research within target countries. Again, there are significant commonalities among the criteria. In each case, the organizations relied heavily upon lifestyle, demographics, attitude, and customer loyalty.

The third decision in the international consumer market segmentation framework, determining the scale or strategy with which segments will be managed, is part of the segmentation decision process for the case organizations. However, selecting the scale of segment management is clearly not a purely marketing-driven decision. Firms in the study have sought to balance the desire to manage segment relationships with the economic reality of having substantial duplication of management structures across multiple markets. A number of case organizations have discovered that duplicate management structures could be consolidated across countries without significantly affecting their ability to customise practices for a market.

The results of this study indicate that the three decision steps presented in the synthesis framework reflect actual practice among the case organizations. However, the assumption of the order of the steps as presented in the literature was not universally supported. Further, the study suggests that the impact of globalization, new technology, and enhanced security concerns has been to heighten, not diminish, interest in segmentation.

While the bulk of the prior work has focused upon single-step segmentation decisions, expanding the international consumer market segmentation decision process to three steps can improve the likelihood of developing a successful segmentation strategy. Country selection is an important decision step because each potential target country will have unique regulatory structures, market dynamics, and population characteristics that present differing opportunities and challenges. As the case results indicate, firms will benefit from using country attractiveness criteria to determine which markets the firm is best suited to serve in terms of resources and managerial expertise. Selection of specific consumer segments within target countries is an important step in market segmentation because of its emphasis on behavioural characteristics.

Utilizing consumer-specific within-country segmentation data allows the firm to target appropriate marketing activities to those consumers with a predisposition toward their product, thereby avoiding the expense of inaccurate targeting. Having identified target countries and within-country segments, selection of the scale or level at which segments will be managed allows the firm to balance the economies that come from centralization of marketing activities with the benefits of hands-on marketing management in important markets. In short, the operational definition of international consumer market segmentation as a three-step managerial decision-making process results in more specific and actionable market segments. In addition, the three-step decision process is more reflective of the 'best practices' of case organizations than simply addressing segmentation as a single-stage decision.

7

Service Recovery

Customer service professionals generally agree that complaint or problem resolution is a key to maintaining client loyalty. Unresolved problems have a particularly negative impact on both continued product use and word-of-mouth recommendations to others. Dissatisfied customers tell far more people about their experience than do routinely satisfied customers.

The bank's response to customer problems can be of critical importance. Data from Technical Assistance Research Programmes (TARP) finds that the majority (63%) of customers who do take the time to complain are not completely satisfied with the bank's response to their problem. Various studies indicate that adequate problem/complaint resolution — or "service recovery" — leads to increased (not merely retained) customer loyalty. Newly satisfied customers are turned into active advocates for the business.

The importance of problem resolution to customer satisfaction was confirmed in a recent study of one bank's retail banking clients. As part of an ongoing improvement programme, a $2 billion-assets locally owned Midwest bank joined with our firm to develop and test satisfaction surveys for both retail and commercial customers. Surveys were mailed to a randomly selected sample of 1,620 customers who used the bank for at least three services (checking, savings, ATM). Many of these customers also had loans from the bank. A three-wave mailing resulted in 973 usable responses.

For the purposes of this report, we are focusing on correlations between the questionnaire items and overall score, rather than on satisfaction scores themselves. Banks differ from one another in performance quality and scores will thus vary considerably from bank to bank. On the other hand, issues of most concern to customers should be fairly consistent across institutions. Issues "of most concern" can be defined as those questionnaire items most highly correlated with overall satisfaction.

In our work in the health-care field, we find that correlations between survey items and overall satisfaction score are remarkably similar across institutions. In other words, although hospital quality and individual patient experiences may vary significantly, what's important to patients does not vary much from provider to provider. Pending additional research, we assume the same holds for bank customers. We feel confident that results from this study of a single bank can be generalized to other financial institutions.

The ordering of items yields several surprises. Accuracy — a characteristic stressed frequently in our bank customer focus groups — is fairly high on the list, yet falls well below other service elements in its relation to overall satisfaction with the bank. Customer experiences that typically yield the most vocal complaints — waiting time, convenience of banking hours, and even teller courtesy — are least correlated with overall satisfaction.

At the same time, one is immediately struck by the fact that those issues most highly correlated with overall satisfaction involve problem/complaint management. Handling problems efficiently, paying attention to questions or concerns, and resolving problems on the phone are clearly of key importance to retail bank customers.

Information issues rank high; this is not to say that problem resolution is the key to customer satisfaction across the board. Obviously, customers will be more satisfied if there are no problems. Note that information issues predominate in the upper part of the correlation list. Answers to questions, and explanations and advice about accounts, products, and services all contribute to the customer's total experience of the bank. Problems in these areas will likely have especially significant influence on satisfaction.

The special importance of problem handling issues derives from the nature of the encounter with a bank. Customer contacts are short and sporadic: A deposit is made one day... an ATM visited another... a check cashed some days or weeks later... a statement received once a month. An account may be opened once in five years. Accuracy, courtesy, convenience information are taken for granted during each contact.

At the same time, perceived errors or service failures stand out sharply in the context of the isolated, brief, focused interaction with a specific bank service.

When these problems are resolved in a timely manner, two positive outcomes result:

- Expectations of service quality are reaffirmed.
- The customer perceives the bank as clearly and actively concerned about keeping his or her business.

Some of the commonly held ideas concerning what's important to retail bank customers may require further research and thought. Error and lapses are inevitable. An emerging principle of customer service in all industries identifies problem resolution as a key to sustaining client satisfaction and loyalty.

The present research indicates that service recovery may be more important to bank customers than other issues typically viewed as drivers of satisfaction. Well-handled problems or complaints produce customers who are actually more loyal than those experiencing no problems at all. As Hart, Heskett, and Sasser observed in their Howard Business Review article: "To err is human; to recover divine."

Given that various researchers find substantial dissatisfaction with banks' efforts at complaint resolution, the implications seem clear. Banks must strengthen complaint management. At the same time, they must also be able to identify problem areas and establish improvement processes before these have a broad impact on clientele. Banks should be actively monitoring customer satisfaction for insight to unresolved or developing service problems and responding aggressively to the data.

Given the breadth and variety of tax relief provisions in the American Recovery and Reinvestment Act (ARRA) of 2009, PL 111-5, one or more could affect your clients' individual returns for the 2009 tax year.

Many are intended to provide relief for taxpayers in financial distress, stimulate consumer spending or provide an incentive for more environmentally friendly living. They cover everything from tax treatment of unemployment benefits to child credits. Tax organizers and client letters should already reflect these measures; the following is a summary of some of the most prominent points to cover in correspondence and discussions with clients.

Income

Net operating losses. The ARRA amended IRC [section] 172(b) (H) to allow eligible small businesses to carry back a 2008 net operating loss (NOL) up to five years instead of the otherwise available two-year limit.

The IRS issued a clarifying revenue procedure because many taxpayers had inadvertently submitted invalid elections to claim a three-, four- or five-year carryback for 2008 NOLs. It modifies and supersedes Revenue Procedure 2009-19. To be eligible for the longer carryback period, the loss must arise from an eligible small business—a proprietorship, partnership or corporation with average gross receipts of $15 million or less for the three-year period ending in 2008 (section 172(b)(1)(H)(iv)).

Under section 172(d)(4)(C), a deduction for losses under section 165(c) from a transaction entered into for profit or from theft or casualty may be treated as a business deduction even if not attributable to the taxpayer's trade or business. Consequently, the Service pointed out in Revenue Ruling 2009-9 in connection with losses from fraudulent investments, this NOL carryback relief is also available to individuals who claim a section 165(c) loss sustained after Dec. 31, 2007, and who are otherwise eligible under the average gross receipts test. The

NOL must have arisen in a tax year ending in or beginning in 2008.

The election for the longer carryback period may be made on the original return by attaching a statement to a timely filed return and specifying the longer carryback period elected. If the tax year for the loss ended before Feb. 17, 2009, the taxpayer must make the election by the later of the due date (including extensions) or April 17, 2009. Alternately, the election can be made by filing an appropriate form and applying the carryback period selected.

The form must be filed no later than the later of six months after the due date (including extensions) for the tax return of the loss year or April 17, 2009. (Note that this date is ear lier than the typical due date for filing forms 1045 and 1139, which is within 12 months after the tax year of the NOL.) The taxpayer does not need to file a statement or label with the form. Taxpayers selecting the option of filing an amended return must file the return for the earliest tax year to which the taxpayer is carrying back the loss.

A taxpayer who elected to waive the carryback was required to file the revocation and new election no later than April 17, 2009. Unemployment compensation. For 2009, $2,400 of unemployment compensation is excluded from tax.

Taxpayers may deduct "qualified motor vehicle taxes," defined as state or local sales or excise taxes imposed on the purchase of a new qualified motor vehicle. The vehicle must be a passenger car, light truck or motorcycle weighing 8,500 pounds or less or a motor home. The vehicle must be acquired after Feb. 17, 2009, and before 2010. The deduction is limited to tax on the first $49,500 of the purchase price.

Taxpayers who itemize and elect to deduct general sales taxes rather than state and local income taxes may not claim the additional standard deduction for the vehicle sales tax. The deduction phases out for individuals with modified AG1 between $125,000 and $135,000 ($250,000 and $260,000 if married filing jointly). The deduction is also allowed for alternative minimum tax (AMT) purposes if claimed as a standard deduction. Guidance is needed on whether the deduction is allowed for AMT when the taxpayer itemizes deductions.

Limitation on Itemized Deductions

In a news release April 7, 2009, the IRS said convenience fees associated with the electronic payment of federal tax, including payment of estimated tax, can be deducted as a miscellaneous itemized deduction (IR-2009-37). This reversed a previous policy Accordingly, taxpayers who are able to file Form 1040, Schedule A, Itemized Deductions, and deduct miscellaneous deductions exceeding 2% of their adjusted gross income (AGI) will get a tax deduction for these fees.

Credit or debit card convenience fees charged for paying taxes electronically vary but average about 2.5% of the tax payment. The fees are deductible in the year they occur. Most individuals still pay their federal tax obligations by check, but last year more than 4 million taxpayers paid their taxes electronically, according to the news release.

CHILD TAX CREDIT

While the amount of the child tax credit remains at $1,000 per dependent child under age 17, under the ARRA, the refundable portion is increased for tax years 2009 and 2010 to the extent of 15% of the taxpayer's earned income over $3,000 (lowered from $8,500). Beginning in tax year 2009, a child who qualifies for the child tax credit must also be the taxpayer's dependent.

Hope credit. For tax years beginning after Dec. 31, 2008, the section 25A Hope credit, renamed the American Opportunity Tax Credit by the ARRA, is increased to a maximum of $2,500 per year (100% of the first $2,000 of qualifying expenses and 25% of the next $2,000), with 40% of the credit refundable.

The credit is phased out for taxpayers with AGI between $80,000 and $90,000 ($160,000 and $180,000 for married filing jointly). The provision extended the credit to all four years of college and expanded the definition of qualifying expenses to include course materials. The Treasury Department is directed to study and report within one year of enactment on how to coordinate the section 25A education credits (including the Lifetime Learning Credit) with the federal Pell Grant programme and the feasibility of requiring students to perform community service in return for the credits.

Energy credits: The ARRA introduced or extended a range of energy tax incentives for individuals and businesses, including credits for energy efficiency equipment and building components, plug-in electric drive vehicles (section 30D) and renewable energy production.

Earned income credit: For tax years 2009 and 2010, the earned income tax credit percentage for families with three or more qualifying children is increased from 40% to 45%.

First-time homebuyer credit: For home purchases after Dec. 31, 2008, and before Dec. 1, 2009, the ARRA increased the amount of the first-time homebuyer credit from $7,500 to $8,000 ($4,000 for married taxpayers filing separately). A first-time homebuyer is an individual who had no ownership interest in a principal residence in the United States during the three-year period ending on the date of the purchase of the home to which the credit applies. Further, taxpayers who remain in the home for 36 months are not required to repay the credit. In any case, no amount is required to be recaptured after the death of the taxpayer. The credit phases out for individuals with AGI between $75,000 and $95,000 ($150,000 to $170,000 AGI for joint fliers).

The taxpayer may elect to treat a purchase during 2009 as made on Dec. 31, 2008, so it may be claimed on a 2008 amended return (the AG1 limitations would then be based on 2008 information). Notice 2009-12, 2009-6 IRB 446, explains how to divide the credit when two or more unmarried individuals purchase the principal residence. The notice provides several examples on how to claim the credit.

MAKING WORK PAY CREDIT

New section 36A allows a credit of the lesser of 6.2% of an individual's earned income or $400 ($800 for married filing jointly). Earned income for these purposes includes net earnings from self-employment that are includable in taxable income, as well as combat pay excluded from gross income under section 112. Effective for tax years 2009 and 2010, the credit is intended to offset an individual's share of FICA on the first $6,452 of earnings. The credit is phased out at a 2% rate for individuals whose modified AGI exceeds $75,000 ($150,000 for married filing jointly). The credit is not available to nonresident aliens, individuals who may be claimed as a dependent by another taxpayer, or any estate or trust. It may be claimed through a reduction in wage withholding or in a lump sum on the tax return filed for the year the wages were earned.

8

Service Development and Design

Research studies abound with information concerning variables with statistically significant influence on worker retention and/or commitment. Despite all we know about the commitment and retention of workers,"many firms (still lack) the capacity to find and keep workers."Financial compensation, although very important; is not the only mason that employees have less than lasting attachments to certain work environments.

More research analysis addressing the relationship between commitment of workers and politics, as well as commitment and value congruency (between workers and their organizations), might provide a better understanding of workers'commitment to work organizations.

Theories and explanations of organizational life are often times based on metaphors that lead us to see and understand organizations in distinctive, yet partial ways. The selected metaphor determines the particular aspect of the organization that will be analysed. For example, the view of an organization as an organism will focus our attention on recognizing the importance of the external environment and the need for organizations to operate as"open systems."Within the context of this metaphor we are interested in how organizations develop, survive, and adapt to changing environments. On the other hand, when an organization is viewed as a brain, a researcher would be more interested in how information is processed. The"organizations as brains"image leads one to focus on cybernetics and holographic systems within the workplace.

This chapter, however, is written with the image of organizations as values (cultures) and political systems. These hypothesized variables are predicted to have strong influences on the commitment of workers.

Politics and power straggles are"woven into the life"of organizations; they are endemic to the structures, processes and behaviours of organizations. Political behaviour occurs for many reasons: ambiguous goals, scarce resources, technology and the environment, non-programmed decisions, and organizational change. Competition over scarce resources is perhaps the most common reason for political behaviour, however.

Contrary to the belief of some organizational theorists, workers are not motivated by one unified goal only. The internal political nature of organizations is a function of diverse and competitive demands. We all come to work situations with many diverse goals, which in turn, cause conflict and competition among workers for the expenditure of scarce resources. Political activity in organizations is associated with the distribution of resources and other advantages for selfish gains.

Organizational politics do not always result in negative consequences. Wamsley and Zald provide a neutral definition of the term. They posit that politics refers"to the structure and process of the use of authority and power to effect definitions of goals, directions, other major parametres of the organization..."Madison et al. also defined organizational politics in neutral terms.

They posited that politics is"a process of influence or the `management of influence'..."Politics can serve a number of important functions, both good and bad. Politics, when used to resolve conflict, is viewed as the art of creative compromise among competing interests, and therefore a good thing. However, this study is concern with the more common and negative image of organizational politics. More often than not, the word"politics"is likely to bring about images of illicit deals, pay-offs, favours, and/or special personal relationships. Concepts of favouritism and nepotism are likewise associated with organizational politics. It is common to describe politics in terms of"games,"involving subterfuge and deceit, played by individuals and/or groups. Such games are played for the purpose of promoting"self-interests"and/or special interests.

Mayes and Allen defined politics as,"the management of influence to obtain ends not sanctioned by the organization or to obtain sanctioned ends through nonsanctioned influence means."Each of these definitions, either in part or as a whole, has some relevance to this research. This author has defined politics as"those activities that are performed for reasons other than organizational efficiency and/or effectiveness."Similar to Mintzberg's understanding of politics, the author's defines the term as a measure of illegitimate, unethical, and arbitrary personnel practices. Mintzberg explained that:

The system of politics... may be described as reflecting power that is technically illegitimate (or, perhaps more accurately `alegitimate')... [Political behaviour in organizations is] neither formally authorized, widely accepted, nor officially certified. As a result, political behaviour is typically divisive and conflictive, often pitting individuals or groups against formal authority, accepted ideology, and/or certified expertise, or else against each other.

In addition to descriptions of illegitimate, unethical, and arbitrary, when studied within a partisan context, politics refers to"that which is in the interest of the strongest party."Partisan politics defines those behaviours that serve special interest. The antonym for the concept of politics is"political neutrality."Political neutrality is a dominant value in public administration and personnel management; it provides for the general interest.

A politically neutral bureaucracy is a value that in public administration theory, at least, is believed to be implicit in the role of public policy implementers--in the role of career public servants. For the most part, the contemporary notion of"political neutrality,"grew out of the civil service reform movement of the late 1800s (which resulted in the Pendleton Act of 1883). Politics in administration or the mixing of partisanship and personnel was believed to not only result in inefficient government, but the fostering of corruption and decay as well. The mixture of personnel and partisanship was seen as the perversion of public interest and thought to result in the promotion of narrow partisan interests.

In public administration, the managerial prospective of government embodies the belief that partisan politics does not have a legitimate place in the vast majority of public personnel and administrative decisions.

The functions of the public administration (for example, transportation, policing, street paving, etc.) have much to do with the public interest and very little to do with the immediate interests of political parties.

Wilson believed that an effective administration is one that is politically neutral. Politically neutrality is a value in federal government. Do senior executives share this value? If so, what weight does this fact have on their level of commitment?

The research questions are:

- Does value congruency between workers, more specifically, senior executive members, and the work environment improve workers' levels of commitment.
- Is there a positive and significant relationship between the degree of importance executives place on their levels of commitment and the concept of a politically neutral work environment?

The "organizations as culture" metaphor is important to understand because an agency's culture and values can have a great affect on the quality of work life experienced by the members, and therefore their levels of commitment. Organizational culture is defined as "the system of shared actions, values, and beliefs that develops within an organization and guides the behaviour of its members."

- Among the three important levels of cultural analysis in organizations (i.e., observable culture, shared values, and common assumptions), the shared value component is of most interest in this study. My hypothesis: "The greater the importance that individual members attach to the politically neutral value, and the greater will be their commitment," is based on the belief that this shared value (between senior executives and the federal government) are the dominant factors contributing to commitment.

The sample population in this research is comprised of both career and political executives. Both political appointees and career executives play significant roles in each Presidential administration.

They both are needed in the federal government to ensure a strong executive leadership system. Political appointees, (also referred as "in-and outers"), who are in government for shorter periods of time, relative to the career executives, are expected to be committed to the President's agenda and philosophy.

Theoretically, they bring new ideas and perspectives to government. However, the short tenure of political appointees is one reason why the ratio of political appointees and career executives must be kept at an appropriate balance. It is important to ensure that the ratio of career executives to political appointees allows for programme continuity and policy advocacy in the management of public programmes. Career executives are needed for expertise and continuity.

The fact that increased numbers of political appointees undermine the managerial capacity of government is a second and more important reason that the number of political appointees and career executives must be balanced. By definition, political appointees have political agendas, as opposed to agendas designed to provide services and programmes for "that which is in the general public's interest." The Report and Recommendations of the National Commission on the Public Service maintained that:

The clear and coherent transmission of the President's policies through his own appointees to the career level becomes progressively difficult as the number of Presidential appointees increases... Layering the civil services with even more political appointees would only serve to widen the gulf between the chiefs and the Indians.

On the other hand, the Career executives, who make-up 90% of the Senior Executive Service (and this sample population), have long tenures with the federal government.

They have institutional memory and a knowledge base of laws and regulations governing the programmes that they must run. Their memory and experiences with the practicality and/or feasibility of programmes can provide very helpful and cost-efficient information for those who might consider implementing similar programmes.

They have been government employees an average of 20 years or more. Their long tenures have allowed them more opportunity to be socialized with the values of government, that is, more opportunity to be embodied with the politically neutral value. Because of the large number of career executives included in this study, it is predicted that the majority will attach great importance to the "political neutrality" value.

A survey questionnaire was developed to measure the effects of politics and values on the commitment levels of members of the Senior Executive Service. A 5-point Likert instrument was used to quantify the respondents' answers for both the independent and dependent variables.

INDEPENDENT VARIABLE: THE "POLITICALLY NEUTRAL" VALUE

It was predicted that the degree of importance that the executives' attached to the concept of political neutrality will be significantly and positively correlated with commitment. The concept of "political neutrality" is inherited in the practices and culture of career executives. As was previously discussed, "political neutral" is an inherit organizational value in government. The degree of importance that executives attach to this value, then, indicates value congruency between federal government as an organization and the executives.

The following three objectives, taken from the goals used to established the Senior Executive Service, under the 1978 Civil Service Reform Act (CSRA), were used to operationalize the political neutrality concept:

- Protecting senior executives from arbitrary and capricious actions.
- Ensuring that the ratio of career executives to political appointees allows for programme continuity and

policy advocacy in the management of public programmes.
- Providing for an executive system that is guided by the public interest and free from improper political interference.

The executives' response scores had a range from 0-3 (meaning "Very Unimportant") to 13-15 (indicating a "Very Important") response.

INDEPENDENT VARIABLE: POLITICS

The research question was: Does politics have a significant and negative affect on the commitment levels of the senior executives? A significant and negative relationship between the politics and commitment variables was hypothesized. The "politics" variable investigated executives' experiences (both personal and those they witnessed) with arbitrary personnel practices.

To answer the question, the researcher employed a Likert scale with responses ranging from "Never Happened to me" (numerical range from 0-5) to "Happened to me many Times" (numerical range from 21-25), which the executives used in response to the following statements:
- Shelving an executive by detailing or reassigning him/her to duties not of an executive nature.
- Trying to force an executive to resign.
- Arbitrarily lowering an executive's performance rating.
- Artificially structuring a reduction-in-force in order to remove a specific executive.
- Arbitrarily demoting an executive.

The "P-EX" variable measured executives' personal experiences with such practices, while the "W-EX" variable measured those negative behaviours that executive members witnessed. Cronbach's alphas were 0.8530 and 0.8558, respectively, for the P-EX and W-EX variables.

DEPENDENT VARIABLE: COMMITMENT

Commitment, the dependent variable, was measured by

using a short version (9-items) of the Mowday, Steers and Porter's instrument. This variable has a reliability coefficient of 0.8957. The concept of commitment is defined as "the strength of an individual's identification with and involvement in an organization."

Examples of statements used to operationalize this variable were as follows: I put forth a great deal of effort beyond that normally expected in order to help this organization be successful. I would accept almost any type of job assignment in order to keep working for this organization. I am proud to tell others that I'm part of this organization.

The "commitment" scale had a possible composite point range from 0-9 (meaning no commitment) to 37-45 (representing extremely strong commitment) for each executive member. The independent variables were politics and a cultural value. Sample Population

A random sample of about 942 senior executives from government's 14 cabinet departments comprised the sample population. The respondents were predominately white males: 90.7% men and 93% white. Approximately, 50% were between 46 and 55 years of age, with the age of 51-55 being the most frequently occurring category. More than 97% of the total sample population held career positions, and less than 3% were political appointees.

STATISTICAL ANALYSIS

Univariate analysis, Pearson's product-moment correlations, and regression analysis were the statistical procedures used to determine the effect of the independent variables on the dependent variable. For each respondent, the numbers representing each response to each independent variable item were added, which resulted in a single summary score for each independent variable. (Each respondent had one summary score for each variable.) The summary scores for all respondents on both independent variables were then correlated with the dependent variable.

On the commitment scale, the respondents had mean and median scores of 34.878 and 36.00, respectively. Most executives (812 or 86%) were either "extremely strongly committed" or "strongly committed" to federal government. Only 102 (or ~11%) were only moderately committed. And although a very few (~2.3%) had a low commitment to government, there was no one who was not committed at all.

The mean, median, and mode for this variable were 5.782, 5.0 and, 5.0, respectively. In terms of their personal experiences, only one (1) person out of 942 reported having many or several experiences respectively, with politics. However there were 11 persons (or 1.12%) who reported more than one personal experience with politics. Although the majority of respondents (593) had not had a negative political experience, 325 (or 35%) responded that they have had at least one personal experience with politics!

WITNESSED POLITICS (W-EX)

To re-iterate, W-EX variable measured the frequency with which executives' witnessed the use of arbitrary personnel practices being used on others within their departments. The mean, median, and mode scores, respectively, were 10.317, 9.0, and 5.0. There were 58 out of 942 (6.2%) executives who had witnessed negative political behaviour targeted toward others either several or many times. Eighty persons (or 8.5%) in the sample had seen such behaviour more than once, while 140 (or 14.9%) had witnessed such behaviour at least one time. What is very interesting to note is the number of executives who simply refused to answer the question (missing information). In response to their personal experiences with politics, only 11 persons would not answer the question, while 598 executives did not share information regarding the witnessing of political behaviour. The 598 missing cases under this category does not mean that the executives never witness others as targets (there were 66 or 7% of the respondents who said that they never saw others being victimized); these 598 missing cases simply mean that those in our sample would not "speak up" about the negative experiences of others! I suspect that this missing information is related to fear of retaliate politics. Confirmation of this hypothesis, however, goes beyond the scope of this investigation. The mean, median, and mode scores for this variable were 13.861, 14.00, 15.00, respectively. Ninety-eight per cent of the sample population felt that this value was either "very important" or "important."

Two facts provided evidence that there was value congruency between the federal government as a workplace and the senior executives. As was previously discussed, in theory, the culture of the federal includes the political neutrality value. Additionally, there was high percentage of executives who felt that political neutrality was important in public administration.

PEARSON'S PRODUCT-MOMENT CORRELATIONS AND MULTIPLE REGRESSIONS

The coefficient correlations (r) between commitment, the politics variables (P-EX, W-EX), and the politically neutral value were all statistically significant. Both hypotheses relative to these variables were supported. There was a negative and significant relationship between commitment and the P-EX variable: $r = -0.2791$, $p = 0.000$. And a similar relationship was discovered between commitment and W-EX variable: $r = -0.3510$, $p = 0.000$. Also as hypothesized, there was a positive and statistically significant relationship between commitment and the importance of the political neutrality value.

The multiple regression analysis resulted in a coefficient of determination (r square) at the 0.2270 level, $p < 0.001$. In other words, the independent variables accounted for ~23% of the variance in the commitment variable. The more politics executives either personally experienced or witnessed, the less were their commitment levels. Those personnel practices, such as "arbitrarily demoting or lowering executives' performance rating," and/or "trying to force them to resign," demonstrates abuse of power.

These practices would, no doubt, negatively affect the self-esteem of these executives and would most assuredly induce anxiety, insecurity, and stress in their lives. Such negative emotional states will not improve commitment of workers. While it is virtually impossible to eradicate political behaviour in organizations, its dysfunctional consequences can be reduced. The reasons that it occurs, as well as the techniques used, must be addressed. Analysis of these two factors can help with the establishment of personnel rules and regulations that are designed to reduce or completely eliminate certain political practices. The negative impact of ugly politics on commitment is not surprising. The most significant contribution of this research has to do with the relationship of public service values and motivation theory.

This study has made two major contributions to the work of Perry and Wise and Wise (2000). First, it has responded to a request for research that develops new methods to operationalize and measure public service motivation. In this study, the "politically neutral" construct provided an operationalization of the three public service motives described by Perry and Wise. Secondly, the author developed a methodology that possibly enhances one's understanding of how public service motivation contributes to organizational commitment. The methodological design is an innovation in and of itself.

The positive relationship between political neutrality and commitment is also significant information because of its implications for organizational productivity. There is a significant and positive relationship between productivity and commitment. Therefore, knowing what influences commitment also helps one to understand what affects performance.

Public service motives of civil servants embody personal and professional values. Perry and Wise identified and categorized three (3) public service motives: rational, norm-based, and affective motives. Evidence of a rational motive was demonstrated by the importance of the one of three 3 variable items that operationalized the political neutrality construct. The variable item that addressed, "protecting senior executives from arbitrary and capricious actions" embodied executives' self-interest (i.e., a rational motive). The implementation of this particular objective could provide protection and security for these managers.

The norm-based motives were measured with the following variable items:

- Ensuring that the ratio of career executives to political appointees allows for programme continuity and policy advocacy in the management of public programmes.
- Providing for an executive system that is guided by the public interest and free from improper political interference.

Those who have a norm-based motive for public service have a sense of responsibility and duty to government. The implementation of the above goals would embody altruistic behaviour, i.e. "a desire to serve the public interest." Based on this study, these goals are important to the executives. It is inherent in their value system.

This research supports Wise's propositions relative to behavioural implications of public service motivation. That is, the greater the strength of ones public service motive (in this case, the importance that executives attached to the political neutrality value), the more likely they are to engage in behaviours that benefit the general public.

The implementation of public service goals is a function of the embodiment of the political neutrality value; that is, those who value political neutrality are more prone toward behaviours that exemplify public interest outcomes. From a psychological perspective, a persons values and beliefs are major determinants of behaviours. Through deductive reasoning then, one can conclude that the executives' embodiment of the political neutrality value will lead them toward public interest behaviours.

In this study, commitment was operationalize as an affective motive. Those with affective motives engage in certain behaviours because of their emotions (e.g., love) and/or commitment to certain goals or programmes. As was previously discussed, most executives (812 or 86%) reported that they had either "extremely strong commitment" or "strong commitment" to the federal government, and the commitment variable was structured to included items that measured love of and loyalty to government. An analysis of the public service motives directs one to question an issue surrounding the individual—organization match: Were the executives embodied with the politically neutral value before coming to the federal government or were they inculcated with this motive by the culture during their longevity in government?

As was previously discussed, Woodrow Wilson, as the "creator" of the public administration discipline, envisioned a politically neutral governmental structure. Secondly, personnel structures, dating as far back as the Pendleton Act of 1883, were designed to reduce and/or eliminate politics from administration. And third, personnel management theorists argue in favour of a political neutral bureaucracy for the purpose of an ethical and effective government.

All of these facts suggest that a politically neutral culture (mission and purpose) is a dominant value influencing behaviours in government. Most of the sample population had been in the federal government between 20 and 25 years, which gave them ample exposure to socialization processes designed to inculcate this value. The culture and value systems of public bureaucracies affect the values of its employees. Wise contends:

Contextual factors related to individual actors, situations, events, and the organization in which behaviour occurs influence the strength of public service motivation. Organizational policies and practices may account for variations within the public sector in the strength of public motives.

Perry and Wise also postulate that "the greater an individual's public service motivation, the more likely the individual will seek membership in a public organization." Oldham and Hackman provided some empirical support for the general attraction-selection framework implied by this proposition. Therefore, arguments can be made on both sides of the questions. Most likely the individual's value system determines his/her initial interest in a particular work situation, then once employed, the organizational culture strengthens these values. In conclusion, the implications of this study are for career planning and placement, and selection and recruitment of workers.

This study has demonstrated strong correlations between value congruency and commitment. Commitment, on the other hand, also strongly correlates with productivity. These two facts suggest value congruency between employees and employers may greatly enhance productivity. Therefore, when possible, organizations should recruit those individuals who share their values. Such persons may be less dependent on utilitarian incentives to motivate their performance. And likewise, in the interest of their own career planning and future level of job-satisfaction, job seekers should include an assessment of their values and pursue those organizations whose cultures embody their professional and/or personal values.

The learning styles of the present generation of students benefit from a concrete, socially contextual learning mode. But it seems a challenge for this same generation of students to transfer learning from one course to another. In response to these findings, interior design students were assigned distinctive problems within the same experiential learning project for two courses, with the aim of connecting the content and coordinating the classes so as to enhance the learning experience.

The Institute for Experiential Learning (IEL) states that experiential learning is composed of three elements: knowledge, activity, and reflection and that it involves students as active and intentional learners. This experiential learning model was incorporated into the problem-solving process for each course.

Moreover, it was thought that an on-campus project could serve as a course transformation tool for future off-campus service-learning activities. This study presents comments on student and team learning and value-added bonuses. The on-campus experiential learning project referenced is the restoration/renovation of a historically significant campus building.

The educational philosophy of experiential learning was first advanced in the late 19th century and has since been expressed through cooperative education, internships, field experiences, and service-learning in many disciplines. It is central in the current renaissance of federal and school interest in service-learning and school-to-work programmes. Furthermore, educational psychologists indicate that the more active our learning, the more we retain. Psychologists go on to confirm that at the heart of experiential learning is the dialogue between theory and practice.

The learning theories of Dewey and Kolb contend that the cycle of learning is composed of these essential components: concrete experience, observation and reflection, forming abstract concepts, and testing in new situations.

David A. Kolb, a contemporary advocate of experiential learning, is most well known on the subject of experiential learning and learning styles. Kolb's scientific model helped move educational thought from the focus on the instructor back to the learner. Experiential learning has become a viable topic of discussion as pointed out by many of the major contributors to the field.

Peter Jarvis used Kolb's model to develop another experiential learning illustration in which nonlearning, nonreflective, and reflective learning were identified as different forms or routes in learning situations. Reflective learning traced out trajectories of contemplation, reflective practice, and experiential leaning in his diagram. Interior design faculties are no strangers to experiential learning.

One cannot learn the complexities of the discipline without extensive design studio projects. Furthermore, graduating students must demonstrate significant skill in the design and development of sophisticated projects.

Faculty support experiential learning opportunities in the corporate world through cooperative education or internship components that allow students to earn academic credit for professional experience.

Where experiential learning is well integrated, students demonstrate a greater understanding of the complexity of real-world problems than those without field experiences. There is a necessity for students majoring in interior design to have a variety of experiences that simulate work-related projects and processes. Such experiences mean that students are better equipped to analyse and respond to the workplace as they move from academia to the interior design profession. "Interior design includes a scope of services performed by a professional design practitioner, qualified by means of education, experience, and examination, to protect and enhance the life, health, safety, and welfare of the public".

Practicing professionals refer to actual experiences when presenting lessons and assignments in the classroom. On the other hand, experiential learning illuminates for students the complexity of real-world situations and the many layers of issues that must be taken into account when designing interior spaces.

The approach of experiential learning through service is consistent with the recent change in paradigm in education from a focus on teaching to a focus on learning. Undergraduate programmes based in service-learning provide a structure in which students and faculty can learn and develop through active participation within a university and its local community.

Wolf contends that the most successful professional programmes are those with experience in service-learning. A service learning philosophy asserts that it is the interface between academic disciplines and the wider community that shapes the future of higher education in the next millennium.

A current trend in education recommends objectives that expose students to experiential learning and challenge them through service-learning.

Eyler and Giles argue that service students became more thoughtful and effective, that they had obtained a deeper, more complex understanding of issues and felt more confident about using what they had learned than students with no service-learning experience.

Servicelearning has become one of the most powerful tools available for integrating experiential learning, professional training, civic responsibility, and responsiveness into higher education. The IEL promotes the application of knowledge, action, and reflection in all experiential learning. So that reflection is not overlooked, Brookfield encourages "praxis," thereby:...ensuring that opportunities for the interplay between action and reflection are available in a balanced way for students.

Praxis means that curricula are not studied in some kind of artificial isolation, but that ideas, skills, and insights learned in a classroom are tested and experienced in real life. Essential to praxis is the opportunity to reflect on experience, so that formal study is informed by some appreciation of reality.

Jacoby stated that reflection is an essential component of service-learning. He defined the goal of student participation in reflection as "promoting [sic] learning about the larger social issues behind the needs to which their service is responding. This learning includes a deeper understanding of the historical, sociological, cultural, economic, and political contexts of the needs or issues being addressed".

The Centre for Public Service and Community Engagement (CPSCE) at Indiana State University (ISU) asserts that service-learning consists of core principles that should engage students in meeting the unmet needs of communities, and enhance students' academic learning, their sense of social responsibility, and their civic skills. In a discipline-based service learning course, students provide service throughout the semester and reflect on their experiences using course content as a basis of analysis.

This qualitative study was prompted by the need for a better understanding of service-learning for the interior design discipline.

The research question is: What are the challenges in making discipline-based service learning education standard practice in interior design? At a 4-year interior design degree programme accredited by the Council for Interior Design Accreditation located in the midwestern United States, three-credit-hour courses in Materials and Finishes of Interior Design and Interior Lighting and Color Theory are taught once a year.

ON-CAMPUS PROJECT

It was believed that a classic historic campus building would capture the students' imagination and was, therefore, selected prior to the beginning of fall classes as the experiential learning project. Situated in the midst of landscaped campus grounds is the original library building. The neoclassical building was constructed of Indiana limestone with the front of the building highlighted by four fluted ionic pilasters and a large projecting cornice capping the structure. The building's interior features a rotunda and colorful dome of opalescent art glass. To study the best use for the building and apply to the National Register of Historic Places both with the National Park Service and the State, the university retained a prominent state architectural firm. The instructor collaborated with the university archivist on the restoration/adaptive reuse of the building.

This arrangement was ideal because the best topics emerge when a community group solicits help in a problem that it has identified. The project was introduced with a description of what was to be accomplished and the students were informed that they were scheduled to give a presentation of their design solutions at the end of the semester. The students were to prepare a design presentation for all architectural finishes for the materials course and a lighting concept and layout for the lighting course. The practicum project description included the restoration of the front steps and the re-creation of the ground entrance as it was in 1910. The restoration was to return the rotunda and dome to the design executed by Alexander and Son, the original architects for the building.

The volunteer sample for this study consisted of 16 students enrolled in the materials course and 15 students in the lighting course in the fall semester of 2001. Of these, eight were enrolled in both courses. Students in each course formed seven design teams for the campus project. Teams in the materials course were composed of one student registered in both courses and one enrolled in the materials class. Student team formations in the lighting course were based on the same criterion. Provided the team formation criterion was in place, students were free to choose their teammates. Teams were directed to be particularly sensitive to the interrelationship between material and color selections, and lamp recommendations for the architectural envelope. Student teams individually interviewed the university archivist, and developed materials, finishes, and lighting concepts in response to key functional areas on two levels of the three-story building.

Goals

The goals of this service-learning experience were to broaden, extend, and deepen the intellectual content by:

- Integrating theory and practice in material specifications and lighting design.
- Increasing students'motivation to engage in academic work through the experience of applying knowledge.

Additional aspirations included encouraging students to develop skills as independent thinkers and researchers, and incorporate team approaches to design solutions (cooperate in research, provide frequent feedback to one another, support one another when blocks arose. Further aims were to include interactions between clients and jurors, demonstrate the understanding of design fundamentals, and theories of human behaviour in interior environments, and link learning, thinking, and doing.

Other expected outcomes included: gain sufficient knowledge of the subject matter in respective courses to solve real-life problems, enhance motivation and active learning, and provide experiences with serving others in the university community. Further anticipated results consisted of: more practical application of interior design principles covered in the courses, sensitivity to the sociological and environmental consequences of design decisions, and application of"good design practice"by treating the participants as"clients"to achieve quality improvement.

Knowledge

Knowledge may be defined as concepts, facts,

information, and prior experience in the context of experiential learning. Throughout the seven weeks allocated for class projects, exams were written based on text content and lectures/presentations on relevant subject matter.

Five manufacturers'representatives provided the industry's viewpoint on a number of products in the materials class. Two principals from a lighting design firm came to the lighting studios, critiqued student projects, and provided perspectives from the viewpoint of the professional lighting consultant. Technical experts are always needed to provide advice during the design process. Arranging for such briefings ahead of time for class proved helpful.

The knowledge variable was measured through the results of three exams per course, one professional lighting critique per team of work-in progress by two practicing professionals, a practicum evaluation sheet, and the researcher's notes.

Activity

Activity may be defined as knowledge applied to current, ongoing events (WII, 2004). Based on interviews with the model client, student teams prepared presentation floor plans, which identified key functional areas, and illustrated material and lighting design applications for the building. Using graphics, written annotations, material samples, and catalogue cuts, recommendations for restoring the facility were organized.

The activity variable was measured through the quality of the practicum presentations as rated on a practicum evaluation sheet. Presentation packages for each course consisted of a specification or documentation booklet, and three presentation boards. Material and lighting solutions were presented on different days; however, teams orally cross-referenced solutions.

Reflection

Reflection may be defined as thoughtful analysis and assessment of one's own activity and its contribution to personal growth. Reflection needs to be a significant element in experiential courses because reflection is the most commonly accepted and used approach to facilitate the conceptual connections of service-learning. Common tools of reflection include journals, daily logs, simulations, small-group discussions, and focused conversations. Because reflection is a critical factor in the discovery and internalization of knowledge, it began at the onset of the programming phase and was integral to the entire problem-solving process for each of the design solutions.

The reflection variable was measured through the researcher's notes on small-group discussions, students'notes on focused conversations, and the results of reading and writing assignments. The learners were provided with a variety of structured and unstructured activities, such as the written and verbal historical justification of material and lighting recommendations.

Qualitative data was collected and emerging themes identified through interviews, focus groups after the completion of each design phase, observations during fieldtrips and professional critiques, self-evaluations, peer evaluation sheets and comments, studio practicum evaluation sheets, videotapes of the students' presentations, and Student Instructional Reports (SIRs) administered at the conclusion of the semester.

Themes looked for included: knowledge, action, reflection, time management skills, aptitude for risk-taking, organization, team performance, professional objectivity versus subjectivity, observation skills, critical thinking, communication, and investigation of designs. For example, each team member evaluated their teammates using five categories on a peer evaluation sheet using a low-to-high range of measure. Time management issues were prevalent in the majority of the findings. The teams worked together either extremely poorly or extremely efficiently, and written comments revealed more personal like or dislike toward their teammates as opposed to objective reasoning.

Practicum projects were evaluated using an evaluation instrument with a rating range of low to high, consistent with the range of measure used in the peer evaluation instrument.

The instructor, students, and jury members completed an evaluation sheet for each student team. The criterion categories addressed all of the themes in this investigation.

Peer and jury evaluations formed a part of the final grade for the practicum assignment portion of these two sophomore and junior courses. The jury was made up of the University Archivist, Director Construction/Planning Services, University Architect, and Associate Vice-President University Facilities Management. The elements of knowledge, activity, and reflection were considered within the on-campus experiential learning project to create a value-added experience. Through self-evaluations and comments, the majority of the students stated that the project was "awesome." This response was part of the qualitative nonscale feedback collected from student comments on their self-evaluations. Integrating experiential learning for an on-campus project into sophomore and junior level design studios for materials and finishes, and lighting problem-solving resulted in the following findings on student and team learning.

The students had valuable lessons on building codes, politics, technology, Americans with Disability Act (ADA), and presentation issues. For example, when working on a historical building, there is an obvious need to balance protecting the historical character of a building and interior space and providing an acceptable level of safety. Some student teams found it necessary to discuss alternatives with the local officials, and other teams proposed a code variance.

This representation addressed the goal of broadening, extending, and deepening intellectual content within this experiential learning activity. Because the students were involved in the designing of a complex environment, they honed their technical and creative skills, and advanced their skills analyzing a problem while addressing a campus community need. Based on the peer evaluations, the students as team members learned to appreciate the complex social dynamics associated with group projects and developed skills to appreciate the importance of oral and visual expression in persuading both teammates and the client.

Each team member brought her/his own ideas into the team, but after discussions and deliberation these individual ideas were commonly reshaped into a strong group solution. This experience taught most team members that the whole (team solution) is stronger than its parts (individual solutions). One student's statement during the team presentation, "Our concept is to implement 21st century technology in such a way that it is sympathetic to the history of the building," supports the understanding of the need for advanced technology in balance with restoration issues.

Activity

The students asked questions and gained presentation practice in a kind of community forum. In an interview for the local city newspaper, one junior student stated that she had no regrets for the extra hours she spent working on her plans for the building.

The process took her and her partner a semester, she said. "We did interviews, walked through the building so many times I didn't even keep track, did lots of sketches, did a lot of math.... It was a big project. It really took up a lot of our time outside of class to figure out how to restore the building."

Reflection

Through small-group discussions, a question emerged: "Why does this university not have a welcome centre?" Both the model client and students concluded that the main floor of the restored project could provide an ideal location for a welcome centre.

As a result of team structure, students began to understand the nature of a cooperative team effort, discovered that defining goals and tasks and meeting deadlines in a team project are very different from the usual experience as independent students.

Students now have experience in working in teams, which has taught them to consider utilizing the strengths and skills of other people. Students were unanimous in their comments, such as: "Too many people don't value historical importance.

There is so much potential here-so many avenues you can take with this building."

Value-Added Bonuses

The local city newspaper wrote a feature article describing a vision for the restoration of the campus building through interviews with the university archivist, course instructor, and interior design students. One team's suggestions for community uses for the project included, "junior high and high school proms, weddings, anniversary parties and all kinds of receptions. The possibilities are endless."

As the existence of service-learning projects has become known in the community, more and more potential clients have approached the interior design programme with suggestions for other projects.

For example, on-campus projects such as renovations to the University Library (Cunningham Memorial Library), Family and Consumer Sciences, Art Department, College of Arts and Sciences buildings, and off-campus projects such as a local downtown historic vaudeville theatre, bookstore, holocaust museum, and two churches have requested input for their projects.

The design studio projects met a university need and provided students with an experiential learning experience. Data was collected from such sources as professional critiques, researcher's notes on small-group discussions, students' notes on focused conversations, and quality of practicum presentations. Reoccurring issues based upon frequency were identified using these sources. Based on the exposure to experiential learning, some of the challenges in instituting service-learning as standard practice included: taking longer than usual to get started (time management issues), students' reluctance to risk the embarrassment of "not knowing," the appearance of chaos, widely varying team performance, subjective rather than objective analysis, and students needing to hone their skills in observation, experience more exercises in reflection, and experiment or test ideas before proceeding to the next design phase.

Coupling experiential learning with design across the curriculum offers an innovative pedagogy to achieving many of the must and should indicators described by the Council for Interior Design Accreditation in its accreditation manual (2006), including perpetuating a cycle of lifelong learning through knowledge, activity, and reflection, and developing the ability to create new kinds of knowledge. Plans are underway to continue experiential learning activities through off-campus discipline-based service-learning projects.

9

Positioning Maps

What is the competitive advantage that a product or a service has over the competitors? What makes it distinguishable from competitor's products or services? One way to identify competitors is through a perceptual mapping. In a perceptual map, products are compared based on how customers view a set of comparable products on quality and cost.

The perceptual map is derived from customer data measuring similarities among brands. Customers are asked to rate each pair of brands on a scale from similar to very dissimilar, which help find out how a product stands in comparison to competitors and decide whether to confront, compete, coexist or cooperate with them.

To be able to sustain in competitive advantage your products must be valuable for customers, not easy to imitate and profitable to sell. Successful products fulfill a high emotional value state, for instance OXO who evolved a single product called GoodGrips to a full line of products penetrating a significant market share. Motorola developed a major presence in the consumer product category with one new product, called the Talkabout.

In evaluating the value impact of these products, it is found that they were successful in communicating 'values' in key categories that connected them to their customers. Product positioning has an important role to play in product development. The product positioning refers to the set of features and value that is valued by the target customer audience, relative to competing products. It is about how you differentiate your product or service in the mind of your prospect.

When you position your product, especially in the established markets instead of creating products and services with distinctive advantage, the company can fall into trap of creating something, which is merely a duplication of the same product with identical characteristics. This is called a majority fallacy, which at the end often results in price wars.

Due to the changes of situation (in the market or internal organization) you may need to reposition your product or service and decide what direction going to move. It is not easy to do, especially when the company has something to lose, such as existing customers or other products.

Positioning is therefore an organized approach for finding a window in the mind of one's prospect in order to position effectively over there a product against its main competitors. This system is based on the concept that communication can only take place at the right time and under the right circumstances. The mind accepts only that new information which matches its current state. It filters out everything else. In other words, positioning is a process by which a psychological"anchor"has been placed into the minds of prospects so that they come to choose one specific person or company over another. The task is however a complex one which explains why so many products attempts fail.

Cagan and Vogel argues that there are three key factors that must be present to guarantee the highest potential of success. Ability to identify product opportunities. - As cultures continue to change, opportunities emerge for new products, which do not just solve existing problems but create possibilities for new experiences.

- Heightened understanding of the customer needs translated into actionable insights that define attributes. - These attributes serve as guides in developing products form and features that consumers quickly recognize as useful, usable and desirable.
- True integration of engineering, industrial design and

marketing which respects and appreciates perspective of each discipline.

The identification of product opportunities should be the core force that drives companies that manufacture products, provide services or process information. A product opportunity exists when there is gap between what is currently in the market and the possibility for new or significantly improved products that result form emerging trends. A product that successfully fills a Product Opportunity Gap (POG) is perceived as useful, usable and desirable. Identifying a POG requires a constant sweep of a number of factors in three major areas; social trends (S), economic forces (E) and technological advances (T).

The social factors include family and work patterns, consumption patterns, health issues, politics, sports and recreation etc. The economic factors focus on income that people perceive they have, or that they expect to have, to give them purchasing power. The technology factors focus on direct and imagined results from new scientific discoveries in corporate, military and university environments.

The process therefore starts with a scan of what Cagan and Vogel call SET factors: Social trends, Economic forces, and Technical advances, which open opportunities for new products. For example, the retro trend (social), ample disposable income (economic), and new materials and processes (technology) opened an opportunity that Mazda capitalized on with its Miata sports car. SET factors change constantly, so they can lead to new insights that were not apparent before. Similarly, changing SET factors explain how products go out of fashion and even how a product can appear before its time.

The next step is to detect in the SET factors some Product Opportunity Gaps. These POGs are a discrepancy between what is currently available on the market and what the SET factors suggest. Discovering POGs is part science and part art. When found, they lead to product opportunities. These SET factors generate opportunities for procuring new products that can have effect on the way people live their lives at any given moment. This goal is to create products and services by identifying emerging trends and to match that trend with the right technology and understanding of the purchasing dynamics.

Successful new products become necessary once they'hit'the market, which when will become instantly desirable. Coca cola has been able to maintain its position as the leading soft drink for the entire century. Baby dolls hitting the children's mind lasted decades. Hit factory in the field of music is another classic example. Once POGs are identified, the challenge become translating the POGs into the development of a new product or the significant modification of an existing product. Positioning maps shows how breakthrough products are differentiated from the competition.

The upper right quadrant of the map integrates the attributes of style and technology and adds a third dimension; Value. Style refers to the sensory and ergonomic elements of a product. It determines how well the product connects with the lifestyle of those in the target market. Technology refers to the functionality that enables the product to operate.

It can include mechanical, electrical, chemical, or software and it includes materials and manufacturing choices as well. Finally, value is"the level of effect that people personally expect from products and services, represented through lifestyle impact, enabling features, and ergonomics, which together result in a useful, usable, and desirable product."Useful means that the product satisfies a human need and is cost-effective, usable relates to ease of use, and desirable means that its attributes combine to make people want to own it.

Upper right products, services and companies merge style and technology in a way that creates strong customer value and promotes positive user experience. Strong brand, corporate values and connection to customer values lead to both short term and long term customer satisfaction. Many breakthrough products stay in the upper right through the constant injection of useful, usable and desirable features of the customer. Each remaining quadrant contains products that emphasize only style, technology or low cost. Through the integration of the attributes represented in the upper right, breakthrough products meet the needs, wants and desires of customers resulting in increased sales, profit and brand equity. This integration results in the creation of breakthrough products that are perceived as having high value.

The positioning maps show how different products in the same category can be located in a matrix with style and technology as the two axes. The third dimension, value, primarily exists in the upper right quadrant where companies make a concerted effort to integrate style and technology by responding to the needs of the customers. While this approach can lead to increased cost in production, the cost can often be easily returned with interest by establishing a higher price for the product, increased sales, increased interest in the company's product lines, or establishing or reaffirming a company's brand recognition. People pay more for quality and value of they feel they connect to their goals and aspirations.

The Motorola Talkabout is an example of product that converted a core technology into a useful upper right product. Prior to Talkabout, there were generic short-range consumer walky-talkies with minimal features, lifestyle impact, and less attention to ergonomics in the lower left. Motorola's core wireless communication technology, which was used for professional applications, was in the lower right. Motorola had to change the performance standards from its professional line to meet projected price points in the consumer market. When consumer's felt the resulting quality is still much higher than the competitors, Motorola had to increase the amount charge for the product over what they had originally targeted. However through careful cost reduction, they still maintained a high profit margin on this highly successful product, which still meets the needs of the market.

Some products possess ideal characteristics which is the characteristics that the target market most desires 'ideal'. The logic here is that whenever a group of consumers has a distinctive "ideal" for a product category, they represent a potential target market segment. A firm does well if its attributes (of the product) are perceived by consumers as being close to their ideal. The objective is to be "more ideal" than the competitors. Each product must provide some unique combination of new features desired by the target market. Instead of allowing the customer to position products independently, marketers try to influence and shape consumers concepts and perceptions.

BMW repositions up to the left and due to the exchange rate, Lexus moves to the right. They reposition because of safety, affordability and the competitors include Infiniti, Lexus, Mercedes Benz and Aurora.

Having said that, some of the conclusions related to the issues of Product Positioning can be summarily laid down as follows:

- Product positioning refers to the decisions and activities intended to create and maintain a certain concept of a product in the customers' minds.
- Marketers try to position a product so that it seems to possess the characteristics most desired by the target market.
- Product position is the result of customers' perceptions of a product's attributes relative to those of competing brands.
- Marketers sometimes analyse product positions by developing "perceptual maps." These are created by questioning a sample of consumers about their perceptions of products, brands, and organizations with respect to two or more dimensions.
- Using a perceptual map, marketers can compare how consumers perceive their brands compared to ideal points representing customer desires.

  Using a perceptual map, marketers can compare how consumers perceive their brands compared to ideal points representing customer desires.
- Positioning can be designed to compete head to head or to avoid it. Head-to-head positioning may be appropriate if the product's performance characteristics are at least equal to those of competitive brands, if the product is priced lower,

or even when the price is higher if the product's performance characteristics are superior. Positioning to avoid competition may be best when the product's performance characteristics do not differ significantly from competing brands, when the brand has unique characteristics, or when marketers want to keep a new brand from cannibalizing sales of their existing brands.

- If a product has been planned properly, its features and brand image will give it the distinct appeal needed. If buyers can easily identify the benefits, they are more likely to purchase the product.
- Evaluating the positions of existing products is important because a brand's market share and profitability may be strengthened by product repositioning.
- Repositioning can be accomplished by physically changing the product, its price, its distribution, or its promotion.

A one concluding remark; In his book 'Crossing the Chasm', Moore says that there is a chasm between the early adopters of the product (the technology enthusiasts and visionaries) and the early majority (the pragmatists). He argues that this is because visionaries and pragmatists have very different expectations. Moore attempts to explore those differences and builds from there to suggest techniques to successfully cross the "chasm", by choosing a target market, understanding the whole product concept including positioning the product.

SERVICESCAPE TYPES, SERVICESCAPE EFFECTS ON BEHAVIOUR

Servicescape is a concept that was developed by Booms and Bitner to emphasize the impact of the physical environment in which a service process takes place. If you were to try to describe the differences a customer encountered when entering a branch of say like McDonald's compared with a small family restaurant, the concept of servicescapes may prove useful. Booms and Bitner defined a servicescape as "the environment in which the service is assembled and in which the seller and customer interact, combined with tangible commodities that facilitate performance or communication of the service".

Servicescape may be likened to 'landscape'. It includes facilities exterior (landscape, exterior design, signage, parking, surrounding environment) and facilities interior (interior design and decor, equipment, signage, layout, air quality, temperature and ambiance). Servicescape along with other tangibles like business cards, stationary, billing statements, reports, employee dress, uniforms, brochures, web pages and virtual servicescape forms the 'Physical Evidence' in marketing of services.

Servicescape is not defined as above. The definition above is the definition for physical evidence. Physical evidence consist of servicescape combined with the tangible elements, so servicescape is a part of physical evidence.

10

Customer Service Strategies

The customer service study revealed that no specific tactic, technology, or mission statement is the key to effective customer service delivery. In fact, what is clear is that effective customer service delivery is organization specific, since services are designed around the targeted customers' desires and the frontline employees delivering the services.

The components of the process for producing effective customer service delivery include appropriately identifying and targeting the ideal customer, establishing a customer-focused vision that is consistent with the prioritized desires of the target customers, establishing the operational procedures and internal infrastructure that support customer service, continuously measuring customer and employee satisfaction, embracing change, and striving persistently to improve.

The customer service literature clearly demonstrates that both profit-seeking and public agencies that implement effective customer service strategies realise financial benefits, either through increased profits or through reduced costs associated with long-term, informed customers; customer referrals; employee retention; improved information exchange; and streamlined service delivery.

Child support enforcement, in this case, is like any other business. In order to implement effective customer service strategies and reap the benefits of good customer service, the Office of Child Support Enforcement (OCSE) agencies will need to implement the process of developing effective customer service.

In an effort to become "more results-oriented and responsive to customers," the Office of Child Support Enforcement (OCSE) contracted with Circle Solutions, Inc. to undertake a study of public and private sector practices and outcomes in customer service. The study included a review of customer service literature, a review of the annual reports and Web sites of 40 companies mentioned in the literature, telephone interviews with companies sited as leaders in customer service in the literature, and site visits to three agencies—two private and one child support agency.

Throughout the study, an advisory group of four State child support enforcement directors provided input and feedback. As a final product of the study, this report summarizes the literature on effective approaches to customer service delivery, highlights four promising practice case studies, conjectures about the transferability of these concepts to child support, and offers future research recommendations. Child support enforcement agencies can refer to this report as a guide for improving customer service, as a resource to learn the costs and benefits of effective customer service delivery, and to inspire future inquiries into effective customer service delivery.

In the 1990s, IBM conducted global research on the question, "What will keep CEOs and senior management awake at night as we begin the twenty-first century?" The study found that, regardless of the industry or geographic location, the most common response was a desire to generate a more customer-oriented culture or business vision.

Customer service is not merely customer relations or how nice frontline workers are to customers. Rather, satisfying or even delighting customers is the goal of excellent customer service. Because customers for different types of services have different needs, customer service strategies will differ and must be tailored to the target customer.

It improves trust and information exchange: In the public sector, including child support offices, good customer service generates satisfied or delighted customers. Satisfied customers lead to increased compliance, improved information exchange, improved relationships, increased trust, and, potentially, decreased workloads or costs. For instance, police departments across the Nation have embraced the concept of community policing. Through community policing, police departments incorporate a customer focus as well as an attitude of partnership with customers, to increase satisfaction and trust and even reduce fear of crime in the community. Customers actually participate in addressing crime and disorder problems, thus reducing the workload on patrol officers.

It saves money and increases profit: In the private sector, good customer service leads to satisfied or delighted customers, which generates customer loyalty, which produces increased revenues and reduced costs. For example, during the early 1990s, IBM transformed itself into a customer-driven organization. From 1994–1999, customer satisfaction increased by 5.5 per cent, revenue increased from $63 billion to over $80 billion, cost and expense savings equaled $7 billion, and stock prices improved over 1,000 per cent.

Upon becoming CEO of Greater Southeast Hospital, a private, nonprofit community hospital, Tom Chapman refocused customer service strategy to save the faltering hospital. Instead of trying to attract more clientele outside the community or turning away the uninsured in the community it served, under Chapman's leadership, Greater Southeast sought to provide better customer service—improving the quality of life and creating community-specific services. The emphasis shifted to treating people when it was cheapest—not in the emergency room but rather when their problems were minor—and to instituting preventative care.

He opened a clinic in the high school to address minor health issues and provide health education resources to teach students about prevention. Additionally, Mr. Chapman improved coordination with the local health clinic and obtained the specific technology from which patients served by the hospital would benefit. Before his arrival, Greater Southeast spent only $20,000–$30,000 a year on a blood pressure programme, although a single stroke victim could cost $30,000 to treat.

The public and private sector customer service literature concurs on the process for delivering great customer service, even if outcomes differ. The current literature supports an outside-in strategy of customer service, rather than the traditional inside-out model for providing services. In the private sector, profit and growth are the *outcomes,* not goals.

Profit and growth are generated by customer loyalty. Loyalty is generated by customer satisfaction. Customer satisfaction is the *goal* that companies should seek and focus on, because high customer satisfaction, as a matter of course, produces customer loyalty and subsequently profit and growth. At this point, the public and private sectors converge—customer satisfaction is the *goal.*

Customer satisfaction is achieved by providing valued services and products, where value is the positive difference between customers' actual experiences and their service delivery expectations. Productive employees also create value.

Employee productivity stems from employee loyalty, and loyalty is a product of employee satisfaction. Satisfaction is generated by high-quality support services (people, information, and technology) and by being empowered to provide value and resolve customer complaints.

This customer service culture must be supported by leadership that emphasizes the importance of each customer and employee. These leaders must be creative and energetic (not lofty or conservative), participatory and caring (not removed or elitist), that is, one who can be a coach, teacher, or listener (not just a supervisor or manager).

Such a leader demonstrates company values (rather than simply institutionalizing policies) and motivates by mission (rather than by fear).

Some components of this model are cyclical. A 1991 study of property and casualty insurance companies found that employees who felt that they were meeting customer needs had twice the job satisfaction level of employees who did not believe they were meeting customer needs. In that study, when a frontline service worker left the company, customer satisfaction levels dropped from 75 to 55 per cent.

In the customer service literature, five guiding principles are adopted by public as well as private agencies delivering excellent customer service:

- Embrace change and persistently strive to improve (be a learning organization).
- Continually ask the target customers what they want and then give it to them.
- Empower, support, and reward frontline personnel.
- Harness the power of information.
- Establish an enabling infrastructure.
- Identify the Target Customer.
  - Begin by identifying the target customers and by considering the point of purchase, point of service delivery or receipt, and point of consumption.
  - Cluster or segment target customers based on their common behaviours, knowing that targeting the wrong customers can have adverse effects on the organization.
  - Determine the priorities of various clusters of customers, knowing that the capabilities of the organization are crucial in addressing these priorities.
  - When possible, focus on customers with high current or future value. (Perhaps in child support this is a custodial parent with many children in the system.) This does not mean that other customers will not receive service, but it may mean that they will receive a different level of service. Consider the frequent flier programmes that airlines and hotels offer to their customers with high current and future value. This does not mean that other passengers will not receive services, but services may not be at the same level.
  - Discourage non-target customers, those who are not likely to be satisfied by the services, and those to whom it is expensive to provide

services, which is a necessary part of a customer focus. A simple example is offered as an illustration. A fire department could discourage residents from contacting the department to remove cats from trees by charging a $20 fee for performing the service and by advertising their busy emergency call load. The equipment and time investment of sending a ladder truck and several firefighters may reduce the effectiveness of the department at responding to an emergency and may not be the most prompt means of accomplishing the task for the customer.

- Determine What Customers Want..
  - Determine what target customers want (not just what they need right now) by asking them in person or as part of a mail or telephone survey or by using other mechanisms (e.g., electronic tracking and researching marketing trends) to determine what they want. Be aware that advertising, word of mouth, and public relations influence customers'expectations. Meeting customers'basic needs or expectations does not always bring high levels of satisfaction. Exceeding expectations produces high satisfaction-therefore, determine customers'ideal desires.
  - Determine how the target customers prioritize their"wants."Generally, customers want convenience, quality products and services, variety or selection, low prices, and protection or security. However, each organization must identify what is most important to its customers.
  - Weigh how important the customer-identified"wants"are to the organization. Are the services something that the organization does, is capable of doing, or wants to pursue?
  - Determine how well the organization can meet the customers'"wants"in comparison with

competitors. The success of other companies at meeting and exceeding customer expectations changes a customer's frame of reference and increases a customer's expectations.
  - Determine which"wants,"if performance delivery were to be improved, would most impact the organization's bottom line (profit, cost, loyalty, trust, or compliance).
- Establish an Organizational Culture Supportive of Customer Service.
  - Utilizing the information gathered, establish the company's customer-focused vision. The vision statement should be simple and may also identify what the company does not want to be. Some examples of simple vision statements include"Absolutely, Positively Overnight"by Federal Express and L.L. Bean's promise "Guaranteed. Period."
  - Live up to what is promised by concurrently developing and applying externally and internally oriented strategic service concepts that reflect the vision. If the organization does not implement both internally and externally oriented service strategies consistent with the vision, the organization will have good intentions but poor customer service (Thompson).
  - Continually reflect on the vision and goals and the way services are delivered to customers. Be creative about the mechanisms used to create and deliver new services. Be willing to change existing practices to integrate improvements.
- Implement an Externally Oriented Strategic Service Concept. The externally oriented strategic service concept establishes how the organization's service is designed, marketed, and delivered to target customers.
  - Take into account the costs of providing services and ways to minimize those costs while

implementing quality control. The service concept must be developed with the frontline worker at its centre. Determine the necessary financial, human, and technological resources necessary, as well as how the organizational structure and flow can enable the frontline worker to delight the customer and deliver the promised vision.

- Use advertising/educational strategies to set appropriate customer expectations.
- When planning, realise that control of information can take the place of assets. For instance, the Rural/Metro Fire Department in Scottsdale (AZ) has reduced the size of its crew and trucks because of technology that allows crews to view microfiche floor plans on the way to a fire. The added knowledge of the building layout allows fewer fire fighters to accomplish the same task that requires more firefighters when they do not have this advance knowledge.
- Provide a feedback loop for incorporating customer comments and complaints into the planning processes. Customer complaints are an invaluable resource and source of information without which organizations cannot be successful. Complaints brought to the organization are one of the most efficient and least expensive ways to obtain information about customer expectations of products and services. Complaints are a more direct means of obtaining information than conducting research studies of customer expectations, conducting transaction studies, or reviewing customer expectations in parallel industries. Another means of soliciting customer feedback that has been implemented by a number of service leaders is to interview lost customers-those who have switched service providers. (Perhaps in child support these

customers were custodial parents who had been making timely payments but who stopped doing so.) Still other options are holding customer meetings, hosting social events, and attending seminars or conferences where customers are present.

Ensure that the complaint resolution strategy supports the customer-focused vision. Most research shows, "...if customers believe their complaints are welcomed and responded to, they will more likely repurchase." British Airways found that 67 per cent of its complaining passengers fly again if their complaints are handled well. British Airways even implemented a creative and convenient way to allow customers to complain by installing video booths at Heathrow Airport so that customers could immediately go into a booth and state a complaint, even during non-business hours. The videotapes are reviewed and addressed during business hours.

- One final element of an externally oriented service strategy is to regularly measure customer satisfaction or delight in the products and services.

- Implement an Internally Oriented Strategic Service Concept.

The internally oriented strategic service concept establishes how the organization's internal processes will support the customer-focused vision. The premise behind the internally oriented strategic service concept is "...capable workers who are well trained and fairly compensated provide better service, need less supervision, and are much more likely to stay on the job. As a result, their customers are likely to be more satisfied...". A study by Sears in 1989 found that "employee turnover and customer satisfaction are directly correlated." Stores with high customer service ratings had a 54 per cent sales force turnover versus 83 per cent in stores with low customer service ratings. This is supported by examples throughout the literature. Taco Bell found that the 20 per cent of stores with the lowest employee turnover rates have 55 per cent higher profits (an outcome of customer satisfaction) than the 20 per cent of stores with the highest turnover rates.

A number of other studies provide convincing evidence as to why companies should avoid employee turnover. Merck and Co. found in 1990 that turnover costs were 1.5 times an employee's annual salary. Clearly this varies based on a number of cost factors (e.g., workers compensation claims, hiring process costs, training costs, and lost business), but it is commonly noted that employee turnover is an expensive problem. Abt Associates studied an automobile dealer's sales and determined that it cost $36,000 to replace a salesperson with 5–8 years of experience with a salesperson with less than 1 year of experience. The economic costs of excessive employee turnover in one trucking company were analysed, and it was determined that the company could increase profits by 50 per cent by cutting driver turnover in half.

- Ensure that leaders of the learning organization exhibit the company values. Leaders must foster the creation and testing of new ideas and be unabashedly willing to change existing practices to integrate improvements.
- Identify employee groups important to implementing the externally oriented service concept. Frontline workers are of central importance.
  - Identify the characteristics and needs of the employee group(s) and how well those needs are met. This may include resources needed to successfully perform the job or needs can refer to compensation, work environmental factors, or personal needs. Understanding employee needs helps an organization to develop successful processes as well as employee retention policies. Learn how targeted employees perceive the proposed customer services. An organization

cannot change without the participation of its employees.

- Focus on recruiting employees who support the customer service vision. The costs of employing people who do not support the customer service vision are considerable. Forum Corporation research in the service industry showed, "...only 14% [per cent] of customers who stop patronizing service businesses do so because they are dissatisfied with what they bought. More than two-thirds defect because they find service people indifferent or unhelpful." Oftentimes, the right employees are those that fit in with the corporate culture's customer service vision, not necessarily those with the most experience in the industry. Additionally, develop career paths that allow successful customer-oriented employees to remain on the frontline.
- Focus on training and employee development throughout employment. A study by Ryder Truck from 1988 through 1989 found that increased training meant lower employee turnover.
- Empower frontline employees to do what it takes to satisfy the customer. Management must support employee empowerment by clearly defining the parametres of the empowerment, while remaining flexible within the parametres. This will encourage creativity. Rules should be simple and few—Continental Airlines actually had an employee handbook burning party to signify the change from a procedural environment to one of empowered customer service. Also, in support of internal customers, the Department of Defence reduced its 230 pages of travel regulations to 17 pages.
- Ensure that management supports employee decisions and judgment calls, even if this means that the cost of satisfying customers initially increases. In positions of high customer contact, quality control is not met by increased supervision, but by the use of

incentives to emphasize quality, making service providers highly visible to customers, and by building a peer group to instill a sense of pride and teamwork.

- In addition to skills and empowerment, equip frontline personnel with the technology, information, and internal resources to do what it takes to satisfy the customer. The literature is replete with examples of how incorporating the latest information technology can improve employee productivity. For example, Charles Schwab developed IWIN, a system that allows an agent to identify and view electronically Charles Schwab literature to respond to customer questions received by telephone. Before this system was implemented, agents who were unfamiliar with the literature in question could not provide immediate and succinct answers to customer questions.
- Ensure that divisions and individuals within the organization communicate. Frontline employees and other employees need information and a support network. A customer should never have to tell one employee what another employee already knows.
- Develop cross-functional teams for operations and improvement tasks. First ask those who are doing the work for suggestions to improve productivity. The Social Security Administration nearly doubled its telephone-answering capacity by implementing automated features, utilizing additional technology to change the way employers' reports of wages are recorded, and cross training its employees to work outside their normal areas of responsibility during peak periods.
- Link all employees' compensation to (and offer rewards for) good customer service performance. Rewards can be money, status, praise, acknowledgement, or perks such as trips or special events. While Charles Schwab does provide monetary

incentives based on the amount of money a broker team brings into the company, if the customer service survey for the quarter does not show strong customer service by the team, the reward is reduced or even eliminated for the quarter. This policy in a profit-seeking environment leaves no doubt that customer satisfaction is the primary goal.

- Finally, measure employee satisfaction regularly. Leaders in the service industry have employed such methods as toll-free numbers, periodic roundtable meetings, and surveys to collect employee satisfaction information.

CASE STUDIES

Four companies/agencies were interviewed in detail, and synopses of these four agencies are included as examples of how customer service concepts may be operationalized. These examples serve as springboards for transferring the concepts to customer service practice in child support. First Interstate Bank and Ford Motor Credit were chosen for intensive review because of their excellence in customer service and because their customer issues are similar to those of child support customers. Cherner Automotive Group was selected because of its excellence in customer service as well as for the opportunity to obtain an in-depth frontline (rather than managerial) perspective on customer service delivery. Visiting Texas Child Support Division provided a successful reality check that the customer service concepts found in the literature can be applied within child support enforcement. Texas Child Support Division was selected because of its excellence in customer service and because it is a model of an agency moving from a non-customer-oriented perspective towards a customer focus.

First Interstate Bank (FIB) is a family-owned and -operated bank that strives to function as a community bank and to be the best service provider.

It operates under three primary goals:

- To make communities better places.

- To serve their customers.
- To make their employees' lives better.

As part of this vision, FIB has created policies and procedures to deliver excellent customer service. The benefits they have reaped by pursuing this vision include market share increases, lower turnover, higher profits, and better communities.

Currently, FIB operates 59 branches in Wyoming and Montana, 14 of which are located in Wal-Mart stores. FIB is the largest bank in each of these States. The primary customer is described as middle-class, middle-aged, stable, and a homeowner. FIB also serves a large population of retired professionals. FIB serves an estimated 150,000 customers each month. The bank works with all customers as long as it is in the best interest of the bank and coincides with the customer's needs. A customer-focused sales and service culture was initiated 4 years ago, when the current Senior Vice President of Branch Administration was promoted to his position:

- *Providing service to customers*: One of FIB's goals is to make customers'lives better. The intent is to"wow"customers. FIB strives to provide customers with what they need, rather than merely trying to make a sale. If an FIB employee knows that a customer can receive a better loan or service elsewhere, FIB will tell that customer to go where he or she can receive the best deal. This honesty and integrity give customers a good feeling about the bank, so that the next time they do business, they will more likely consider coming back to FIB. The"mirror test"has been the golden rule for FIB. In their interactions with customers and other employees, FIB staff are told to ask themselves whether they can look in the mirror and tell themselves that they have made the right decision.

  Customer input is formally solicited every 2 years via mailed surveys. Additionally, customer comment cards, customer exit interviews, and customer complaints are a resource to FIB for what customers want. Complaints are tracked and analysed for patterns.

- *Making employees'lives better*: At FIB, employees have opportunities to advance. They have a sufficient amount of vacation/sick time off, and managers are committed to mentoring and developing their staff. FIB focuses on hiring and maintaining customer-oriented employees. Employees are supported, rewarded, and granted discretion. Employee input is solicited through focus groups, conference calls, workshops, and one-on-one visits. Advisory boards composed of various bank staff provide feedback to each division leader. FIB has never laid off an employee.
- *Making communities better places*: FIB believes that communities have changed as a result of the way FIB conducts business. Additionally, employee contributions to charities (except religious organizations) are matched by FIB.

According to FIB management, resistance to change and toward a customer-focused culture should be expected. A customer-focused culture can be developed only when it is embraced and supported at the top. When supervisors and managers are sold on customer focus, their attitude, as well as policies and procedures, will flow down to the frontline. At FIB, one-on-one discussions worked well to ascertain and address reasons for hesitation and subsequently to gain buy-in at the executive level. Having secured top-level buy-in, management strives to operate as a team and model customer-oriented behaviour. Accountability must be maintained from the top-down.

During the transition to a customer-focused culture, supervisors may feel as if they have lost some control and autonomy. Trust must be built at this level to reduce the fear of hidden agendas. In order to increase supervisor morale, managers and executives spend more time face-to-face with supervisors and line staff and maintain open communication. Upper management travels to the branches and conducts focus groups and conference calls to build the customer culture. With open communication and honesty, trust is built.

Managers are constantly working with their employees and looking for ways to improve services.

Under the philosophy that management must "inspect what they expect," managers conduct check-ups with branches by:

- Visiting with a checklist (e.g., asking open-ended questions),
- Performing formal audits,
- Conducting loan reviews, and
- Hiring mystery shoppers (an external company is hired to pose as customers and report back on the service received).

Using these routine check-ups, managers offer fast and quick decisions concerning improvement and strive to provide feedback to the branches immediately. FIB is striving to eliminate non-customer service functions from frontline employees'roles. In so doing, they have centralized check processing and implemented timesaving technology.

FIB endeavors to consistently provide great customer service. Whether a customer calls on the telephone, approaches the teller line, or approaches a loan officer, standards of conduct and greeting have been created to guide the interaction. FIB employees are to properly greet all walk-in customers or customers who call on the telephone. FIB operates zero tolerance for"ducking and hiding"when employees see a customer. FIB believes that it is essential that interaction with customers is positive for continued payments and good customer service relationships.

During in-person interactions, FIB staff are directed to smile, stand and greet the customer, shake hands, introduce themselves, learn the customer's name, initiate non-business conversation, give the customer their full attention, and stand and thank the customer for his or her business upon concluding the interaction. Similarly, telephone calls are answered within three rings, and callers are thanked for contacting FIB. Call takers ascertain and use the customer's name, strive to minimize holds to no more than 30 seconds, and always thank the customer at the conclusion of the call. Even voice mail greeting protocols follow these principles.

Frontline employees are given clearly defined discretion to satisfy customers. Tellers are provided with a dollar amount for discretionary use. Employees are encouraged to err on the side of a customer. However, if a customer becomes verbally abusive to an employee, this behaviour is not tolerated. A senior employee will intervene, and in extreme cases, the customer may be asked to find a new financial institution. Frontline personnel receive newsletters that inform them of FIB's operations; the goal is to keep them informed, as well as to generate team spirit.

Hiring

FIB hires on attitude first. Bank officers feel that with the right attitude, a person can be trained to deliver good banking service. The goal is to hire an individual because of his or her service philosophy and desire to help people, rather than hiring someone who is focused only on salary. FIB's recruiting strategies sometimes even include soliciting employees from retail services when staff identify someone with a great service attitude. Prospective managers are required to take personality tests. Internally, managers are mentored via a 2-year training programme—even while serving in a frontline position.

Training

FIB maintains a customer focus through continual training. All personnel are taught their roles and responsibilities within a customer-focused culture. During the last 4 years, FIB has spent $1.5 million on external training in customer service. Ongoing training costs approximately $350,000 annually. Cross training is used to provide staff with the "big picture."

Managers are taught how to supervise and mentor staff. For example, a recent coaches' newsletter article offered tips for encouraging employees to implement skills and attitudes resulting from attending a training session

These tips included:

- Allow the employee to implement a new idea or skill that came from the training.
- Ask the employee to present the training information at the next departmental meeting
- Use informal conversations and praise to reinforce the skill development.
- Role model the behaviour.

Frontline personnel are taught to ask open-ended questions to gather the most information from customers. Debt collection personnel are taught communication skills and proper telephone techniques, as well as skills in collecting money. As part of this training, staff are taught to ask questions as early in the delinquency process as possible, because as time passes and the delinquency becomes more serious, customers will no longer be receptive to freely providing information.

FIB incorporates creative training strategies to make learning enjoyable. One example implemented in one branch is the TUFS programme (Teaming Up For Success), which utilizes employee teams to make presentations to all branch staff on customer-focused service issues. A recent presentation utilized the Jeopardy theme to create a skill drill competition. Still another team presented a role-play of improper customer service versus FIB customer service.

MOTIVATING AND REWARDING EMPLOYEES

FIB employees are motivated by understanding their role within the customer-focused culture, through one-on-one coaching, accountability at all levels, performance evaluation and performance-based rewards, and employee and team incentive programmes. Additionally, the bank strives to maintain high employee morale and retain employees by offering them flexible time for doctor visits, childcare, etc.

The most successful incentive programme thus far has been non-monetary. Employees nominate a coworker who has gone out of his or her way to assist an internal or external customer. The nomination is posted on a banner in the break room. The winner or MVP of the week receives a traveling trophy. The trophy is a football with the executives'signatures on it. Another programme, the"I"Team incentive programme, involves service bucks. Service bucks are obtained by a point value system. The award is given in front of peers.

An employee can receive service bucks in one or more of four categories:

- Going out of his/her way to help a fellow employee.
- Going out of his/her way to help a supervisor with a special project
- Going out of his/her way to help a customer.
- Going out of his/her way to help him/herself improve a process and make the job easier.

Under a different initiative, employees/branches are awarded prizes for doing their best and for increasing deposits and checking accounts. Every employee has an opportunity to gain points and eventually select a prize from a catalog.

Each year, FIB employees are evaluated on their performance. FIB uses pay performance management guidelines.

The emphasis of the performance evaluation has been on customer relationships. Performance evaluations incorporate statistical information contained in management reports, customer feedback, and management's observations. Employees can also be awarded performance-based bonuses, which adhere to a scale so as to eliminate any appearance of favouritism. FIB is automated-anyone within FIB can view an account. As information is entered, standard abbreviations are utilized so that anyone can understand the status and nuances of any account.

The system that tracks loans and collections automatically queues accounts for a loan officer's attention, based on a pre-established prioritization protocol. Largest delinquency amounts are the top priority, followed by frequency of broken promises of payment, bounced checks for payment, highest limit past due, and number of days past due. The system is set up to accept notes, so that the substance of a loan officer's conversation with the customer can be captured for review and follow-up.

This system enhances productivity and the employee knowledge base of contracts when interacting with customers. The system is set to inform all employees of the status of each contract.

FIB has a number of automated forms and letters. In the debt collection department, the bank uses an automated system to produce uniform letters. This system includes merged fields that insert the name, address, and account number on the letter. Another bank employee, not the debt collector, stamps, signs, and mails the letter. This system frees up time for the debt collector and provides him/her increased opportunities for customer contact.

MARKETING

The marketing department responds to (and tries to predict) market trends, focusing on the financial needs of FIB. Marketing staff gather information through interviewing, trial and error, and customer surveys.

They have found that particular marketing yields particular customers-not all products are needed/wanted by all customers. The marketing department focuses on how to better serve the community. The goal is to maintain customers for the long haul.

FIB uses a number of mechanisms to share information about services with customers and prospective customers. Word of mouth has proved most effective. Additional media have included radio, television, trade show booths, Internet, I-Beetles (Volkswagen beetles that advertise FIB's Internet site), and employees wearing FIB apparel while in the community.

Defining Good Customer Service in Debt Collection

The debt collection department uses a standard set of procedures for working with debtors and delinquent customers. The uniformity of implementation of these procedures is seen as critical to good customer service. By standardizing the process, FIB believes that all customers will be treated equitably.

The department is organized so that one person handles all loans purchased in-house. Loans purchased from other lending institutions are handled by personnel with various levels of expertise and experience, depending on the level of complexity or level of delinquency. Early in the collection process, employees and customers are educated about customer responsibilities. Customers must expect that they are obligated to make the required payments. Debt collectors are trained in how to approach customers who are first-time delinquents versus repeat delinquents.

Before interacting with a customer, the loan officer reviews the customer's history. When a contract is 10–30 days late, the loan officer makes several telephone and mail contacts but retains a degree of flexibility with the customer. At this point, a loan officer may change a payment due date, extend the loan for up to 30 days, or accept partial payment (although this is discouraged) and restructure the loan.

When two payments are outstanding and the customer is 30–45 days delinquent, the loan officer becomes sterner when communicating with the customer. Senior debt collectors handle these customers, and customers receive a certified form letter and a follow-up telephone call.

At this point, the options are:

- Restructure the account,
- Terminate the credit line, and
- Collect the collateral.

Within debt collection, management utilizes a number of procedures to ensure that all customers are receiving high-quality service and that employees are held accountable for results. Two persons are required to be present when cash is tendered.

Loan statistics and management reports are reviewed as a double check on delinquency amounts and numbers of delinquent customers. This information is used to review the seriousness of delinquent loans for each debt collector. If there are any problems within the debt collection department, the Central Collections Manager notifies everyone in the department during the staff meeting.

Problems are addressed through training. FIB recognizes that debt collection can be personally taxing for employees, and therefore, is proactive in preventing employee burnout or turnover in the debt collection department.

- Debt collectors are not expected to become personally involved with the customer, nor are they expected to provide social services. The primary objective is to work with the customer to collect payment.
- Within debt collection, a person generally is not kept in one position for more than 2–3 years. Rather, a person may be moved to a different classification of contracts (e.g., from personal to dealership accounts, or from accounts delinquent 30–45 days to accounts delinquent up to 30 days, or to recoveries rather than telephone follow-up with delinquents).
- Debt collection personnel are required to leave the office for lunch (which is also required). Breaks are taken every few hours.
- Employees are encouraged to use vacation time.
- Staff alternate going into the field, for a change of pace.

Creative Ideas:

- During November and early December, in anticipation of Christmastime spending, as well as winter weather layoffs for outdoor laborers, the debt collection department is particularly proactive with customers who have a history of delinquency.
- Customers may make payments with credit cards. The use of credit cards for payment was pilot tested with customers who lived more than two States away. This sampling was intentionally designed to address the "check lost in the mail" syndrome. Due to the success of the pre-test, all FIB loan customers may use credit card payments.
- Debt collectors solicit information early in a customer's delinquency as a means of keeping a current address and other information. Otherwise, due to the Privacy Act, if the customer relocates, it becomes more difficult to obtain a current address.
- In an attempt to embody one-stop shopping, FIB

operates 14 branches in Wal-Mart stores. In particular, during weekday morning hours, retired customers utilize these branches.

- FIB implemented 24-hour banking and Internet access to accounts.
- The bank is excusing frontline employees from responsibilities that are not related to customer service. For example, check processing is completed at a central location.

The benefit to FIB of providing great customer service is their continued reputation as a customer service-oriented organization. This reputation attracts more customers while retaining old ones, resulting in a larger local base of customers. Additional benefits of great customer service include high employee morale, resulting in a low turnover rate, gains in market share, increasing profits, lower unemployment, and better communities.

The costs of delivering great customer service are difficult to estimate, but they can be attributed to training, salaries of certain people, and incentives. FIB estimates spending over $3 million over the past 4 years to create a customer-focused service culture. There is a high level of commitment to provide good customer service through training.

Ford Motor Credit (FMC) operates as the flagship for Ford Financial by providing financing and leasing for Ford, Lincoln, and Mercury customers. Ford Financial focuses on providing value and service and continually seeks out new ways to increase customer satisfaction. Their first value is "Winning with Our Customers." This value is embraced, communicated, and rewarded.

Ford Financial serves more than 10 million customers in 40 countries. Primary customer interactions are through call centres, operating in Omaha (NE) and Nashville (TN) in the United States and in Ottawa (Ontario) and Edmonton (Alberta) in Canada. These call centres receive an estimated 1.5 million customer calls each month. Their customers want quick service, knowledgeable employees, written confirmation of action taken, and professional and courteous treatment.

WORKING FOR CUSTOMERS

FMC stresses the importance of creating a holistic customer service culture by beginning with upper-level management and actualizing this goal among all staff including frontline personnel. The framework for the customer service culture at FMC includes learning what the customers want; implementing steps to provide for those wants for which a business case can be made; equipping frontline employees with training, information, empowerment, and motivation; and monitoring success through customer and employee feedback mechanisms.

When the U.S. call centres were being developed, the director researched other call centres to find a model for their design. In favour of economies of scale (related to technology, resources, and personnel), FMC implemented call centre access on a national scale at four sites. Even with this consolidated design, FMC is committed to providing personalized service.

Call centre management utilizes customer telephone and mail survey results as well as focus group findings to guide implementation. Once analysed, this information is provided to the areas within the call centre for which it applies. (For example, customer feedback about loan rates goes to employees responsible for making policy decisions about rates. Customer input about experiences and interactions with personnel are provided to staff in training and human resources.)

Call centre managers are expected to coach and mentor call takers, based on performance during quality control checks. FMC management utilizes formal feedback initiatives to ensure that communication between the frontline and management remains open. One of these programmes is the Voice of the Customer Committee. On this committee, frontline workers meet with management during a monthly meeting at which staff relay what customers want, based on their interactions with customers that month and over time. Another mechanism, the Ideas Programme, offers an opportunity for frontline personnel to submit a proposal to management on how to improve customer service. Employees are rewarded for submitting proposals, and when ideas are implemented, a gift card is provided.

Frontline employees, especially through the Voice of the Customer Committee, have made important contributions to improving customer service at FMC. For example, frontline staff identified necessary changes in the voice menu wording, suggested options that should be added and some to omit from the phone tree menu, and identified customers' information needs. Frontline personnel are encouraged not only to report to management any processes that are not working, but to offer potential solutions.

The key to hiring someone on the front line, according to FMC management, is to hire staff with a passion for customer service. Training for FMC staff includes training on teams, as well as learning how to give and receive feedback, how to be a good team member, and how to improve telephone communication skills.

One important motivator for employees is the policy within the company that includes customer satisfaction as a determining factor in employee compensation. Quarterly, customer telephone survey results are tabulated, and employees receive bonuses that are tied directly to their scores. Also, prizes are offered for customer letters or phone calls of praise. Lunches are offered to teams who perform well in customer service.

In an effort to make the payment process as convenient as possible for customers, FMC piloted a phone pay system through Western Union. Currently, this programme produces 350,000 transactions each month. Other pay options include direct electronic payments from a bank account or payroll deduction and Internet-based payment processing. Twenty-two per cent of FMC payments are processed electronically. At the time of this report, they are also considering whether to permit credit card payments.

During a month when the customer simply cannot pay, FMC works with customers who struggle to make full and timely payments. For example, a customer may be permitted to skip a payment and add that payment to the end of the loan.

Another option is reducing the amount of the monthly payment and extending the length of the loan. Accountability is enforced through late payment charges and reports made to the credit bureau.

Customer service is key to the day-to-day operation of Cherner Automotive Group (Cherner). This sentiment is echoed from the frontline employee to the upper-level executive. The Cherner philosophy of customer service delivery is customer satisfaction through continued friendly communication and interaction, coupled with accessibility and responsiveness. Cherner's approach is very individualized, and they believe that customer service is relative to the customer being served. In no case did a Cherner employee claim to be in the business of selling vehicles; rather, employees view themselves as"in the people business."Building customer relationships is underscored. Cherner employees realise that exemplary customer service brings in new customers, as well as repeat customers. This is accomplished by reputation or referral.

Cherner operates two dealerships, both of which are located in the Northern Virginia technology corridor. Cherner has a wide customer base that includes retired persons, business professionals, members of Congress, and community residents. Many Cherner customers are repeat customers or referrals.

Cherner is a family-owned and -operated business. The corporate culture embraces change; strives to learn what customers want and gives it to them; and seeks both customer and employee loyalty. Cherner considers customers'first impressions to be important and strives to create a warm and inviting environment. Cherner employees attempt to make customers feel welcome and to provide individualized attention.

The only"formal"policies for making this occur include the"10-foot rule,"whereby employees who are in the area should acknowledge customers within this range and ask to be of assistance, and a policy that all customers who enter the dealership are acknowledged within 30 seconds. Cherner employees understand the value of smiling and being pleasant to all customers.

According to Cherner staff at all levels of the company, customers deserve responsiveness. The ability to individualize service is, in their opinion, what sets them apart in customer service delivery. There are no written guidelines, but employees have a degree of autonomy in making decisions.

For example, the service advisor has the latitude to refund money or to adjust a charge ticket. The core ideology is that each employee is encouraged to do whatever it takes within reason-based on the situation-to serve a customer immediately. Employees are discouraged from having a"this is my job or that is not my job"attitude. Rather, all employees work for the same company and every employee is responsible for serving customers and making them happy.

Integral to Cherner's customer service delivery is the need to understand customer expectations. Cherner listens to their customers and provides convenient forums for customer feedback. The most widely used method is their customer satisfaction survey. Each customer who purchases an automobile receives a questionnaire from Ford Motor Company. The results are shared with the dealer. Also, Cherner hires an outside company to phone a sample of their service customers to collect data on customer satisfaction. These findings are presented in the monthly report"Viewpoint."The service area also has a customer feedback/suggestion box, posted beside the cash register.

Staff at all levels of the organization articulated their customer service orientation as:

- Being pleasant and smiling at customers.
- Being a good listener (and being empathetic to customers'situations).
- Doing the job right the first time.
- Being accountable.
- Building trusting relationships with customers.
- Treating people fairly.
- Making customers fully happy.
- Being willing to apologize.

Cherner's owners and managers set the tone for the company. Managers are expected to"lead by example."The general manager adheres to a policy of"Management by Walking Around."In other words, he and other managers try to stay connected with employees throughout the organization by working side-by-side with them. Senior-level executives have an open-door policy and solicit employee input during staff meetings. Calls are not screened, so customers also can contact managers directly.

Managers attempt to empower employees by providing a supportive environment in which employees are encouraged to make decisions. Managers are expected to coach frontline staff. During interviews, frontline personnel indicated that if a frontline employee were experiencing difficulties, managers would speak with that individual and coach him/her. However, frontline staff felt that improvement would be expected and that the employee would be held accountable for improving, or the employee would be terminated. As an employee's experience increases, so does the amount of discretion allotted to the employee.

Cherner frontline personnel perceive that they are supported by management in that whatever they feel they cannot handle can be turned over to management, with frontline staff confident that the situation will be addressed. Management also listens and responds to the needs of the employees. This is handled in different ways. For example, when employees in service determine that they need some training or equipment to do the job better, they can write the request on a white board designed for this purpose, and a member of management will address the request (and keep the notation on the board until the request is resolved). The white board is also an information-sharing tool for frontline employees. Employee meetings are an another forum for raising and addressing issues.

Most of the dealership's employees have longevity with the company. During each discussion with Cherner employees, regardless of organizational level, the interviewee acknowledged that to deliver great customer service, a company must hire and retain the right people. Managers added that "the right person" is one who can get along with others, possesses good judgment, can work on a team, is motivated, and possesses the desire to grow and learn. Cherner wants to hire sales personnel who are motivated not by money, but rather by the desire to help people.

Cherner offers multifaceted, ongoing training for employees. In order to continually provide effective customer service, employees are trained both in-house and by the manufacturers. Ford Star Satellite training, Ford's training facility in Centreville (VA) and printed training materials from KIA and ISUZU are designed to keep employees current on various features and aspects of the products being sold and serviced. Other training offered is designed to enhance selling techniques and customer service and to update technicians on vehicle and repair technology. In the past, employees received gender sensitivity training that was offered to improve customer service for female customers.

Among the most creative training strategies is Cherner's frontline mentoring system, whereby a senior salesperson mentors a new salesperson for 90 days. The senior salesperson is responsible for teaching sales basics, orienting the new employee to Cherner culture and attitude, describing Cherner products, and detailing processes. One frontline employee stated that this type of mentoring is a key component to great customer service that is transferable to other organizations.

At all levels of the organization, employees reported being very self-motivated—driven by personal pride and the desire to do a great job. This may be a result of Cherner's hiring policies as well as employees' positive perceptions of their work environment.

Most of those that were interviewed commented that separate and distinct from the actual family ownership of the dealership, the working environment feels like a family environment. Employees know and talk with one another, even across departments; employees support one another; employee picnics and gatherings allow families to get to know each other; and employees simply "get along." This family environment proves to be a strong motivator for Cherner employees at all levels.

Another motivator that was mentioned comes directly from individual customers. Employees reported receiving Christmas cards, gifts, notes, and personal appreciation and friendship from satisfied customers. Cherner, as well as the vehicle manufacturers, offers incentives to foster and sustain employee motivation. Cherner sponsors contests, and the winners are given free tickets to sporting events or dinner coupons, monetary awards, and other "per's" (e.g., use of a vehicle, recognition, etc.) Rewards are also offered based on customer survey scores, reported by Ford. At times, there are luncheons or dinners.

Rather than a point-in-time formalized evaluation process, employees are continuously recognized for good service. Similarly, management addresses negative behaviour as it is observed or identified via customer surveys or complaints and seeks to correct this behaviour through mentoring and coaching.

Technology is a resource primarily used for training and in the service area. Service employees are linked to each of the manufacturer's databases and have access to sophisticated on-line reference manuals. They are connected to nationwide databases that have background information on the history of the car, as well as customer history. This allows for a more detailed, efficient, and expedient service call and better customer service.

Ford Star is a satellite training initiative that allows employees to remain at the dealership while receiving training. Employees can even take the required tests and receive their scores via the Internet. This lends convenience for employees being trained.

The attitude of customer responsiveness holds true for complaints. Employees echoed the same sentiment: "If you receive it, handle it. If you can't handle it, find someone who can until the problem is solved." Employees explained that complaints are an information resource for them, and that they utilize the information to improve services.

Cherner boasts a low turnover rate, estimated at approximately 10 per cent. In fact, an average employee will remain with Cherner for 10 years. The General Manager has been with Cherner for 29 years. This low turnover is attributed to the family-oriented atmosphere, competitive wages, and knowledge that the jobs at Cherner are secure (as Cherner does not have a history of layoffs).

One challenge to this positive environment has been a recent decision to respond to customer and manufacturer desires to operate on Saturdays. As such, employees who used to be off each weekend now find themselves working on some Saturdays. In an effort to reduce employee burnout or turnover that such a change may produce, Cherner offers special incentives to these employees. For example, an employee who works on Saturday may choose to take the following Monday off (service advisors can take Friday) or to be paid for an extra day of work at overtime rates. Management also provides lunch for employees who work on Saturday.

Cherner focuses on outcomes rather than the process. Cherner offers its vehicle repair customers a shuttle back to work, within a reasonable distance, or to the transit station. However, Cherner recognizes that because of local traffic conditions, offering this service during evening rush hour is counterproductive. Therefore, customers are reimbursed for cab fare back to Cherner when traveling from the transit station to Cherner to pick up a vehicle during evening rush hour. While Cherner could have told customers that the shuttle does not run during rush hour and that transportation would have to be arranged on their own or during non-rush hours, Cherner went the extra mile with customers and found a mutually beneficial way of providing this service.

Cherner aims to exceed customer expectations. When customers have their vehicles at Cherner to be serviced, they are provided with complementary car washes. Cherner proclaims that the benefits of customer service delivery are happier customers, high employee morale, employee and customer loyalty, free advertising (word of mouth), and sales generation. "If you do it right the first time, you won't have to do it again." This is the premise from which they operate. Satisfaction the first time results in not having to spend more labour hours rectifying a situation. This, in turn, makes daily business operations more fluid and service more efficient. Satisfaction the first time also enhances the dealership's community reputation as that of a professional, people-oriented business. This business stance generates a larger customer base. High employee morale is also a benefit of good customer service. Employees take pride in their work.

The costs to Cherner for delivering great customer service include employee incentive costs, salaries, and bonuses; training costs; car wash expenses; shuttle service expenses; and write-off costs for services performed but not charged to the customer.

As part of its external customer service strategy, the Child Support Division in Texas has developed a programme called *Compact with Texans,* which outlines the vision, guiding principles, and goals of the division and explains how external customers can continue to provide feedback on child support.

The guiding principles are:

- Always do what is best for the child, by putting children first.
- Treat everyone with dignity, respect, honesty, and courtesy.
- Walk in the customer's shoes—have empathy.
- Be a leader in doing the right thing, not just in doing things right.
- Participate and contribute in finding solutions—work as a team.
- Maintain objectivity and be nonjudgmental.
- Respect customer' privacy.
- Bear in mind that the customers' perceptions of reality are their reality.

These principles are designed as the framework for action at the agency and individual levels when serving both internal and external customers. Everyone in the division is provided with a copy of these principles to hang on their office walls, and these principles are also posted in conference rooms and hallways throughout the office. To advance these principles, the customer service action plan addresses:

- Improving access to services and staff by implementing regional call centres; expanding and publicizing the Office of the Attorney General (OAG) Child Support Web site—including online application for services; publicizing the complaint process on posters and the Internet; considering a plan to increase office hours; and putting computers in six office lobbies, on which customers may access some case information as well as conduct job searches.
- Ensuring comprehensive, accurate, and easily accessible information that is easy to understand by recording information about billing and interest, credit bureau reporting, and license suspension laws on a toll-free line; providing telephone access to information about mail-out dates; providing call takers with screen pops; providing parents with an information packet and video (and also including it on the Web site) about customer expectations, services, procedures, and timeframes when they first enter the system; providing presentations in public forums or for selected groups regarding child support; comprehensively training new employees; and providing staff with information online.
- Ensuring prompt action on new case information and responses to customer requests and inquiries by instituting several policies, including: the service delivery process must begin within 20 days of receiving an application for services; telephone messages must be addressed within 2 business days, and action must be taken within 2 business days of information receipt; actions taken on a case or information received must immediately be documented; responses must be made to written inquiries within 10 days; follow-up efforts to telephone inquiries must be undertaken within 15 business days; automated wage withholdings must

be acted upon within 2 business days of receiving information about a new employer; either customers are seen when they walk in or appointments must be scheduled to occur within 10 days of the customer's request. Additionally, prompt action is actualized by improving the automated computer system and allowing parents to make address changes on an automated toll free line.

- Improving accuracy and quality by revising forms, standardized letters, and publications as necessary to ensure that they are clear and current and that they use plain language; training all central office staff in writing techniques; training managers in leadership development; creating a compliment-tracking system; establishing an employee recognition programme (including revising performance plans and defining merit raise criteria); providing automated management reports; conducting a workload study; sharing best practices; and creating a customer service advisory team.
- Treating customers professionally, courteously, and respectfully by pilot testing privacy measures in waiting rooms, providing customer service and other professional training to all staff, creating individual staff training plans, attaching information about court procedures to court notices (including expected wait time), and instituting a regular customer feedback process.

The Child Support Division of the Texas OAG works with mothers, fathers, and legal guardians of children to locate absent parents; establish paternity; establish, enforce, and adjust child and medical support orders; and collect and distribute the money associated with these orders. They have over 1 million active cases.

In 1997, the Texas legislature mandated the Sunset Advisory Commission to review the OAG Child Support Division to determine whether the OAG should continue to administer the State's child support programme. Legislators were receiving too many complaints about the Division from constituents. The Sunset Commission conducted its review in 1998 and recommended that the OAG continue to administer the programme for a 2-year probationary period. The Commission made a number of recommendations for improving the programme. The highest priority was improving customer service and, in particular, accessibility. Too often, customers needing information about their cases could not get through to staff for information. Of the 1.5 million calls a month that child support received, only 14 per cent of those who wished to speak with staff could do so. Thousands of calls each day were abandoned. A customer service survey revealed that 48 per cent of customers were dissatisfied.

Shortly after the Commission issued its report, a new Attorney General took office. He hired a new Deputy Assistant Attorney General for child support, and they both made customer service a top priority, with answering the phones as the number one objective. A full-time staff person was hired to develop the customer service strategy and action plan. The process included focus groups with internal and external customers, a customer satisfaction survey, and an employee satisfaction survey, as well as and soliciting input from various special interest groups.

Customers said that they were most concerned with obtaining timely and accurate information, preserving their personal dignity, and being respected. Employees wanted empowerment and discretion.

To make the plan "stick," the administration realised that they needed to communicate, improve staff development, measure performance, and increase employee accountability and recognition. Quarterly, the regions report on their progress through action plans.

In the quarter from March through May 2001, regional progress reports revealed that regions:

- Maintained telephone answer rates at approximately 95 per cent.
- Implemented external customer surveys and suggestion boxes.

- Sought employee input through surveys, suggestion boxes, and staff meetings.
- Rewarded employees with merit increases, promotions, donated food, gift certificates, tickets, and special events, as well as via a recognition board or e-mail commendations.
- Implemented flex and optional work schedules.
- Focused on improving relationships with other agencies/individuals within the system, especially court personnel (one region instituted court greeters).
- Instituted a job pool to reduce hiring delays.
- Implemented quality control procedures such as "mystery callers."
- Maintained on-the-job training efforts.
- Improved office appearance.

Overall, after the first year of implementation, a general customer satisfaction survey revealed a statewide increase in customer satisfaction to 63 per cent (up from 52 per cent in 1999). Furthermore, in Spring 2001, a survey of custodial parents who had recently had an establishment performed reported an 82 per cent satisfaction rate. Intuitively, management claims that staff stress levels are down and that morale and job satisfaction are on the rise.

Efforts to improve customer service are continuing through the undertaking of the "e-degree" project (in which employees use educational leave and agency computers to take up to 3 hours of online college-level courses per semester) and the WorkSMART model office-reengineering project. The WorkSMART project is in the planning stages. WorkSMART embodies an ideal for service in which customers gain empowerment over their cases through increased access to online information online.

Customers will be able to electronically enter their case into the child support system via a streamlined application process, use a graphical roadmap to know the status of their case, and review frequently asked questions and answers while experiencing shorter processing times. Much of the detailed development of these action plans has been pushed down to the regional level (e.g., training strategies, measurement strategies, reward systems, and customer input mechanisms). Texas is working on maintaining consistency in these procedures while allowing each region some discretion. This strategy was designed to increase buy-in and ownership at the regional level. As a result of this autonomy, different offices may vary in their customer service strategies and levels of success. While executive management has found this autonomic setup effective, the downside is that its varied measurement strategies do not lend themselves to easy statewide assessment.

At the beginning of the customer service implementation, the Director closed the central call centre and created regional call centres. At the regional level, managers focus on getting the phones answered and supporting employees—through training and cross-training, by clearly outlining expectations, through consistent management, by serving as role models, by rewarding good work and good customer service, and by encouraging open communication.

A regional call centre manager stressed the importance of his own attitude (attitude filters from the top down, according to this manager) as a means of setting the tone of the office and keeping employees productive and willing to provide the best services possible. In support of this belief, every day he walks around the office and greets each employee, offers assistance, provides answers to questions, and maintains an open-door policy.

He emphasizes results and delivering a consistent message. As long as the center's goals are being met, he offers flexibility (e.g., in scheduling lunch breaks and requests for time off). He has instituted strategies to cope with the unit when it is not fully staffed, by flexing lunch schedules and by having management serve as backup. He tries to handle most problems by talking with all of the staff instead of isolating an individual. However, individual accountability does play an important part in the management strategy. This particular call centre succeeds both in meeting its telephone answering goals (staff and managers answer 96 per cent of all incoming calls) and in maintaining low employee turnover (approximately 22 per cent in the region, but of those who have left, every person still works within the Texas Child Support Division via transfer or promotion).

Call centre management has trained employees that their role is to accurately handle as many incoming phone calls as possible. The purpose is to free up time child support officers (CSOs) to be able to process cases. Brief interviews with frontline call centre staff suggested that call centre employees and managers share a rapport and can rely on one another for help or answers to questions. Two people said that the best part of their job is the feeling of helping someone. Another person took pride in thoroughly addressing all of the callers' issues so as to deflect calls for CSOs. One call taker even assigns "ticklers" on his calendar so that he knows to check the system to make certain that appropriate action has been taken on a call he has received.

Call takers reported some challenges, including balancing the target talk time (about 4 minutes) with providing thorough information to the caller, dealing with callers who are not truthful, and handling concerns that caseworkers may not be able to perform requested follow-up. However, the call centre statistics show that 95 per cent of calls are answered, the average wait time since inception of the regional call centres is approximately 30 seconds, and that call takers spend an average of 3 minutes of talk time per call.

Management places the same emphasis on hiring call centre staff as they do in hiring CSOs. Call centre staff are paid at the CSO level. Some call centre staff were hired from field offices, as well as from county child support offices, and others were hired with customer service backgrounds but with no child support experience. Management for the six call centres includes personnel from the central office, some of whom had worked in field offices and others from general hiring pools.

All child support staff receive 2 days of basic training in customer service, even those personnel serving internal customers only. New staff also receive this training. During this training, instructors stress that the Division's guiding principles apply to both internal and external customer service. Managers receive advanced customer service training on how to support staff to deliver great customer service. Training is offered regionally, and therefore staff from all levels train together. In addition to customer service training, staff are trained in how to deal with hostile customers. The next initiative is to design and implement a follow-up course in customer service.

Motivation is addressed on a number of levels:

- Staff participated in the internal focus groups that led to the Compact with Texans. This participation generated introspection, and executive personnel believe that this introspection may be a positive motivation.
- Additionally, some regions cross train and cross work. For example, personnel in Dallas train on both call centre and field office tasks and then, depending on the workload, staff can assist in either location. This additional knowledge helps the employees in one location understand the impact of their actions on their coworkers.
- The call centre manager sets high expectations of staff and strives to provide employees with the training, information, and resources needed to meet them.
- The customer service culture has clearly been established as a permanent priority. Executive staff stress the importance of adhering to the customer service philosophy and individual accountability, and staff are aware that they can be dismissed for a lack of customer service.
- Performance plans include customer service measures and clearly outline performance expectations and standards.
- Staff are rewarded with merit increases, promotions, food, gift certificates, tickets, and special events, as well as via a recognition board or e-mail commendations. (Worth noting: during one office recognition celebration, staff from another field office

came to offer phone support so that everyone could attend the event.)

According to Texas Child Support Division executives, one of the keys to the improvement of customer service in Texas child support is technology. In particular, six regional call centres were established and were equipped with technology and systems to improve efficiency, information availability, and information exchange. The call centres handle approximately 25 per cent of all customer service contacts.

First, a model- the Erlang C Formula-was used to understand the relationship between the amount of incoming calls, time taken to handle those calls, wait time for callers, and number of call centre staff. With this formula, executive personnel determined the number of staff needed given call volume, target maximum wait times, and handling times for calls. Initially, the number of required staff calculated by this method was higher than that of actual staff available for the effort. As a result, Texas had to address another factor in the formula-handle time.

Efficiencies in call handling have been gained through a number of innovations:

- Calls are automatically disseminated to call takers based on availability of their lines. Once a call taker hangs up, the call taker has a pre-set amount of time to perform call wrap up activities, and then the line automatically becomes part of the call queue once again. (Previously, call takers had to proactively re-set their "ready" buttons.) The system includes a way to put a line on "break" as necessary.
- Screen pops were designed to utilize the incoming phone number to pull up a case, rather than requiring the call taker to obtain a case or social security number upon answering the call. This feature saves an average of 15 seconds per call.
- A Graphical User Interface ("GUI") screen was developed to contain the core information used on typical calls to child support. This feature was created so that call takers spend less time flipping from

screen to screen. This feature also can save an average of 76 seconds per call. Additionally, data entry options on GUI save additional data entry time-about 92 seconds per call.

The database of cases (TXCSES) includes a diary function that permits staff members, whether in a call centre or field office, to make a notation on the case so that anyone who opens the case will be current on action taken or contact made on the case. It also allows staff to e-mail one another directly. Another useful feature allows call centre staff to mark the correspondence or case so that the call taker receives a reminder notice to perform follow-up.

Still other call centre technology allows call centre staff to be acutely aware of the number of calls coming in and the length of wait time. First, a digital light board posted in the office provides this real-time information. Additionally, a computer tracking system provides aggregate statistics on the calls and is located in the break room.

Intellicenter software is used by call centre managers to provide quality control by periodically screening calls and coaching staff, as appropriate. At the call centre, everyone agreed that technology has made their jobs easier.

Another technological improvement for customer service has been the interactive Web site. On the site, customers can provide information, obtain payment information, and make complaints. Customers are using the site for all of these things. The Web site was designed to reduce the number of phone calls, while increasing information access for customers. Web site use has been increasing since inception. In August 2001, there were 196,403 transactions from individuals who had entered their pin number and were actually accessing case information. On average, the site receives 3,967 hits daily. Ten per cent of all customer service contacts are over the Web site. The Web site won an award from Computer World Magazine.

An intranet Web site provides internal customer service information for staff. Texas also utilizes an automated telephone system that addresses 65 per cent of all customer service contacts.

MARKETING

Marketing the new regional telephone numbers to child support customers is critical to the success of the call centres. The information campaign has included public service announcements; news service announcements; fliers inserted into the mail for paying cases; coordination with courts, probation, volunteer coordinators, child support field offices, and special investigators to distribute the new regional numbers; providing the number to arrestees during a large"round up"operation; and by word of mouth.

One of Texas's principle debt collection tools is the Special Collections Unit (SCU). The SCU works with both financial institutions and non-custodial parents (NCPs) to collect past-due child support from the financial accounts of the NCPs. Prior to taking legal action, an SCU employee contacts the financial institution's legal staff to develop a rapport on a staff-to-staff level. During the initial conversation, the SCU employee explains the lien/levy process used by child support and provides a telephone number for use in the event of questions or problems during future transactions. SCU staff also work with the NCPs, listen to concerns, and explain applicable laws supporting the collections efforts. At this time, SCU staff also explain to NCPs the financial and moral advantages of paying child support debt in full. Many times the NCP will not have calculated the impact of the compounding interest rates on his/her debt or the problems associated with being reported to the various credit bureaus. Throughout the process, SCU closely monitors the liens/levies. If an error is made by the SCU or financial institution during the lien/levy process, staff of the SCU act promptly to release the lien/levy and explain the error to the NCP. Staff of the SCU has received numerous comments from NCPs praising their professionalism and personal concern, even after the NCPs have paid substantial sums toward their child support debts.

Regional Call Centres: The regional call centres were created to eliminate busy signals and long wait times on hold. When customers call the local number, an automated feature of the telephone response system directs all custodial parent callers (90 per cent of all callers) to the call centres. NCPs, attorneys, and other members of the public and officials (10 per cent of all callers) are routed to the field offices because these calls tend to be more complex and lengthy in nature. With the call centres, Texas also strives to establish a system in which the first person that a customer speaks with can address the issue rather than having to transfer the call. In customer service terms, the call centres strive to provide one-stop shopping. Customers want to be able to contact one person to obtain answers and action on their case. At the call centres, personnel are taught to identify the caller's question and what needs to be done at the moment to address it. These strategies, combined with the creative technological strategies that save precious seconds and help to direct calls appropriately, have increased calls answered from 14 per cent to 95 per cent within a 2-year period. An additional cost savings has been achieved because in lieu of one toll-free statewide number, customers can now call locally.

- *Frequent-Caller Programme*: A Unique Telephone Number Study determined that 100 of the most frequent callers generated 5 per cent of total calls. These individuals were proactively contacted by child support staff and asked what could be done to address their questions or issues, so the customer would not be compelled to keep calling back.

  This effort revealed that frequent callers tended to repeatedly call for three primary reasons:
  - Callers were seeking any adult with whom to converse.
  - Callers were frustrated with the agency and wanted to complain.
  - Callers were"shopping"for answers from different call takers. During this effort, the child support representative attempted to focus the caller on a

specific problem or issue with which the Child Support Division could assist and about which it was responsible. Frequent"shoppers"were provided the answer noted in the log of contacts, so as to reaffirm the consistency of the message.

- *Customer Education*: At least one of the field offices has utilized a proactive approach to customer education. As parents become a part of the child support system, they are requested to participate in an informational presentation at the local child support office. This allows child support caseworkers to explain the processes, timelines, and what is expected from the parents. Additionally, it is an opportunity to have a caseworker assists the parents with the paperwork, to ensure that it is properly completed the first time and, therefore, can be processed without delays.
- *Ombudsman Programme*: Texas has established an ombudsman programme to receive, track, and investigate customer complaints. Ombudsmen are located in every field office as well as in the central office in Austin. Complaint information is entered into a central database so that it can be analysed for trends and utilized as opportunities to improve service.

The data are not intended for use in performance evaluations, but individuals who are the subjects of complaints are notified, and the complaint is addressed. Advertisements about the ombudsman programme are hung in courthouses and child support offices, and the information is available on the Web site. The implementation of the ombudsman programme created a mechanism by which child support personnel can address complaints, and the programme has reduced the amount of dissatisfied customers filing complaints with their legislators about child support.

The costs easily identified with the shift toward customer service have been training costs, the expense of 210 new call centre staff salaries, and the performance incentives (e.g., merit increases, promotions, donated food, gift certificates, tickets, and special events). Conversely, however, collections have increased, and paternity establishment has improved. Nontangible benefits have included improved employee morale, decreased legislative inquiries, and improvements in customer satisfaction ratings.

Since the effort began, a survey of custodial parents has shown considerable increases in:

- Customer satisfaction overall.
- Ability to contact the local offices by telephone.
- Satisfaction with responses and explanations received from staff.
- Satisfaction with action taken on cases.

Texas is continuing to explore opportunities for quantifying the benefits of improved customer service. Child support agencies benefit from providing excellent customer service because excellent service in child support will lead to increased information sharing, increased trust, improved relationships, and ultimately increased compliance. The literature suggests that child support agencies should make customer service their goal and anticipate that increased information sharing, increased trust, improved relationships, and ultimately increased compliance will be the outcomes of excellent customer service. The evidence suggests that low child support officer turnover will lead to high customer satisfaction and that employees who perceive that they are meeting customer needs will have high job satisfaction.

Some readers may presume that becoming customer oriented is more difficult in the public sector than in the private sector. Perhaps the motivation for doing so may be less in the public sector. However, the degree of success achieved has been relatively equal. The American Customer Satisfaction Index is a standardized measurement of customer satisfaction that is implemented by the University of Michigan Business School. This survey is used in both the public and private sectors. Year 2000 survey findings demonstrated an average public sector score that was competitive with the average scores of private sector businesses (65.7 out of 100 points for local government, 68.6 for Federal Government, and 71.2 across the private sector). In particular, in 2000, the Administration for Children and Families (represented by the Head Start Bureau) received one of the highest Federal scores at 83.

A number of elements can be put into place within child support that will increase the opportunities for excellent customer service delivery. An initial set of possibilities is offered below. First, identify the customers in child support enforcement. The OCSE purports that both custodial parents and NCPs are the customers in child support, whereas the child is the ultimate beneficiary.

Minnesota Child Support Enforcement has analysed its customers and outlined five primary categories of parents whom they serve: complying, uninformed, unable, reluctant, and evading. Minnesota defines these categories by levels of readiness, willingness, and ability to comply with child support obligations. The purpose of these categories is to systematically modify the child support system's response to the parents, based on each parent's place on this continuum. In other words, Minnesota is attempting to individualize its child support services, while treating parents equitably. This strategy also allows for the inevitable shifting in parent category:

Complying parents are defined as those parents who are "knowledgeable of expectations and are ready, willing and able to comply. Custodial parents are willing to give information. Non-custodial parents are willing to fulfill orders. Both are willing to form economic partnership in support of their children." Minnesota plans to respond to these parents by reinforcing these behaviours and rewarding willing compliance.

Specifically, parents are provided with feedback on their compliance and trends; success stories are shared among customers; parents' opinions are sought about how obligations may be more easily met; ongoing financial transactions are automated for ease of service; expedited and non-adversarial processes are available to both parents; face-to-face services are available; and amicable resolutions are pursued and celebrated.

Uninformed parents are defined as those parents who "may or may not know [that] they are a parent, don't know of their responsibilities and rights, and are not familiar with the child support system or processes." The response to be implemented with these parents is to educate. Specific responses include public awareness campaigns; forming partnerships with programmes having compatible purposes; linking welfare reform and child support messages; addressing incoming questions promptly, completely, and accurately; avoiding acronyms; and focusing outreach efforts on expectant parents, pre-teens, teens, and separating or divorcing families through schools, churches, employers, local governments, and advocacy and community groups.

Unable parents are defined as those parents who "are knowledgeable and willing, but unable to pay or participate. The non-custodial parent may be financially unable due to being unemployed, underemployed, impaired, imprisoned, or otherwise rendered unable. The custodial parent may have information but is unable to provide it to the system due to language or other barriers." The response to this category of parents is to strive to enable parents. This is attempted by identifying the reason for the inability by listening to parents, connecting the parents with services (employment, training, school grants, or financial management), addressing individual barriers (through peer support groups, safety plans, etc.), encouraging non-cash contributions when financial contributions are unavailable, establishing and modifying orders that reflect the changing ability to pay, and offering delayed or deferred financial payment when necessary and when the lifetime financial contribution can be increased overall.

Reluctant parents "are knowledgeable and able to comply, but reluctant; they wish to avoid the system or other parent." This reluctance may be driven by a perceived or real threat, such as domestic violence, fear, anger, or cynicism. The system response in Minnesota is to motivate and prod these parents into complying by setting clear expectations; using visible, predictable, and automated collection tools; addressing underlying issues through services such as referrals for counseling, assistance on custody or visitation, and financial management; providing cross-language and cross-cultural alternatives; allowing parents the opportunity to correct mistakes; and cultivating staff who are skilled at diffusing emotionally charged situations.

Evading parents "are knowledgeable and able, but refuse to comply. They act affirmatively to avoid obligations, such as flight or willful refusal to work with [the] system or other parent." The system response in Minnesota is to compel compliance by locating these parents quickly; using automated actions to start compliance; outsourcing these cases to a collection agency; applying enforcement tools early (before a full year of noncompliance has passed), including contempt proceedings, professional license revocation, liens against real and personal property, and State or Federal criminal prosecution; imposing noncooperation penalties; and emphasizing during publicity about arrested evaders that the losers in these situations are the children.

By identifying these five categories, Minnesota is recognizing that parents have different situations, motivations, and needs and is attempting to design a system that is adaptive to these differences while maintaining an overall goal of obtaining financial support for children.

In child support, agencies cannot select to whom services will be provided. To complicate matters, custodial parents and NCPs may seem to have competing or at least different needs. This same phenomenon is experienced by Home Depot, which serves contractors as well as"do it yourselfers."In Home Depot's case, the company has been able to cope because it found that contractors and"do it yourselfers"require services and materials at different times of the day and so the stores tailor staffing and store hours to be able to provide good service to both.

For child support, one option may be to direct most efforts or the most-appropriate efforts toward the best return. If most customers are parties to complying cases, instituting low-cost efforts to reward or reinforce this behaviour in an effort to maintain it (e.g., certificates to fathers who have not missed a payment over a 1-year period; instituting a policy of thanking the custodial parent when that parent calls and has made the payment for that month, or sending confirmations of payments received with a statement about the significance of that parent as a responsible parent) is appropriate and could be cost-effective.

Similarly, a fairly low-cost response for educating uninformed parents (e.g., explaining the process upon entry into the system, via a video, a class, or written materials) may be cost-effective as well.

However, the agency could take a banking approach toward those customers who become delinquent (those unable, reluctant, or evasive).

First Interstate Bank stresses the importance of early identification of those customers who have missed payments and of prioritizing among these customers in an effort to organize the workload. Speaking with customers who have missed payments by up to 15 days accomplishes a number of things; the customer is more open to providing information and may have more options available.

The philosophy behind this process is that working with someone soon after the missed payment is likely to be less costly than allowing the debt to build before making contact. Prioritizing customers by the amount of the payment missed or number of children to whom the payment is applied or any other possible mechanisms will allow those frontline personnel who make contact with parents to begin gaining control over the workload and will help to reduce the"squeaky wheel phenomenon."A different tone and set of possibilities are extended to customers who are 30-45 days late because there is a point of diminishing returns.

Collecting payment from customers who have missed two payments is probably going to require more effort on the part of child support, so the best offense is to try to prevent two payments from being missed.

DETERMINE WHAT CUSTOMERS

Want and Give It to Them

A number of child support agencies, including those in Texas and California, have implemented customer surveys. Customer surveys can and should be used to determine what child support customers most want from child support services and to seek input on improving services, collect baseline information by which to measure results of improvements to the system, and to reinforce a customer focus. The Urban Institute prepared a sample customer survey for OCSE from which questions could be gleaned, and child support agencies also may use one another as a resource for samples.

Implement an Externally Oriented Strategic Service Culture

Establishing an externally oriented strategic service culture in child support follows the same process as similar procedures in the private sector. In this culture, management places an emphasis on minimizing costs, increasing quality control measures, educating customers, establishing a customer complaint mechanism and resolution strategy, and measuring customer satisfaction.

Both First Interstate Bank and Cherner Automotive Group offer creative quality control procedures. At Cherner and FIB, frontline supervisors serve as coaches or mentors and are trained to serve in this capacity. FIB has a policy to"inspect what they expect."In child support services, rather than relying only on statistics or monthly reports about the quality of services at field offices, central office management could regularly visit child support field offices.

The visit would include discussions with field office managers regarding operations, observations of customer interactions with staff, auditing and reviewing measures identified as important to customer service, addressing patterns of complaints, brainstorming on improvement opportunities, and rewarding excellent customer service practices.

A creative customer education tool used by FIB is the I-Beetle. Employees of FIB drive a Volkswagen Beetle painted with an advertisement for FIB's Web site. This takes the message to the customers-during traffic jams, on trips to the supermarket, while shopping at the mall, etc. Opportunistic marketing may be something worth considering in child support.

Messages about responsible parenting or a new child support Web site or call centre telephone number could be distributed where child support customers are already going-whether at the supermarket, on downtown streets, at shopping malls, at job placement centres, or at the town ball field.

California Child Support Services has automated its complaint tracking and established an Interagency Agreement with the Department of Social Services, State Hearing Office, to conduct State hearings when appropriate.

Implement an Internally Oriented Strategic Service Culture: Implementing an internally oriented strategic service culture in child support means hiring the right people; continually training employees in customer service; seeking input from employees; empowering, rewarding, and supporting frontline personnel; utilizing technology to reduce the workload on CSOs and other frontline personnel and to provide easy access to information; creating an enabling environment where discretion is clearly defined and frontline judgment calls are supported by management; utilizing cross-functional teams; and measuring employee satisfaction.

©This may mean hiring staff with an aptitude and attitude for customer service, even if child support skills must subsequently be learned. Such a culture may also be actualized through software that categorizes and automatically queues cases for attention by CSOs, based on the status of the case. This means instituting incentives for providing great customer service, whether perks, recognition, or merit raises. It also means that divisions or departments within child support services must communicate and cooperate with one another. It includes proactively attempting to deter burnout of CSOs and call takers by encouraging staff to take appropriate breaks and eat lunch away from work, use vacation time, and modify the work that a person does.

What Recommendations or Lessons Learned Do the Model Agencies Interviewed Offer to OCSE?

- Understand that good customer service takes time, patience, persistence, consistency in message at all levels, accountability, courtesy, respect, and emphasis on team players.
- Make sure upper management and executives at the top are sold on a customer service culture.
- Put a human face on customers—treat them with a personal touch, rather than as a collective.
- Make it easy for customers to do business with the service.
- Listen to customers to learn what they need and want.
- Address the immediate needs of the customer.
- Hire the right people by hiring on attitude and training on the skill.
- Mentor new employees.
- Manage by staying close to the frontline.
- Train the frontline on how to address customer problems.
- "Inspect" what you "expect."
- Don't focus energies on the bad apples—put energies and resources into those employees that want to work in customer service.
- Ensure that management/executives listen to their employees' complaints (without interruption) and have trust in their employees.
- Ask open-ended questions.
- Have uniform expectations of the customers.
- Establish uniform processes, policies, and procedures to collect payments. Customers must be able to expect the same expertise, collection efforts, production, recovery, and professional delivery regardless of which branch or individual is working.
- Develop working relationships with other partners

(e.g., courts, credit card companies, vendors, or other banks) that play a role in debt collection.

- When working with a customer complaint, try to understand the customer as well as those available to help address the problem.
- Frontline employees should mentally separate themselves from problems in an effort to address the issue so that the outcome is positive for all involved.
- Maintain an orderly work atmosphere.

The results of this study provide a glimpse of how child support agencies may be able to strategically plan and implement a customer-focused culture and the benefits that child support agencies should expect from successfully implementing excellent customer service. The study also suggests several possible areas for future study:

- OCSE may consider selecting one or several elements of the process for further study. For example, what specific performance measures may be appropriately implemented for child support officers when the agency has a customer focus? Circle Solutions, Inc. (Circle) has recently received a contract from the Department of Justice to conduct a school resource officer performance measures study and pilot programme with four police agencies that are implementing community policing in schools. Under this programme, customers and stakeholders in school safety are participating in the development of the performance measures. A similar pilot programme could be adapted and utilized for child support agencies.
- OCSE may consider studying the effectiveness of specific customer service strategies in child support enforcement in pilot states that implement the customer service process outlined in this study.
- OCSE may wish to highlight many more promising customer service practices in child support across the Nation. Case examples or a compilation of examples

within the structure of the customer service process could offer States a point from which to brainstorm.

- OCSE may wish to create a toolkit for developing a customer-focused culture. Circle Solutions recently completed a"Collaboration Toolkit"for the Department of Justice. The Toolkit is a nuts-and-bolts guide for law enforcement and their partners to develop, fix, and sustain productive law enforcement-community partnerships to support the advancement of community policing. The Toolkit offers worksheets and exercises for working through pitfalls and organizing these efforts, and it refers the reader to resources to learn more. A similar toolkit presentation of the customer service process may be useful for State child support agencies.
- OCSE may also wish to explore in more detail some creative strategies of serving customers related to co-location of child support with other offices or businesses, payment choices, call management, training strategies, etc.

Certainly, this study lends itself to a great deal of further exploration. The study revealed that no specific tactic, technology, or mission statement is the key to effective customer service delivery. In fact, what is clear is that effective customer service delivery is organization specific, since services are designed around the targeted customers' desires and the frontline employees delivering them. The components of the process for producing effective customer service delivery include appropriately identifying and targeting the ideal customer, establishing a customer-focused vision that is consistent with the prioritized desires of the target customers, establishing operational procedures and internal infrastructure that support customer service, continuously measuring customer and employee satisfaction, embracing change, and striving persistently to improve.

The customer service literature clearly demonstrates that both profit-seeking and public agencies that implement effective customer service strategies realise financial benefits, either through increased profits or through reduced costs associated with long-term, informed customers, customer referrals, employee retention, improved information exchange, and streamlined service delivery. In this case, child support enforcement is like any other business. In order to implement effective customer service strategies and reap the benefits of good customer service, child support agencies will need to implement the process of developing effective customer service.

11

Managing Demand

The challenge of meeting the demand for public services that are free at the point of use is increasing. Examples, in increasing order of complexity and controversy, include water, higher education, road space, and health care. These services are perceived as important to society in general, and demand is rising rapidly and unsustainably. Such increases in demand can be managed either by reducing the demand—for example, by charging, as for water or road space—or by increasing the supply—for example, via increased funding, as with student loans. In health care, perversely, we do the opposite of both these approaches: we fuel demand by failing to manage it—for example, by not curbing expectations—and we are often forced to cut supply through lack of resources.

Demand for health care is undoubtedly rising. The average number of consultations for children in each of the first years of life (even after excluding surveillance and immunisations) has, in one general practice, risen from 3.73 per child in 1960 to 17.2 in 1990. We need to understand better how this ever increasing demand for health care is initiated and expressed and use this understanding to manage the whole system better. Professionals have the same increasing expectations from the service as the public does. Managing the pressure on the health service is as much about managing the expectations and rights of professionals to treat as it is about managing the expectations of patients to be treated.

To many, managing demand for health care sounds like a euphemism for rationing via restricting supply. However, it is a broader approach: the consumption of any product or service is determined by the relation between supply and demand, and different tools are used to influence supply and demand. Historically, supply management has been the most potent tool in coping with the challenges in health care. In the past 15 years this has been supplemented by processes for assessing need. We now need to add demand management to these approaches.

Demand management is the process of identifying where, how, why, and by whom demand for health care is made and then deciding on the best methods of managing this demand (which might mean curtailing, coping, or creating demand) such that the most cost effective, appropriate, and equitable health care system can be developed.

Critically, it depends on understanding how the behaviour of those who express the demand—citizens and professionals—is changing. It is concerned with making more appropriate use of the health services (not necessarily reducing it or making it cheaper). More specifically, demand management "is the support of individuals so that they may make rational health and medical decisions based on a consideration of benefits and risks." This definition comes from North America, where managing demand is an established discipline.

The many causes of a demand for health care need a variety of responses. For instance, some pressures may be best met, not by curtailing demand but by coping with it and meeting it in a radically different way. Recent examples include the use of helplines as a first point of access to health care in the home. The assumption that better informed people demand ever more health care may be unfounded. Studies of interactive information sources that allow patients to understand the advantages and disadvantages of prostate surgery show that increased information may persuade some people to avoid surgery. In a country with relatively high activity levels, such as America, this has been shown to reduce activity by up to 40%. In countries with lower activity rates it is not clear that the proportionate decrease would be the same, although it is important to find out.

The figure shows the way in which people travel through the healthcare system. Most healthcare needs are met without recourse to formal healthcare services, so a vital part of demand management is supporting this self care. Similarly, most problems presented to primary care are dealt with without referral. Again, efforts to manage demand at this stage will be most rewarded. At the interfaces between successive parts of the system important decisions are made about how the expressed demand might be best met.

Traditional reasons for increasing demand:

- Cultural and behavioural (a much larger, informed and demanding middle class—consumerism, where the concept of rights is outpacing that of responsibility).
- Technological (specifically information technology and health technology).
- Epidemiological (long term care is now increasingly common relative to short term cure)

Ultimately, the best place to manage demand is before it meets the service-that is, through promoting self care. This needs more than simply exhortations not to use the service for minor complaints, but meaningful education and true empowerment of individuals, households, schools, and workplaces so we feel more competent and confident to meet simple health-care needs ourselves. This involves a bigger investment in advice lines, nurse practitioners, and self care manuals, and the continued enhancement of the roles of pharmacists and other health care professionals. NHS Direct, as proposed in the recent white paper on the NHS in England, has much to offer.

SELF CARE

In helping people make more appropriate decisions about their own health we must not compromise safety but instead explicitly share risk. This involves assessing the best content and format of information in self-care manuals that integrate consistently with the advice from health care professionals over the telephone or other forms of technology. There is much to be learnt from the experience of health maintenance organisations in America, many of whom issue comprehensive manuals and free phone numbers on enrolment. Importantly, a high degree of consistency exists between the advice in the manuals and from the professionals.

PRIMARY CARE

In primary care general practitioners need to be supported to manage demand more extensively. Gatekeeping (more recently and appropriately called filtering) can be done much more successfully if primary care is supported with more knowledge sharing, more risk sharing, and a more graduated access from primary care to secondary care (or other statutory and voluntary services).

THE POWER OF KNOWLEDGE

The knowledge that underpins primary care (and the way it is used) is essential in managing demand. This can be divided into the fears, understanding, and expectations of the patient; the evidence from valid, relevant, and accessible research knowledge; and an up to date knowledge about the facilities and support available from fellow healthcare professionals (especially in secondary care). Access to research knowledge has been undergoing most change recently and has the potential to help manage demand more rationally and consistently. Knowledge sources for both professionals and the public need to change from being there "just in case" to being there "just in time."

Managing demand in secondary care and beyond needs another set of tools. Although fewer patients are seen than in primary care, many more resources are consumed. The ability to manage the pressure on the hospital's front door is intimately related to the extent to which the healthcare professionals in the hospital are prepared to support colleagues in primary care. This support involves decision support, explicit knowledge on generalisable research (on effectiveness and cost effectiveness) and localised knowledge on availability, access, pre-referral support, and outreach services.

It is important be able to be explicit about, and share the risk of, all decisions between the patient and the professionals (including the legal consequences). For the general practitioner to refer and the physician to admit on increasingly smaller tolerances will cripple the system even more quickly. We need to be able explain and share risk between doctor and patient, between primary and secondary care. This implies having senior people on the front door, not only to manage acute illness quickly, but also to see the patient at the front door, and sometimes refer home again, as a practice acceptable to both patient and general practitioner. "If in doubt, admit" may become an unaffordable policy.

PRACTICAL WAYS OF MEETING THE SAME NEEDS

Coping with demand is about exploring better ways of meeting the same need-that is, increasing the efficiency and convenience of the system without compromising quality. Creating demand may be an appropriate way of managing demand if there is a poor uptake of a preventive service-for example, breast screening-where early intervention would reduce the demand for alternative and less successful interventions later on.

We need to turn the consequence of the changing expectations in society into a fundamental part of the solution. We need to find the best ways of helping people make the most efficient and fair use of a service that will never have enough resources to do everything. Understanding of the ways of managing demand is in its infancy, though there is some evidence on their effectiveness.

MANAGING CAPACITY

Capacity Management is a process used to manage information technology (IT). Its primary goal is to ensure that IT capacity meets current and future business requirements in a cost-effective manner. One common interpretation of Capacity Management is described in the ITIL framework. ITIL version 3 views capacity management as comprising three sub-processes: business capacity management, service capacity management, and component capacity management.

As the usage of IT Services change and functionality evolves, the amount of processing power, memory etc also changes. If it is possible to understand the demands being made currently, and how they will change over time, this approach proposes that planning for IT Service growth becomes easier and less reactive. If there are spikes in, for example, processing power at a particular time of the day, it proposes analyzing what is happening at that time and make changes to maximize the existing infrastructure, for example, tune the application, or move a batch cycle to a quieter period.

These activities are intended to optimize performance and efficiency, and to plan for and justify financial investments.

Capacity management is concerned with:

- Monitoring the performance and throughput or load on a server, server farm, or property
- Performance analysis of measurement data, including analysis of the impact of new releases on capacity
- Performance tuning of activities to ensure the most efficient use of existing infrastructure
- Understanding the demands on the Service and future plans for workload growth (or shrinkage)
- Influences on demand for computing resources
- Capacity planning – developing a plan for the Service

Capacity management interacts with the discipline of Performance Engineering, both during the requirements and design activities of building a system, and when using performance monitoring as an input for managing capacity of deployed systems.

12

Services Marketing Strategies

Perhaps the most significant difference between systems that produce products and systems that produce services is that product manufacturers can buffer their manufacturing processes from customers through use of inventories. In fact, a major category of inventory is called "buffer" or safety stock as we will see in the next module of this course.

On the other hand, in pure service systems, where the customer receives services directly from the service provider, the customer is in the "boundary" of the provider. In this case, when demand for service exceeds the capacity for service, one or more waiting lines form or customers leave the system unserved. Medical doctors cannot "inventory" medical care; lawyers and other professional counselors cannot "inventory" consultations; and airports cannot "inventory" aircraft parking positions at terminals. Waiting line models helped me determine how many parking positions we would need (the waiting line) to avoid holding aircraft on the runway (also the waiting line), until cargo handlers (service providers) could unload and turnaround the aircraft. The models worked fairly well, although I should have done more sensitivity analysis to handle increases in the arrival rate as things got a little "hot" the last day of the evacuation in Libya.

Enough nostalgia - on to the basic structure of waiting line systems. Waiting line systems, also called queuing systems from the underlying modeling basis of queuing theory, involve a *population source*, an *arrival process*, a *waiting area*, and a *service area* or *channel*. Waiting line systems also have *costs*, *operating characteristics*, and *management response strategies*.

WAITING LINE SYSTEM COSTS AND MANAGEMENT STRATEGIES

There are basically two costs that must be balanced in waiting line system - the cost of *service* and the cost of *waiting*. Note that I am not considering another possible cost component - the cost of a scheduling system. Theoretically, a scheduling system is a management strategy designed to avoid waiting lines (meaning you should *never* wait in the doctor's office - yeah, right!) and is not covered in this module. Scheduling systems are useful when the customer is known to the system and the short and long run costs of waiting are relatively high. We will study scheduling system applications in linear programming later on in the course.

Rather, in this module, we will study the more interesting scenario where customer arrivals to the system are random - that is, the customer is not known before arriving to the system and the arrival process is random as we will discuss later. In this case, to avoid longer than desired waiting lines, the service provider may exercise management strategies to increase the service rate by using faster servers, more servers, automated service, or some combination of strategies. Each of these strategies increases the cost of service, but produces the benefit of reducing the cost of waiting.

When the cost of service and the cost of waiting are known and measurable, the waiting line models in this set of module notes help us determine the optimal, or close to optimal waiting system configuration and rate of service. This can be tricky because the cost of service has a positive relationship with the rate of service, whereas the cost of waiting has a negative relationship with the rate of service. That is, the faster the service rate (or the more service), the higher the cost of service; whereas the faster the service rate, the lower the cost of waiting. Of course, the opposite is true: the slower the service rate, the lower the cost of service but the higher the cost of waiting.

The cost relationship can be sketched out in a graph, with dollars on the vertical axis and the rate of service on the horizontal axis.

We will examine the cost of service and cost of waiting components as we examine the main waiting line models later. It should be cautioned, however, that it is often difficult to measure the cost of waiting for customers that are external to the service provider's company or organization. For example, if customers in a car repair waiting line system are defined as mechanics waiting for tools from a tool crib to repair a car, it is fairly easy to measure the cost of mechanic waiting since the repair company employs the mechanic. The cost of waiting may simply be the time spent idle in the line times the employee's salary for that time unit.

However, if the owner of the car being repaired is defined as the customer of the waiting line system, the cost of waiting may be more difficult to measure. Retired "snow birds" may have discretionary time to spend in a waiting room and their cost of waiting may be relatively low. On the other hand, for someone who is employed and depends on their car to get to work, the cost of waiting may be relatively high, depending on their income level.

If the cost of waiting also incorporates the cost of losing a customer because long waiting time drives the customer away, measurement becomes even more difficult. As an alternative to managing the waiting system by measuring, analyzing and minimizing its combined total costs, the service provider may try to manage the service system by setting threshold parametres for system operating characteristics, and then use faster servers, more servers, automation of the service activity or some combination of strategies to achieve those parametres.

The Population

The population that generates customers to waiting line systems may be infinite or finite. In most cases, populations can be considered infinite, even though they are really finite. For example, if we were to study the characteristics of waiting lines forming at the Fort Myers side of the Cape Coral Bridge at morning rush hour, we know that the population generating the arrivals is the finite population of Cape Coral, around 100,000. However, since there is no actual limit placed on the customers arriving at the toll booths, we assume the population is infinite. All but one of the models we will study make this assumption. The finite model is the appropriate model to use when the population is relatively small, such as 20 total computers in a network office that feed a computer repair person server.

Arrival Process

Arrivals to the waiting line system from the population source may be on an individual or batch basis. We will assume arrivals are on an individual basis. The difference is best illustrated by the arrival of a car to a parking lot at a restaurant. One driver leaving the car to enter the restaurant would represent the arrival of one unit or customer to the waiting line system. If a bus pulls in, there could be a batch arrival of 30 customers. Did you ever notice that the bus stalls are behind the Cracker Barrel Restaurants on the interstate highways - just so you can't see all those batch arrivals before you pull off!

It is also assumed that the arrivals are nonscheduled, and the arrival of one unit is independent of, or does not impact, the arrival of other units. Whenever these assumptions are made, arrivals are assumed to follow the Poisson Probability Distribution, a member of the family of discrete probability distributions. The Poisson Probability Distribution is completely described by its mean, which is given the Greek symbol lambda. In a waiting line system, the mean we are referring to is the mean arrival rate. For example, we may say that the mean arrival rate is 4 calls per hour to a catalog company's telephone bank.

Another way of representing the mean arrival rate is to take its inverse, which gives us the mean time between arrivals. So, if I invert the mean rate of 4 calls per hour, I get ¼ hours. The mean time between arrivals is $1/4^{th}$ of an hour, or one arrival every 15 minutes.

Mean Time Between Arrivals = 1/Mean Arrival Rate

The probability distribution that is used to describe this time between arrivals in a waiting line system is the

Exponential Distribution. The Exponential Distribution is used to model the probabilities of continuous variables such as time, in the case of waiting line systems. The Greek Symbol Mu, is used to describe the mean of the Exponential Distribution.

If you have the mean time between arrivals, you can find the mean arrival rate by the similar procedure - taking the inverse. For example, what if we knew that the average time between arrivals to a bank teller was 5 minutes.

The mean arrival rate would be computed as follows:

- Mean Arrival Time = 5 minutes = 5/60th hours
- Mean Arrival Rate = 60/5 = 12 customers per hour

Customers arriving from a population next join the waiting line in the waiting line system.

WAITING LINE CONFIGURATION

Waiting lines may be infinite or truncated. For all of the models we will examine except one, we will *assume infinite line length*. One of the models we will examine is designed to model situations where no waiting is allowed - the ultimate of truncated systems. My telephone allows no waiting - if I am talking to someone, the next caller gets a busy signal. However, airline reservation systems allow callers to a busy reservation agent to wait in a queue.

The waiting line system may use a *single line/single server channel* configuration which means one line forms in front of a single service channel. The word *service channel* is used rather than server to avoid confusion. A single service channel may have many servers, but room for only one customer. That is called a single service channel. Grocery stores have multiple single line/single channel configurations. Banks, on the other hand, employ a *single line/multiple channel* or teller configuration.

Customers *discipline* in the waiting line configuration may vary from *patient*, to *balk* (view the line, then leave), *renege* (join the line, then leave), *jockey* (join the line, then move to another line when you think it is moving faster - that's me!), or collude (give your groceries to another customer - scum of the earth to students of quantitative methods)! Waiting line models *assume that the customer is patient*. Departures from the waiting line to the server are *assumed to be first in, first out* or first come, first served rather than last in first out, or like my deli - service in random order!

SERVICE CHANNEL

The main feature of a service channel in a waiting line system is the service time, also *assumed to follow the Exponential Distribution* when the time to perform service for one customer is independent from the time to perform service for others. If the average time to serve one customer is 10 minutes, then the mean service rate in hours may be found by converting 10 minutes to hours (10/60th of an hour), then taking the inverse:

Mean Service Rate = 60/10 = 6 customers per hour

Note that rates are always stated as per hour, ... per minute, ... or per whatever time unit; where as service times and times between arrivals are stated simply as hours, minutes, or whatever time unit. Once service is completed, it is assumed that customers *exit the system* and return to the population. Of course, they may exit one system and feed another. If the second system is independent of the first, then there may be two separate and distinct single line/single server systems.

That finishes our coverage of the basis structure of the waiting line system. Waiting line models have been designed as quantitative methods to analyse the operating characteristics and costs of waiting line systems. The models are categorized by the probability distributions that describe the arrival rate and service time processes, the number of channels, and whether the population is infinite or finite. The first model we will examine is one which follows the structure of a single service/single channel system.

Single Server/Single Channel System

The title of this section is a long way of describing a very common waiting line system: a single line forming in front of a single server. The quantitative methods described in this section are used to compute the operating characteristics and costs of this system.

Pause and Reflect

The assumptions needed for using quantitative methods to analyse operating characteristics of this single server/single channel system include an infinite population, Poisson arrival rates, infinite line length, patient customer discipline, FIFO departure from the waiting line, Exponential Service times and customer departure to the population.

Let's examine the following example problem. A document clerk earns \$15/hour, processes an average of 5 documents per hour throughout the workday, and receives documents at the rate of 4 per hour. There is a cost of waiting for the documents (by an office paralegal) of \$25.00 per hour. For this problem, the mean or average service rate is mu = 5 documents per hour, and the mean or average arrival rate is lambda = 4 documents per hour. The law firm is interested in knowing the operating characteristics of this waiting line system, such as average time a document spends in the waiting line, number of documents in the waiting line, the utilization rate of the document clerk, the probability of 3 documents in the system, and the cost of the system. The following formulas are used to model the operating characteristics of the single line/single channel waiting line system with Poisson Arrivals and Exponential Service time.

- *The probability of an idle system (no documents in the system, P0):*

  P0 = 1 – (lambda/mu) = 1 – (4/5) = 0.20

There is a 20% chance that the system will be idle at any one point in time.

Look at the formula carefully to see that we divide lambda, the mean arrival rate, by mu, the mean service rate. Recall that the arrival rate must be less than the service rate or the waiting line explodes. This can be shown mathematically in the formula. If lambda were greater than mu, the probability of an idle system would be a negative number greater than one which is infeasible.

- *The average number of documents in the waiting line (Lq):*

  Lq = lambda/[mu(mu – lambda)] = 4/[5 (5–4)] = 3.2 documents

- *The average number of units in the system (L):*
  L = Lq + (lambda/mu) = 3.2 + (4/5) = 4 documents

From the formula, you can see that this includes the documents in line as well as in the service channel.

- *The average time a document spends in the waiting line:*
  Wq = Lq/lambda = 3.2/4 = 0.8 hours or 48 minutes.

The initial time units of this and other time-related operating characteristics are the same as the input units. If input arrival and service times and rates are in hours, then output times will be in hours. I converted 0.8 hours to minutes for ease in interpretation.

- *The average time a document spends in the system:*
  W = Wq + (1/mu) = 0.8 + (1/5) = 0.8 + 0.2 = 1 hour

As with the number of units in the system parametre, this time includes the time a document spends in the line, plus the time in service.

- *The probability that an arriving unit has to wait for service:*

Pw = lambda/mu = 4/5 = 0.80

This operating characteristic is also known as the utilization factor for the service channel. A critical requirement for single line/single channel service systems is that the utilization factor be less than one. Otherwise, the waiting line would explode. In fact, queuing systems are not very efficient anytime the utilization factor exceeds 75 or 80% due to the interaction of the two probability functions. We will illustrate this later.

- *The probability of n documents in the system. Let's say we are interested in knowing the probability of n = 3 documents in the system:*

Pn = (lambda/mu)n * P0 = (4/5) * 0.2 = 0.1024

Since we are working with discrete probabilities, to find the probability of three or less documents in the system:

Pn < 3 = P0 + P1 + P2 + P3
= 0.20 + (4/5)* 0.2 + (4/5) * 0.2 + 0.1024
= 0.20 + 0.16+ 0.128 + 0.1024 = 0.5904

...and we follow the law of probability that says all probabilities of the distribution must sum to one, so the probability that there will be more than 3 documents in the system is:

$$P_n > 3 = 1 - 0.5904 = 0.4096$$

Costs Of The Waiting Line System

The total cost of this waiting line system is the sum of the cost of waiting and cost of service.

Total Cost = Cost of Waiting + Cost of Service

= $(c_w L) + (cs\ k)$ where

k =number of channels

c_w = cost of waiting = $25.00 per hour for 1 paralegal

c_s = cost of service = $15.00 per hour for clerk

Total Cost = ($25 * 4) + ($15 * 1) = $115

Sensitivity Analysis

Recall that I said with purely random arrivals waiting line systems are most stable with utilization rates less than or equal to 75%. That may seem unusual to you, that we only want to work our employees at 75% utilization. The problem is that the arrival rate and service time parametres are averages. The variation is always what kills us.

For example, the average arrival rate is 4 documents per hour, and the service rate is 5 documents per hour. At any point in time, the system may experience an arrival rate of 5 documents per hour and would be at the verge of explosion unless at the next point in time, the arrival rate slows down to 3 documents per hour.

And, this considers that the service rate remains constant, which it doesn't in this model. The service rate could slow down to 4 documents per hour with an arrival rate of 4, and we have the same problem.

Of course, we could also have a speed up in the arrival rate and a slow down in the service rate to result in chaos. To buffer against explosion, which occurs when the waiting grows and grows and we never catch up, waiting line systems with purely random arrivals are generally kept to a maximum utilization rate of 75%. Note that the above example illustrated a system with a utilization rate of 80%. What if the arrival rate increases to 4.5 documents per hour, which represents a 12.5% increase.

The new utilization rate is:

Pw = lambda/mu = 4.5/5 =.90, a 12.5% increase as well.

The line length now increases to:

Lq = lambda/[mu(mu - lambda)] = 4.5/[5 (5-4.5)] = 8.1 documents, a 150% increase!

That's why we don't operate at utilization rates above 75%. I really find this interesting from my operational experience. People who say they are working their people at 100% utilization are not working in random service systems - they can't be or the system would be pure chaos all the time. The formulas for the operating characteristics and costs of this model are relatively simple. As we begin to change the assumptions and develop more complicated models, it is important to understand relationships and concepts, and then rely on the software to do the number crunching, in my opinion.

USING THE MANAGEMENT SCIENTIST SOFTWARE PACKAGE

We will be using The Management Scientist Waiting Line Module to do the actual operating characteristic and cost analyses. To illustrate the package for the first example, click Windows Start/Programmes/The Management Scientist/The Management Scientist Icon/Continue/Select Module 9 Waiting Lines/OK/File/New and you are ready to load this example problem.

A couple of comments are in order. The operating system characteristics are reported similar to those calculated earlier in the module notes. However, the only cost given in the programme output is the total cost. If you wanted to get the components, you would have to work the formulas. Also note the probabilities are the probability of exactly n units in the system. So, the probability of exactly 1 unit in the system is 0.16. To get the probability of 1 or less units in the system, you would have to add the probability of 1 unit in the system to the probability of 0 units in the system. Printing follows the same format used in the other three modules we have used in the course.

MANAGEMENT STRATEGIES

With The Management Scientist Software, management can quickly analyse the impact of continuous improvement strategies. For example, suppose management could train the document clerk to be more efficient and process a document in an average of 10 minutes, versus the current service time of 12 minutes. This change should not impact the arrival rate of 4 documents per hour, at least in the short run. Let's also keep the cost per document waiting at $25.00 per hour, and the cost of service at $15.00 per hour.

PAUSE AND REFLECT

In this example, the service rate was: The document clerk can process 5 documents per hour. Remember to get the service time, take the inverse of the service rate. The inverse of 5 is 1/5th hour, and 1/5th hour is 12 minutes. So, what is the service rate for a service time of 10 minutes? First, convert 10 minutes to hours to keep the time units the same as the arrival rate. That gives 10/60th hours. Now take the inverse of 10/60 which is 60/10 or 6 documents per hour.

Now we are ready to go to The Management Scientist. Note again that all we need as input parametres are the arrival rate, the service rate, the number of servers, and the costs if we are going to perform an economic analysis.

By the way, this analysis took five minutes, including getting a cup of coffee! Seriously, the time consuming part is gathering the data. Every waiting line analysis I have done means getting out a clip board and a watch, and timing how many arrivals come into the system in an hour (or a day, or a month - whatever the appropriate time unit). Repeat this to get at least 30 observations of the arrival rate. This could take some time if there are arrival rate differences throughout the day. For example, a bank teller operation experiences a different arrival rate between 4 and 5 p.m. on a Friday payday than that which is experienced between 9 and 10 a.m. on a slow Tuesday. If the bank wants to study the arrival rate on Friday paydays, they need a lot of Fridays to gather enough observations to get the average arrival rate. After you get the arrival rate, then you have to use your watch and clipboard to measure the service time of the teller, the document clerk, the aircraft unloading team - whatever your server is at 4 p.m. on a Friday payday, do this for maybe 30 observations (30 hours).

Back to management strategies, Suppose instead of training, management decides to hire another document clerk. If we make the assumption that documents can randomly arrive in a line in front of each document clerk (actually would probably go into a file basket) and the clerks allow the documents to be patient (one clerk doesn't steel"easy to process"documents from the other's in basket, for example), then we can use the models of this section to compute the operating characteristics. The only adjustment we need to make is to assume that the arrival rate is cut in half to 2 documents per hour for each clerk. This assumption makes sense if we assume that adding the clerk does not impact the arrival rate of documents to the system in the short run. So, our arrival rate is 2 per hour, the service rate is 5 per hour (for each clerk), and the costs remain at $25 for waiting and $15 for service.

We have to be a little careful since these results are for the single server/single channel system, meaning for one document clerk. We can assume that the average time a document spends in line and in the system are representative for both servers if both document clerks operate at the same service rate (if this assumption isn't t true, then we simply run two different analysis, one for each of the two different service rates). However, we would have to double the average number of units waiting in line and in the system since there are two systems in our new configuration. The cost of this system looks favourable, but remembers, we have to double it since we have two systems. That gives a new total cost of $63.34 - just a little better than the training solution.

But wait a minute! This isn't the best way to add a server,

although this is what grocery stores do - when a new server is added (that is, another cash register opens), a new line is forced to form in front of that server. However, rather than adding a line in front of each server in a waiting line system, it is more efficient to keep a single line that feeds the multiple servers as is done in banks and at Disney. Single line/multiple service channel systems allow the line to discipline the slowest server; and keep customers patient and happy. Every time I go to Dunkin Donuts or the Publix Deli, I try to talk the customers around me to form a single line saying,"it will minimize your average waiting time in the queue compared to the chaos of haphazard clustering around the counter - trust me."Most of the time they just look at me with an expression that says,"you need a hobby or something."We are going to look at the single line/multiple server channel system next.

OTHER WAITING LINE MODELS

Single Line/Multiple Channel System

My favourite waiting line model is this one: I wish more service activities would adopt it. Everything is the same as with the Single Line/Single Channel System except there are multiple service channels.

So, for our example, the arrival rate is 4 documents per hour, the service rate is 5 documents per hour, the cost of waiting is $25 per hour, and the cost of service is $15 per hour per server channel. Let's go to The Management Scientist to get the operating characteristics and costs for a single line/two server channel system.

As anticipated, this configuration gives the best results of all alternatives tried so far. Sorter waiting times and fewer documents in the line and system result in lower costs. Can we improve on the single line/two service channel configuration by adding a third server? Just go back to The Management Scientist, input 3 as the number of service channels, and rerun the solution. The results show the waiting time decreasing but the total cost increasing to $65. This means, 2 servers with a single waiting line is the optimal solution to this problem. While the waiting time did decrease, the decrease from 2 to 3 servers is less than from 1 to 2 servers; but the cost of service goes up at a flat rate of $15 per hour. The net effect is that the total cost curve is beginning to rise when we go to 3 servers. I hope you are getting as excited about waiting line models as I am! We've just scratched the surface but the remaining models just respond to changes in the assumptions. Let me summarize other popular waiting line models.

POISSON ARRIVALS, DETERMINISTIC SERVICE TIME, ONE CHANNEL

The Management Scientist Waiting Line Module includes the model used to analyse single line/single service channel systems that assume deterministic service times. This is the case of automated service, when there is no variation in the time to serve customers.

POISSON ARRIVALS, ARBITRARY SERVICE TIME, ONE CHANNEL

The Management Scientist Waiting Line Module includes the model used to analyse single line/single service channel systems that assume service times are not random and independent. Recall that when service times are random and independent, we can model them with the Exponential Distribution. But what if your service times for your project follow the Beta Distribution like in Pert/CPM. Recall that activity times are represented by three time estimates: optimistic, most likely and pessimistic. Recall also that we can compute the mean and standard deviation for this distribution with no trouble at all. To work this model in The Management Scientist, just select Poisson Arrivals/Arbitrary Service (1 Channel) in the Model selection screen, and the next screen asks you for the mean and standard deviation of the service time.

Poisson Arrivals/Arbitrary Service (No Waiting)

This waiting line system is like a telephone system that

does not allow customers to wait if the telephone server is busy. The Management Scientist has this option but don't expect a lot of operating characteristic output. That is obviously because with no waiting, there is no average wait time, average number of units in the line, etc. Multiple channels are allowed.

Poisson Arrivals/Exponential Service (Finite Population)

This waiting line system is designed for scenarios in which there is a finite customer base, where finite is defined as less than 30 customers - sometimes referred to as the machine repair problem. At Ramstein Air Base we had a detachment of 8 C-130 cargo aircraft. The aircraft maintenance operation was really a waiting line system with the average arrival rate being the number of aircraft that would go into maintenance per day. The service time was the average time to repair or inspect/maintain the aircraft. But since there were only 8"customers", we would use this model to analyse the operating characteristics of the system.

CUSTOMER SERVICE FUNCTION

Customer Service Representaives provide a valuable link between customers and the companies who produce the products they buy and the services they use. They are responsible for responding to customer inquiries and making sure that any problems they are experiencing are resolved. Although most customer service representatives do their work by telephone in call centres, some interact with customers by e-mail, fax, post, or face-to-face.

Many customer service inquiries involve simple questions or requests. For instance, a customer may want to know the status of an order or wish to change his or her address in the company's file. However, some questions may be somewhat more difficult, and may require additional research or help from an expert. In some cases, a representative's main function may be to determine who in the organization is best suited to answer a customer's questions.

Some customer inquiries are complaints, which generally must be handled in accordance with strict company policies. In some cases, representatives may try to fix problems or suggest solutions. They may have the authority to reverse erroneous fees or send replacement products. Other representatives act as gatekeepers who make sure that complaints are valid before accepting customer returns.

Although selling products and services is not the primary function of a customer service representative, some customer services representatives may provide information that helps customers to make purchasing decisions. For instance, a representative may point out a product or service that would fulfill a customer's needs.

Customer service representatives use computers, telephones, and other technology extensively in their work. When the customer has an account with the company, a representative will usually open his or her file in the company's computer system. Representatives use this information to solve problems and may be able to make specific changes as necessary. They also have access to responses for the most commonly asked questions and specific guidelines for dealing with requests or complaints. In the event that the representative does not know the answer or is unable to solve a specific problem, a supervisor or other experienced worker may provide assistance.

Many customer service workers are located in call centres, where they spend the entire day speaking on the telephone. Companies usually keep statistics on their workers to make sure they are working efficiently. This helps them to keep up with their call volume and ensures that customers do not have to wait on hold for extended periods of time. Supervisors may listen in on or tape calls to ensure customers are getting quality service.

Almost every industry employs customer service representatives, and their duties may vary greatly depending on the nature of the organization. For instance, representatives who work in banks may have similar duties to tellers, whereas those in insurance companies may be required to handle paperwork, such as changes to policies or renewals. Those who work for utility and communication companies may assist customers with service problems, such as outages. Representatives who work in retail stores often handle returns and help customers to find items in their stores.

Work environment. Although customer service representatives work in a variety of settings, most work in areas that are clean and well lit. Those who work in call centres generally have their own workstations or cubicle spaces equipped with telephones, headsets, and computers. Because many call centres are open extended hours or are staffed around the clock, these positions may require workers to take on early morning, evening, or late night shifts. Weekend or holiday work is also common. Because peak times may not last for a full shift, many workers are part-time or work a split shift. As a result, the occupation is well suited to flexible work schedules. Many companies hire additional employees at certain times of year when higher call volumes are expected.

Call centres may be crowded and noisy, and work may be repetitious and stressful, with little time between calls. Also, long periods spent sitting, typing, or looking at a computer screen may cause eye and muscle strain, backaches, headaches, and repetitive motion injuries. A growing number of employers are hiring telecommuters, who provide customer service from their own homes. Although this remains somewhat rare, it can be a major advantage for workers who need to remain in their homes during the day.

Customer service representatives working in retail stores may have customers approach them in person or contact them by telephone. They may be required to work later in the evenings or on weekends, as stores are generally open during those times. Evenings and weekends tend to be peak hours for customer traffic. Customer service representatives may have to deal with difficult or irate customers, which can be challenging. However, the ability to resolve customers'problems has the potential to be very rewarding.

13

Services Management Trinity

Service Management is integrated into Supply Chain Management as the joint between the actual sales and the customer. The aim of high performance Service Management is to optimize the service-intensive supply chains, which are usually more complex than the typical finished-goods supply chain. Most service-intensive supply chains require larger inventories and tighter integration with field service and third parties. They also must accommodate inconsistent and uncertain demand by establishing more advanced information and product flows. Moreover, all processes must be coordinated across numerous service locations with large numbers of parts and multiple levels in the supply chain.

Among typical manufacturers, post-sale services (maintenance, repair and parts) comprise less than 20 per cent of revenue. But among the most innovative companies in Service, those same activities often generate more than 50 per cent of the profits.

Traditionally overlooked as a'necessary evil', Service Management is moving to the forefront as a business strategy. To maintain growth and customer loyalty in a competitive environment, leading companies are now recognizing the need to improve Service and Service Parts Management capabilities.

Benefits

The main drivers for a company to establish or optimize its Service Management practices are varied:

- High service costs can be reduced, i.e. by integrating the service and products supply chain.

- Inventory levels of service parts can be reduced and therefore reduce total inventory costs.
- Customer service or parts/service quality can be optimized.
- Increasing service revenue.
- Reduce obsolescence costs of service parts through improved forecasting.
- Improve customer satisfaction levels.
- Reduce expediting costs - with optimized service parts inventory, there is no need to rush orders to customers.
- Minimize technician visits - if they have the right part in hand, they can fix the problem on the first visit.

An impressive body of literature on the management of service companies has emerged since G. Lynn Shostack advocated, in 1977'that services"break free". The unique characteristics of services have received acceptance, while related issues of service design and production, services marketing, and services management have been given an impressive amount of attention in books and leading journals.

Despite this progress, a number of issues mandate continued scrutiny. There is the growing recognition that the boundaries between goods and services have become increasingly blurred and that the majority of goods contains significant service components and vice versa. For example, some commentators have noted the potential for competitive advantage that is inherent in correctly leveraging the service components of products. This fluidity is perhaps best captured in Shostack's molecular model, which views all market entities as containing some tangible and intangible elements with services being defined as intangible-dominant entities. The outcome of this dialogue has been an increase in the number of services management perspectives that are applicable in what were traditionally considered manufacturing domains and, conversely, an increase in the level of attention given to the strategic management of service firms.

Central to this debate is the issue of how service companies can attain a sustainable competitive advantage.

"Service businesses generally are noted for their high level of mimetic or imitative behaviour. Innovations, such as new types of bank accounts or investment vehicles, are invariably quickly imitated by competitors. Innovative airlines, which sought to use frequent flyer programmes to build switching costs for customers, found that, very quickly, many other major airlines were offering similar incentives. This level of imitation has focused attention on what kinds of resources and capabilities a service firm might leverage in order to gain a competitive advantage.

Gaining positions of competitive strength has become more important in an environment that has become increasingly global and competitive. Competition in industries such as air travel and transportation is inherently more global than in many manufacturing businesses. Deregulation in the likes of financial services has ushered in a new era of global competition and quick competitive reactions. The size and importance of the service sector has grown considerably. This sector accounted for 74 per cent of gross domestic product and about 79 per cent of national employment in the United States in 1992. In addition almost 60 per cent of total value added in the U.S. economy in 1992 came from private (nongovernment) services.

This chapter responds to these developments by proposing a model of competitive advantage in the international services sector, which is designed to help managers evaluate the potential sources of such advantage. It draws heavily on an existing foundation of literature spanning the disparate fields of services marketing, strategic management, international business, and industrial organization economics. At the intersection of these strands of thought is the resource-based view (RBV), which is the conceptual premise of this chapter. The next section outlines the perspectives provided by the RBV for international services firms. Subsequently, a conceptual model is presented, and selected sources of international competitive advantage are outlined. Finally, conclusions are drawn and implications discussed.

COMPETITION IN INTERNATIONAL BUSINESS: INSIGHTS FROM THE RESOURCE-BASED VIEW

Organizational strategy has long been viewed as the challenge of matching internal resources and strengths with the opportunities existing in the environment. This is perhaps best summarized in the seminal framework of Learned, Christensen, Andrews, and Guth. Thus, the task of strategic management is viewed in terms of the interplay of the personal values of management with the firms'skills and resources, and of how these are matched to environmental opportunities/ threats and broader societal expectations.

Throughout the early 1980s, the broad thrust of strategy research focused on the second quadrant. This research is best demonstrated by the work of Porter. It posited that a firm's performance was largely a function of the structure of the industry and the firm's position in the industry. However, empirical research toward the end of the decade increasingly began to show greater performance differences among firms in the same industry than across industry boundaries. Allied to this was a conceptual swing toward the end of the decade back to a forgotten portion of the LCAG framework, namely quadrant 1. Building on earlier work by Penrose and Nelson and Winter, what has become known as the resource-based view is illustrated by the work of Barney, Conner, Dierickx and Cool, Grant, Mahoney and Pandian, and Peteraf, to name but a few.

The resource-based view focuses on heterogeneity among firms in the same industry. It views firms in terms of unique bundles of resources and capabilities that provide the basis upon which a competitive advantage can be pursued. The normative implication of this view is that the firm should base its strategy on its own resources and capabilities. Irrespective of the markets or combination of markets served, firms should seek to leverage the resources best suited to those markets. This may even lead to a situation where the firm will choose to compete in inherently less structurally attractive markets if it possesses resources that are valuable in serving those markets. Of course, in an international context, there may be other motives for competing in structurally unattractive markets, most notably defensive foreign direct investment or cross-subsidization, where firms try to preempt the strategic moves of international rivals.

CONDITIONS NECESSARY FOR COMPETITIVE ADVANTAGE

The potential to confer a competitive advantage is not inherent in all resources but, rather, in only those that meet a rigorous set of conditions. The first condition is that the resource must be valuable--it must provide the opportunity to exploit some environmental opportunity or neutralize some threat. Resources are considered valuable when they enable a firm to conceive of or implement strategies that improve the firm's efficiency or effectiveness. Some authors construe value in terms of meeting a key buyer need.

In addition, resources must have the characteristic of rareness. If valuable resources are possessed by a large number of competitors or potential competitors, they no longer represent a source of competitive advantage. This is the key issue of heterogeneity underlying the resource-based view--firms possessing unique bundles of skills and resources can attain a sustainable competitive advantage. Third, there must be the condition of imperfect mobility of resources.

Where resources are easily traded between competitors, no competitive advantage can be maintained. Imperfectly mobile resources include those that are idiosyncratic to the firm, those for which property rights arc not well defined, or those that are co-specialized assets. The imperfect mobility of assets is a critical factor in service businesses as people are the key assets in many cases, and their high mobility frequently results in the loss of accounts and the emergence of new competitive threats as in the case, for example, with personnel employed by advertising agencies and moving to other ones.

Finally, for an advantage to be sustained, resources must be imperfectly imitable or provide some ex-post limits to competition: That is, subsequent to a firm gaining a superior position and earning rents, forces must exist that limit competition for those rents. It was noted above that innovations such as the development of a new type of account by a retail bank or a new advertising style by a creative department frequently results in a host of imitations from competitors.

For a firm to be in a position to exploit a valuable and rare resource, there must be a resource position barrier preventing imitation by other firms. Sustaining a competitive advantage over a period of time requires the presence of isolating mechanisms that prevent imitation. Several such barriers that have been cited in the literature include causal ambiguity and uncertain imitability, where the drivers of success are difficult to identify. Imitation may also be prevented by the process of asset stock accumulation within the firm.

Where these stocks possess the characteristics of time compression diseconomies (accumulation has taken place over a long period of time), asset mass efficiencies (a critical mass of stocks has been developed), and interconnectedness (stocks are interrelated), then imitation is difficult. Indeed, the significance of asset stock accumulation in the services sector has been demonstrated elsewhere, when the"reservoir of organizational and managerial expertise that has been built up over the years can provide branch offices with information at a cost very much lower than a de novo indigenous firm would have to incur"--in other words, an ownership advantage in international competition.

Thus, service firms must seek to identify the skills and resources they possess and that meet the above criteria, and to leverage such resources to attain a competitive advantage. For service firms trading internationally, there is the added dimension of the location of such resources, which may be in the home or host country, or both. The traditional international-business literature and the more recent global strategic management literature have identified that the success of a multinational firm is likely to be based on some combination of three sets of advantages, namely, firm-specific advantages, country-specific advantages, and internalization advantages. In resource terms, this effectively amounts to the combination of country-specific and firm-specific resources since internalization or coordination can be viewed as a managerial capability and hence a firm-specific resource.

The conceptual lens of the RBV demonstrates important differences between these two sets of resources. Country-specific resources derive from the resource endowments of countries or, in neoclassical economics terms, its comparative advantages. Country-specific resources are available on equal terms to all firms competing in an industry. Therefore, there are no barriers to prevent competing firms from imitating a given firm's portfolio of country-specific advantages. It is recognized, however, that a given firm's ability to gain access to these resources or to preempt their usage may be dependent on firm-specific political competences. In addition, some authors suggest that country-specific advantages are dynamic and change over time--for example, Japan's move from a low-labour-cost country to a high-labour-cost country. However, firm-specific resources are considered unique to the firm, and, therefore, are likely to possess greater barriers to imitation, which suggests that they will be a more important source of competitive advantage.

RESOURCES VERSUS CAPABILITIES

Authors have recently sought to distinguish between the potential rent-generating assets of an organization. A variety of distinctions have been suggested, including assets and core competences, resources and capabilities, intellectual assets and nonintellectual assets, tangible and intangible resources, and assets and skills. Despite the range of nomenclature, the issue being addressed by the various authors is similar, namely, that the rent-generating assets of an organization can be broadly classified in terms of two basic types. On the one hand, there are the organization's resources, which are tangible, can be either inputs or outputs, and possess two key attributes: ownership and value. Ownership can be legal in terms of title deeds to land, property, or equipment, or in intellectual property such as patents, trademarks, licenses, or trade secrets.

In addition, the firm may own assets that are not legal in nature, such as reputation with customers, organizational or personal networks, and databases. The most acceptable measure of value from an accounting perspective is exchange value. Thus, resources in the main are viewed as relatively easy to trade between firms.

On the other hand, organizations also possess capabilities or competences--that is, the capacity to deploy resources, usually in combination, in order to effect a desired end. The key characteristics of capabilities are that they are firm-specific and developed over time, but, unlike resources, they are not easily tradable between firms. In general, capabilities are information-based or intellectual assets. In addition, they tend to be cross-functional or arise from the integration of individual functional capabilities and thus are sometimes referred to as"intermediate goods"in the production process. Therefore, by definition, capabilities meet the requirements of rareness and inimitability and are a strong basis for competitive advantage. The normative implication of this logic is that service-firm capabilities are likely to be the most sustainable source of competitive advantage.

HOME- AND HOST-COUNTRY FIRM-SPECIFIC RESOURCES AND CAPABILITIES

The issue of potential synergies between home- and host-country firm-specific advantages has been a central issue in the vast body of work that broadly falls within the gambit of globalization. The globalization debate began in the early 1980s and has continued with intensity ever since. One of the primary hypotheses of globalization was that markets were converging. Reaching back to the marketing-standardization literature of the 1960s, this meant that companies could be successful by selling standardized products throughout a global market at low prices due to the resulting economies of scale, in effect utilizing only home-country firm-specific advantages. This was in sharp contrast to the earlier view of the multinational corporation as a collection of autonomous subsidiaries tailoring resource use and strategy to particular local market needs. However, even some of the early proponents of globalization conceded that this hypothesis might be a little simplistic, and began to suggest that standardization was a matter of degree.

From this recognition of complexity emerged the view that, to be successful in the global marketplace. The firm must organize itself to achieve the benefits of global integration, national responsiveness, and learning. In resource terms, this meant that the firm should not rely solely on the resources of the parent company (global integration) or the subsidiary (national responsiveness), but must seek to emphasize both and successfully transfer learning in both directions (i.e., from the home-country headquarters to the subsidiary and vice versa). So, while several authors contend that a company should pursue a global strategy on the basis of the globalization potential of the industry, there is a contrasting view that firms need to combine both global and local dimensions, sometimes known crudely as""localization".

Stated in resource terms, this"transnational solution"suggests that superior performers in international business will combine both home- and host-country firm-specific resources and capabilities. This suggests that service firms must consider extensive foreign direct investment and create an opportunity for the successful combination of home- and host-country firm-specific resources and capabilities. However, other"nonequity"forms of organization, with origins largely in the services sector, such as licensing, franchising, and management contracts, equally present an opportunity for the successful integration of home-and host-country resources. Their effectiveness in achieving such integration seems to be greater in consumer services than in industrial or business services.

COUNTRY-SPECIFIC AND FIRM-SPECIFIC RESOURCES

Porter highlighted that many firm-specific resources were rooted in the firm's country of origin. This is illustrated by the strength of German companies in engineering, of U.S.

companies in consumer goods and services, and of Italian companies in craft-based industries. Kogut extended this analysis to show that long cycles of country leadership in international competition can be explained by differences in country capabilities embodied in the firms in these countries.

In addition, many of these capabilities are sticky and diffuse slowly across borders due to four factors: technological opportunities, selection forces, identifiability, and institutional lock-in. In terms of technology, many firms have established relationships with country-specific research centres, trade associations, educational institutions, and skilled individuals. These relationships are built up over a long time and are not easy to replicate in other countries. In many cases, these are the clusters of organizations identified in Porter's "diamond"framework. Equally, selection pressures are analogous to Porter's concept of domestic rivalry, an essential requirement to the development of globally competitive firms.

Identifiability refers to domestic firms having a better understanding of the sources of success of domestic competitors than do international competitors. This understanding can have numerous reasons and results in a greater propensity to imitate domestic competitors that leads to greater national rather than international diffusion of management capabilities. Institutional lock-in is analagous to the notions of administrative heritage or strategic commitment at a national level where the change and adoption of new techniques are impeded by previous investment, past practices, and perceived wisdom. The immediate implication of this analysis is that the firm-specific advantages underlying service-firm strategy are likely to vary from country to country, reflecting the fact that such advantages derive largely from the country of origin and diffuse slowly across borders.

Kogut, however, noted that long cycles of country leadership are driven not only by technological investments resources) but also by the efficiency of the dominant organizing principles (capabilities). Foreign direct investment is the extension of the organizing principles of domestic firms to foreign markets. Organizational types, such as the global firm, provide a vehicle for the diffusion of capabilities across borders due to the high level of integration or coordination of its activities.

Close interaction between parents and subsidiaries is also a central aspect of the transnational firm, which has been advocated as the organizational type most suitable, given the current complexity of international business though not necessarily in every industry. Most major multinational firms have at various times experimented with increasing the integration of their operations. The learning that has accrued from these integration efforts suggests that the firm-specific advantages underlying the strategy of leading international competitors will not vary from one host country to another, thereby reflecting the diffusion of management capability.

TOWARD A RESOURCE-BASED MODEL OF COMPETITIVE ADVANTAGE IN INTERNATIONAL BUSINESS

The process by which resources and capabilities are translated into a competitive advantage for the multinational firm, which demonstrates that superior performance is likely to be attained through the adoption of strategies based on a combination of home- and host-country firm-specific resources with host-country location-specific resources. It highlights that management plays an essential role in leveraging this resource pool in ways that enable the firm to gain advantage. Management must make choices regarding which product markets to compete in, whether to try to attain a position of low-cost leadership or differentiation, or both, and which resources and capabilities to use in order to attain these positions of competitive leadership. Superior performance, which can be measured in the conventional terms of market share leadership or return on investment, accrues to firms achieving a competitive advantage. Sustaining the advantage over time requires reinvestment on the basis of competitive strength.

This model is an extension of the model of competitive advantage that can be found in the strategic-management literature, but it clearly sits very comfortably with the extant international business literature, as well as the"transnational solution"proposed by Bartlett and Ghoshal to help managers deal with the complexity of international business.

SOURCES OF COMPETITIVE ADVANTAGE FOR INTERNATIONAL SERVICE FIRMS

The model is designed to assist managers of service firms in building a sustainable competitive advantage on the foundation of the resources and capabilities inherent in the company. It also helps managers identify which skills and resources are most likely to be an important source of advantage and to realise the importance of being able to combine potential advantages from both home- and host-country locations. In specific cases, the actual skills and resources underlying competitive advantage are likely to be contingent on the characteristics of the service itself, the service firm, and the service industry as well as of the country of origin of the firm.

However, sources of advantage in service industries identified elsewhere can be seen to meet the requirements outlined in the model. For example, Stalk, Evans, and Schulman contend that the growth and subsequent market dominance of WalMart resides in the company's unique logistics capability, which confirms the importance of capabilities as a potential source of competitive advantage. The logistics system known as"cross-docking"ensures that goods are simply moved from one loading dock to another in forty-eight hours or less, resulting in minimal inventories and shaving between 2 per cent and 3 per cent off the cost of sales. The system is a source of competitive advantage because it meets all of the criteria outlined earlier. It is used in a value-generating way-creating cost savings in a business where tight margins are critical and low costs are a key success factor.

It is a rare system, and, because it combines people, delivery vehicles, and communication systems, it is clearly immobile. But it is its inherent barriers to imitation that help to confer a competitive advantage on WalMart. It is extremely difficult to duplicate the required constant communication between suppliers, distribution centres, and sales outlets achieved through the company's investment in a private satellite communications system.

Similarly, Pleval, Nellis, Lane, and Schuler attribute the success of AT&T's Global Business Communication Systems (GBCS) division to its unique human resource capability. Its human resource strategy is linked to overall business strategy, and review and reward mechanisms are designed to increase personal motivation while simultaneously achieving company goals. The company views its employees as"its only sustainable competitive advantage."

Again, this division of AT&T has been successful because it utilizes a set of resources/capabilities that meet the criteria necessary for competitive advantage. GBCS uses people in a value-generating way by explicitly connecting their efforts with key company goals such as using a total quality management approach, being a leader in customer-led applications of technology, and being the best value supplier. People can always leave an organization, so why do many firms contend that their people are their only sustainable advantage?

In the ease of GCBS, mobility of personnel is not a major concern, as its success resides not in individuals but rather in a complex set of relationships among individuals reflected in performance management, recognition, compensation practices, and communication programmes. Furthermore, even though individuals who are hired away by competitors are able to describe them, these systems prove difficult to imitate because of the levels of reaming that occur while these"asset stocks"are being accumulated.

The key role of people, as a source of competitive advantage in internationally traded services, is demonstrated by the high level of foreign direct investment by firms in industries like financial and management services in order to maintain control over this resource.

This chapter contends that competitive advantage for service firms lies in the unique resources and capabilities possessed by the firm. Not all resources or capabilities are a source of competitive advantage-only those that meet the stringent conditions of value, rareness. immobility, and barriers to imitation. The actual sources of competitive advantage are likely to vary depending on the nature of the service, the particular traits of the firm, the nature of the industry, and the country of origin.

The normative implication of this analysis is that service managers conduct a rigorous analysis of internal resources and capabilities. What eve resources and capabilities does the firm have, and which of any of these strengths are unique? What scope is there for making investments to develop unique resources and capabilities that would yield competitive advantages in the future?

The analysis also raises the question of control of key sources of competitive advantage. Foreign direct investment arguably creates the greatest potential not only for control but also for the effective integration of resources across national boundaries. More traditional forms of organization in the services sector, such as licensing, franchising, and management contracts, have been shown to be effective control mechanisms in consumer, though not in business, services.

14

Interfunctional Conflicts

Working relationships between functional areas are critical to firm performance. Most business initiatives require the active participation of an array of functional areas; consider me team effort involved in successful product launches or the complex organizational coordination needed to open a new retail store.

Priorities must be aligned across various functional areas and operations coordinated to gain the greatest benefit and exploit opportunities. While the interdependence involved would seem to mandate working together, functional silos and isolationism often create significant barriers. Thus, many firms face a substantial challenge as they struggle with internal misalignment. Ideally, internal relationships should help focus individual and organizational efforts to encourage cooperation and achieve objectives.

The current research was undertaken to examine the influence of internal relationships on firms'logistics performance. More specifically, the research centres on relationship effectiveness between marketing and logistics and how it influences the development of capabilities (information capabilities and firm-wide integration) and ultimately - logistics performance. It is our contention that effective marketing/logistics relationships can help to create, develop, and maintain critical capabilities to support long-term firm success. Coordination within a firm is generally considered a prerequisite to supply chain coordination extending across companies. Effective relationships can serve as a coordination mechanism.

The following sections briefly review the theory base for the research and introduce a conceptual model. Relevant literature is presented and synthesized to support research hypotheses. Then research methodology and analysis/results are detailed. Finally, managerial implications along with limitations and suggestions for future research are detailed.

The resource-based view (RBV) of the firm provides the tiieoretical framework for our research. The resource based view of the firm attributes superior performance to organizational resources and capabilities.

Resources are assets a firm owns or has access to. Resources can be considered strengths that firms can use to develop and implement strategies. Firm resources are often classified into three categories: physical capital resources, human capital resources, and organizational capital resources. Physical capital resources include physical technology used in a firm, plant and equipment, geographic locations, and access to raw materials. Human capital resources include the training, experience, judgment, intelligence, relationships, and insight of individual managers and workers. Organizational capital resources include a firm's formal reporting structure, formal and informal planning, controlling, and coordinating systems, as well as informal relations among groups within the firm and between the firm and its environment. In the current research, we are most interested in relationship-oriented resources. Relationship-oriented resources can actually fall under both the human capital and organizational capital resource categories.

Capabilities involve an organization's ability to assemble, integrate, and deploy resources. Similarly, Hunt refers to capabilities as"repeatable patterns of action in the use of assets to create, produce, and/or offer products to a market". In other words, capabilities are what firms do with assets; how they make use of their assets. Firms attempt to transform assets into something (e.g., better service, innovative products) that will give them an edge in the marketplace. The intent is to identify and build capabilities that set them apart from their competitors. Differences in resource allocation, in corporate focus, and in how firms leverage their resources, result in differentiated capabilities. Because of resource constraints, firms must select the most opportune areas for capability development that offer the most defensible competitive position.

Two types of capabilities are examined in our research - information capability and firm-wide integration capability. Again, capabilities deal with an organization's abilities. Thus, information capability refers to an organization's ability to acquire, process, and transmit information to support decision-making. The complexity and fast-paced nature of today's business environment make high level information capability more important than ever.

Integration capability is the organization's success in, or ability to get, separate work parties (departments, functional areas) to work together in a cooperative manner to arrive at mutually acceptable outcomes. Integration capability is defined at the firm level, not the dyadic level. Integration capability is critical to coordinate business operations and focus resources. Both capabilities are related to logistics performance, as described in detail in the subsequent sections. Our model depicts the relationships between resources, capabilities, and firms'logistics performance. The next section presents rationale for the proposed relationships.

RESOURCE-CAPABILITY LINKAGES

Interfunctional interactions are required if personnel are going to effectively work together to achieve corporatelevel strategic objectives. Employees in various functional areas have the potential to contribute a variety of skills and expertise that ideally can be blended together for the good of the organization. However, conflicts can occur due to differences in individual goals. Therefore, it is essential that personnel recognize the value of working together.

Our research examines the effectiveness of marketing and logistics relationships, specifically, the perception of personnel interacting with others in the two functional areas that their relations are worthwhile, equitable, productive, and satisfying.

Marketing and logistics were selected because of the vital roles they play within firms and extending to the supply chain. They directly interact with customers and impact value creation for customers.

Innis and La Londe's study found that both logistics and marketing significantly contribute to customer satisfaction. Marketing assumes responsibility for creating and managing demand; logistics assumes responsibility for fulfilling demand. The product must be where customers want it, when they want it, in order to close the sale. The relationship between marketing and logistics can provide a foundation for broader organizational gains, including firm-wide integration.

Integration is generally considered to involve interaction and collaboration. Previous studies have mainly focused on dyadic internal integration - involving only two functional areas. However, at an optimal level, integration should bring all departments together into a cohesive organization. Such firm-wide integration extends across functional boundaries of a firm and requires a system view of all the business processes within a firm.

Thus, firm-wide integration, instead of dyadic internal integration, is examined in the current study. As discussed above, marketing and logistics are critical to creating customer value; however, they cannot work in isolation and achieve long-term success.

This is clearly indicated by Porter's value chain framework, which identifies both marketing and logistics as primary functions and points out that they need to be linked with other functions to create superior customer value. Other areas ranging from manufacturing to finance and customer service ideally must supplement the efforts of marketing and logistics. As both marketing and logistics are highly customer-centred, effective coordination and focused attention by these two functions can provide the platform for the broader integration to develop a truly market-oriented firm.

Thus, it is argued that if the relationship between marketing and logistics is effective, it will have a positive influence on firm-wide integration. Within the RBV framework, marketing and logistics relationships are considered a resource. That resource can be leveraged to create a capability in the form of firm-wide integration.

H1: Marketing/logistics relationship effectiveness has a positive impact on firm-wide integration.

Marketing/logistics relationship effectiveness as a resource is proposed to be related to another type of firm capability - information technology capability. Information technology (IT) capability refers to the ability to acquire, process, and transmit information for effective decision-making. Information technology capabilities, as will be discussed subsequently, are generally believed to be associated with enhanced performance. However, there have also been examples where IT extensions failed to yield productivity/quality improvements. The literature refers to this as a"productivity paradox."

With respect to IT results, some studies have shown IT to have a strong positive impact on specific performance measures while other studies have provided contradictory findings. The implication is that management sometimes fails to leverage the full potential of IT. It is proposed that input from marketing and logistics can help to leverage IT to better advantage. Previous researchers have reported instances in which information technology applications were not relevant to industry and/or firm information needs.

As Tippins and Sohi noted, managers have"begun to realise that there is still much to learn about how to best strategically position IT to ensure the greatest positive effect". Marketing and logistics personnel, who are typically closest to the line of action, can help to determine the best information systems, and allocate resources to the areas of most need. Marketing and logistics groups that have developed effective relationships and work well together, will be better prepared to guide IT strategies and decisions than are marketing and logistics groups mat are less interactive and less collaborative. Thus it is proposed mat:

H2: Marketing/logistics relationship effectiveness has a positive impact on information capability.

CAPABILITY TO CAPABILITY LINKAGE

In addition to the impact of the marketing/logistics relationship on two types of firm capabilities (firm-wide integration and information capability), the relationship between these two capabilities is also examined in the current study. The free flow of information across the supply chain enables effective integration and"serves as me key that unlocks the power of supply chain integration". Integration whether internal or external - is predicated on the exchange of information.

The positive causal relationship between information capability and firm-wide integration can be explained from two perspectives. First, from a relational point of view, better information capability can reduce conflicts among various functional areas, which in turn can make firm-wide integration possible. Ruekert and Walker suggest that communication difficulty can cause significant conflicts among different functional areas because of differences in backgrounds, objectives, and values. Cross-functional conflicts resulting from communication breakdowns will make the implementation of firm-wide integration difficult to achieve. Conversely, smooth communication among functional areas facilitated by superior information capability can minimize potential conflicts and allow different departments to work together.

Second, from an operational perspective, information capability is a necessity for implementing firm-wide integration. Firm-wide integration involves coordination and collaboration among all relevant functional areas. Shared information must be relevant and useful. Thus, IT has been argued to be the backbone of supply chain structure because it allows for the transmission and processing of information necessary for synchronous decisionmaking. Williams, Nibbs, Irby, and Finley also noted mat IT provides critical support for strategic and operational decisions. While me importance of information systems cannot be overemphasized, the current study focuses more specifically on a firm's information capability. As discussed previously, advanced information systems do not guarantee attaining desired firm gains. Instead, me emphasis needs to be placed on developing superior information capability with the support of efficient and effective information systems. High levels of firm-wide integration can only be achieved when the information systems are designed to improve the speed, accuracy, and sharing of information needed within the firm as well as with external constituencies.

H3: A firm's information capability positively enhances firm-wide integration.

CAPABILITY-PERFORMANCE LINKAGES

Some of the previous research found no direct linkage between information technology and performance. This is not surprising - information technology is a commodity. As such, it is neither difficult to transfer or to imitate. Barney suggests that it is difficult for a firm to develop sustained competitive advantage or superior performance purely based on information technology. Instead, information capability - not information technology per se - has a positive impact on logistics performance.

When a firm successfully transforms its information capability into a distinctive capability, it is not readily matched by rivals, it makes disproportionate contribution to customer value creation, and it is robust and can be used in different ways. A high level of information capability allows dissemination of needed information throughout an organization (or across organizations). The dissemination and sharing of information can provide support for decision-making, lead to consensus regarding the meaning of the information, and generally allow members of the firm to act on the information in pursuit of organizational goals.

The ability of a firm to effectively share information plays an important role in overall firm performance. This is due, in part, to the fact that application of information technology has the effect of reducing levels of complexity.

In general, distinctive capabilities can contribute significantly to superior performance. For example, previous research has shown that firms with higher levels of information technology capabilities outperform other firms on financial measures. Information capability is especially critical to logistics performance because logistics operations are heavily dependent on effective and efficient information sharing. Logistics activities typically involve the sharing of very timely and very sensitive demand and sales data, inventory data, and shipping status data.

Although some studies have argued the positive relationship between information technology and logistics performance, Droge and Germain's study yielded an interesting finding: EDI (a type of information technology) doesn't have a positive impact on a firm's inventory management (a type of logistics performance) unless the firm's JIT reaches a sufficient level. Droge and Germain's result implies that information technology can only contribute to better logistics performance (inventory management in their study) when it is used to develop necessary information capability (to support JIT in their study).

Similarly, Daugherty also suggests that EDI as a type of technology is necessary but not sufficient to guarantee strategic linkage. Thus, instead of focusing on the IT itself, it is more important for firms to develop high levels of information capability, which can improve logistics performance. Developing IT as a capability is the key. From me practitioners' perspective, many managers have also stated that information technology capability is the most important factor influencing logistics performance improvement.

H4: A firm's information capability positively impacts logistics performance.

Integration is a cornerstone of supply chain management. The Council of Supply Chain Management Professionals' (CSCMP) definition of supply chain management clearly states:"In essence, supply chain management integrates supply and demand management within and across companies."The locus of our study is internal integration - firm-wide integration.

The literature strongly suggests that integrating processes, at all levels, should increase firm performance. Giménez and

Ventura found that companies achieving higher levels of internal integration enjoy higher absolute performance than those with lower levels of internal integration.

Internal integration has also been shown to improve performance in the areas of customer service, better management of inventory, higher forecast accuracy, and greater customer and employee satisfaction. In part, the enhanced performance comes about because linking internal activities helps to reduce duplication and redundancy while meeting customer demand at lower costs.

The interest of the current study is the link between internal integration and logistics performance. Giménez and Ventura attribute integration-related improvements to achieving cost, stock-out, and lead time reductions because of collaboration among the internal process areas. Gustin, Daugherty, and Stank found that integrated firms are more likely to achieve significant tangible logistics benefits including substantial inventory savings, lead time reductions, customer service enhancements, and improved forecasting and scheduling capabilities. The rationale behind this link is simple but very important: logistics cannot be managed in a vacuum, and superior logistics performance can only be achieved when all relevant functional areas work closely together. Thus,

H5: Firm-wide integration positively impacts logistics performance.

The following section details the data collection and research methodology. Hypothesis testing and results are also presented.

Survey research was used to collect the data, while multi-item scales were deemed appropriate to measure the constructs. The questionnaire was subjected to a thorough review by six highly qualified professionals, including three academicians with relevant research experience, two consultants, and one executive from the electronics industry. These experts evaluated the scales and survey draft from the perspectives of representativeness, specificity, clarity, readability, content validity, and face validity. Modifications were made based on their feedback.

A total of 434 prospective respondents were selected from logistics/supply chain executives of Fortune 500 companies and members of the Council of Supply Chain Management Professionals. The selection of potential respondents was based on involvement in the areas of interest as indicated by job title. The study used a key informant approach. Executives selected are in a unique position with sufficient information to provide the input needed. Other researchers have provided justification for utilizing key informant reports.

After initial telephone contact, 253 executives agreed to look at the survey and consider completing it. Potential respondents were provided with the option to complete the survey either through a survey web site or in a paperbased format. A cover letter was enclosed with the survey to explain the purpose of the research, and a drawing for $500 was offered as an incentive to increase response. Two weeks after the initial wave of mailings and emails, a follow-up postcard or email was sent as a reminder. At the end of the designated response time, 125 usable surveys were received, representing a 28.8% response rate. Out of these responses, 111 were completed online and the balance in paper format. Griffis, Goldsby, and Cooper found no differences in the nature of data gathered by web-based and mail surveys. Our responses are in line with their findings; a comparison of responses (web-based vs. mail) showed no significant statistical differences. Thus, it is believed that these 125 responses can be analysed as a single data set.

Non-response error was tested in two ways: The first test compared early and late respondents for all study constructs. There were no significant differences found between the last quartile of responses, and the first three quartiles of responses. As an additional test of non-response bias, 15 non-respondents were randomly chosen from the sample to complete an abbreviated version of the questionnaire online. Telephone calls were made to help ensure all completed the survey. Again, comparison of the responses to the same items in both the full and short versions revealed no significant differences between respondents and non-respondents. Thus, non-response bias is not considered a problem in the final sample.

CONSTRUCTS AND SCALE ITEMS

The items from Stank, Daugherty, and Ellinger and Ellinger, Daugherty, and Keller, which originated with Van de Ven and Ferry's research on organizational assessment, were adapted to measure the effectiveness of marketing/logistics relationships. Respondents indicated moderate levels of effectiveness in marketing/logistics relationships within their firms. The means of the five items ranged from 4.12 to 4.62.

The measure of the information capability construct was adopted from Bardi, Raghunathan, and BagChi. Four Likert scale items were anchored with 1 = Strongly Disagree, 4 = Neutral, and 7 = Strongly Agree. Again, responses showed moderate levels of information capabilities within surveyed firms with means ranging from 4.18 to 4.96.

Items from Rodrigues, Stank, and Lynch and Zacharia and Mentzer were utilized to measure firm-wide integration. Respondents were asked to indicate level of agreement with statements regarding the current level of internal integration within their firms. The mean measures for the six items ranged from 4.84 to 5.54, indicating moderate to slightly higher levels of integration.

The logistics performance scale was adapted from Stank, Keller, and Daugherty. The original scale had seven items. However, based on expert review and content analysis, two items -"The ability to respond to the needs and wants of key customers"and"The global judgment regarding the extent to which perceived logistics performance matches customer expectations"- were dropped because they did not match other items very well. Respondents indicated somewhat higher levels of relative logistics performance compared to their competitors. The means of the five items used range from 4.90 to 5.26.

SCALE ASSESSMENT

Statistical tools used to analyse the data include SPSS and AMOS 5.0. Following the approach suggested by Mentzer, Flint, and Kent, a basic analysis of the collected data, including examination of incorrect coding, item normality (skewness and kurtosis), means, standard deviations, and outliers, yielded acceptable results.

Confirmatory factor analysis (CFA) using maximum likelihood estimation (MLE) was conducted to assess and validate the operational constructs. All latent variables were allowed to correlate with each other. The major fit indices examined include Chi-square, Chi-square/degree of freedom ratio, comparative fit index (CFI), and root mean square error of approximation (RMSEA). The insignificant probability associated with the Chi-square indicates a close fit between the hypothesized model and the perfect fit. The relative Chi-square value of 1.187 also falls into the recommended range of 3 to 1. Because CFI accounts for sample size, a common bias in index calculations, it has been argued to be the"index of choice". The current model has a CFI value of 0.981, which is above the stringent cutoff threshold of 0.95 suggested by Hu and Bentler. RMSEA has been recognized as one of the most informative criteria in covariance structure modeling because it takes into account the error of the approximation in the population and is sensitive to the number of estimated parametres in the model. The RMSEA value of 0.039 is within the suggested range (less than 0.08) for good model fit. The above critical indices examined all demonstrate superior fit between the measurement model and the data.

Other AMOS outputs of CFA were used to examine the constructs'unidimensionality and validity. Standardized regression weights showed that all items loaded on appropriate factors (constructs) as expected. Critical ratios (CR) of these regression weights are all significant at 0.05 level, supporting the unidimensionality and convergent validity of the constructs. Discrimant validity was tested with the approach suggested by Fornell and Larcker-comparing the average variance extracted (AVE) of each construct with the shared variances between each of the constructs. All average variances extracted were in excess of the shared variances between constructs for each of the two-factor models, demonstrating discriminant validity. More stringent Chi-square tests were also conducted. Nested models were examined for each pair of constructs, where the inter-factor correlation was fixed to 1. All Chi-square differences were significant, indicating the proposed measurement models have better fit with the data. This again supports discriminant validity of the constructs.

Finally, a test of internal consistency reliability was performed utilizing Cronbach's coefficient alpha. The range of Cronbach's coefficient alphas was from 0.796 to 0.942; all are greater than the suggested 0.70. Therefore, all scales were considered reliable. Together, the above results support the overall reliability and validity of the scale items used to measure the hypothesized constructs.

Hypothesis 1 suggests that marketing/logistics relationship can improve firm-wide integration. Firm-wide integration involves all the different functional areas within a firm, but this finding suggests that marketing/logistics relationship effectiveness plays a special role to facilitating and enhancing firm-wide integration. Hypothesis 2 proposes that there is a direct causal relationship between the effectiveness of marketing/logistics relationships and a firm's information capability.

This path is supported with a significant standardized regression weight of 0.265, supporting the argument that better marketing/logistics relationships can significantly improve a firm's information capability by designating the most suitable information systems for the firm. Hypothesis 3 examines the link between a firm's information capability and its firm-wide integration. This result confirms previous research suggesting that strong information capability is an important prerequisite of firm-wide integration. However, it should be noted that Hypothesis 3 was not as strongly supported as the other hypotheses. Hypothesis 4 is supported, confirming that information capability can improve a firm's logistics performance. In line with the results of previous studies, the current study posits that firm-wide integration can improve a firm's logistics performance. This path is supported in the current model.

Further, multiple squared correlations for all the endogenous latent variables were examined to check the effectiveness of the proposed model. The value results indicate that 7% of information capability's total variance is explained by marketing/logistics relationship effectiveness, 36.2% of firm-wide integration's total variance is explained by information capability and marketing/logistics relationship effectiveness, and 28.9% of logistics performance's total variance is explained by the other three variables. Considering the limited number of variables involved, the proposed structural model is effective.

Our research highlights the importance of marketing and logistics relationships and the broader ranging impact they have on firm performance. If the marketing and logistics groups work well together, they can provide the focus that is so important to adequately deploy firm resources in a manner that is responsive to the needs of the market. Marketing and logistics relationship effectiveness was shown to impact firm-wide integration. These two groups are usually the ones closest to customers. The information they obtain in their boundary spanning positions can be shared with other functional areas. As such, they should be able to develop an appreciation for internal capacity and a"feel for the market"that can guide both day-to-day operations and their firms'strategic directions.

The key is, of course, that they must cooperate, collaborate, and generally work well together if such a platform is to be built. In contrast to traditional us/them approaches where each of the functional areas fights for its own turf, effective marketing and logistics relationships create a synergistic environment of working together. It may also be a situation where that by working together they create a system of checks and balances. For example, promises made by marketing must be lived up to by logistics. If the two groups have conferred in advance, logistics will know what will be promised and will either work to see that is done or request adjustments as necessary. Thus agreement can be reached before customer expectations are set and many potential failures/problems can be avoided.

Marketing and logistics relationship effectiveness was also shown to impact IT capability. This, no doubt, reflects the fact that marketing and logistics can provide input to customise systems and design output that will be relevant and of practical value. In the typical company, a myriad of reports are automatically generated and often only a fraction of those reports are actually used. Marketing and logistics can help to tailor output reports that are useful in day-to-day operations as well as tracking longer term, strategic data.

This study also augments previous research verifying that information capability and firm-wide integration positively impacts logistic performance. Accurate information on customer requirements and orders places logistics in a position to meet customer demand. Additionally, when different divisions of an organization work together and share information it can help optimize the entire organization instead of yielding fragmented, individual improvements.

The current research makes an important contribution to the literature by identifying a critical driver of firmwide integration-marketing/logistics relationships. However, certain limitations need to be recognized to help advance future research on integration.

First, as a preliminary study on the crucial role of marketing/logistics relationships in achieving firm-wide integration, the proposed model focuses on a limited number of constructs. While meaningful results were found, especially marketing/logistics relationship's direct and indirect impacts (through information capability) on firmwide integration, some interesting research questions remain unanswered. What are the important factors that can contribute to better marketing/logistics relationships? Besides information capability, is the link between marketing/logistics relationship and firm-wide integration mediated by other constructs? Future research could also examine marketing/logistics relationships and other potential drivers of internal integration in the same model to provide a more holistic view.

Second, integration in the current study is measured with relatively general items. Integration is a multidimensional construct that consists of various components. Marketing/ logistics relationships might have particularly strong impacts on some of these components and less of an impact on others. Thus, future research examining marketing/logistics relationships'influences on different sub-dimensions of firm-wide integration may yield greater knowledge.

Third, me current study emphasizes the importance of marketing and logistics functions to internal integration because of their unique cross-boundary characteristics; their potential impacts on external integration also deserve examination. In fact, because both functions interact with customers and other external partners extensively, it can be expected that better marketing/logistics relationships may also contribute significantly to external integration. Thus, it is suggested that future research could explore the importance of marketing/logistics relationships by including internal and external integration in the same model.

Fourth, while statistical analysis confirmed the expected relationships, only limited variability in responses was noted. This suggests that more precise measures are needed. Future research should focus on developing better methods of measuring the constructs.

Using one key informant from each responding firm in the current study can be justified, but must be acknowledged as a limitation. Inputs from managers from both sides of the relationship (including supply chain partners) could provide greater insights. Additionally, future research should examine the level of integration across a variety of firm departments or divisions. Research should also explore the issue of whether strategic integration among senior levels of management versus operational-level integration at the departmental level influences performance differently.

A global economy requires business organizations to cultivate their international holdings by respecting the national differences of their host countries and coordinating efforts for rapid innovation. In this chapter we first review relevant literature in the areas of communication and innovation and explore how efforts toward innovative practices are directly related to globalism and business strategy. We then focus on issues associated with national culture, corporate culture, and professional culture that are relevant to strategies for researching business communication in global contexts. Finally, we suggest directions for future work.

Prior to the dawning of the new millennium, much was written about innovation, culture, globalism, and strategy. Commentaries on organizational vision, effectiveness, direction, and mission usually noted the necessity to innovate and expand beyond normal limits and borders. Inherent within discussions of innovation and globalism are issues relating to national and organizational culture, and to a lesser extent the professional cultures of members of innovative, globalized business firms. What are the forces precipitating such concerns? What role does intercultural communication play in formulating visionary and strategy revolutions?

In this chapter, we begin by examining issues relating to the critical and dynamic nature of innovation, globalization, and strategy-concepts that have become increasingly ambiguous from their excessive use in trade and scholarly literature. We review some of the more prominent research. We then sample the literature on three concepts of culture that are critical to the task of researching global and innovative business communication: national culture, corporate culture, and professional culture. In our final section, we offer some directions where future business communication theory and research could profitably proceed.

EMERGING REALITIES FOR BUSINESS COMMUNICATION

We will argue, along with others, that many of the emerging realities for business (e.g., continual innovation, global markets, strategic planning, and technological change) have become so interrelated that in the fundamental process of developing a vision or mission, organizations often treat these realities as interrelated strategies rather than separate issues. It is no longer accurate or appropriate to strategize about innovation without an accompanying integrated discussion of global markets, foreign subsidiaries or alliances, and cultural issues related to international involvement.

Businesses in the 21st century face a wide array of complex opportunities including, but not limited to, expanding into global markets, developing internal and external innovative products and practices to remain competitive, and attracting and retaining the most talented workforce possible. International markets have become enticing prospects in companies'efforts to increase market share and diversify offerings. Market potential becomes especially salient with international trade alliances emerging across the globe such as NAFTA, the European Union, ASEAN in Southeast Asia, and Mercosur in South America. Beyond market considerations, innovation efforts in the United States increasingly rely on foreign resources. Even research and development dollars that were previously spent almost entirely in the United States now find their way into foreign nations to the tune of $15 billion a year, 10% of the total spent on R&D. As organizations research, innovate, and market goods and services in foreign nations, the level of competition from both domestic and international firms becomes more intense.

Maintaining a competitive edge in a global, innovative, and dynamically evolving environment produces substantial pressure to redefine how business is conducted. A hierarchical, bureaucratic structure is less responsive in such an environment, and a flatter, more responsive organizational pattern is required. As organizations reengineer their structures to become more proactive and accessible, new patterns of communication emerge. Organizations find it necessary to push decision-making authority to lower levels, employ cross-functional teams, and encourage organizational learning. It is also essential for firms to increase and improve external communication with international suppliers, subsidiaries, alliance partners, and customers. The interrelationships of innovation, culture, globalization, strategy, and communication are unmistakable and become more visible with time. Each new start-up company, regardless of location, will view these forces a s supportive components of a larger scheme.

Much of the research focusing on issues of innovation, globalization, strategy, and communication historically has examined these factors in isolation, without the benefit of triangulating their processes and implications. Furthermore, a number of theoretical assumptions have been made in each area that may no longer hold as organizations change their communication patterns and practices in response to changing conditions and new opportunities. Communication scholars face multiple obligations, responsibilities, and opportunities as the focus shifts from paradigms privileging one-company, one-country studies to research approaches informed by multilevel theorizing and more gestalt and inclusive forms of problem conceptualization. The remainder of this chapter identifies previous research in innovation, culture, and strategy and suggests new perspectives that better reflect the true nature of these interrelated phenomena.

INNOVATION AND COMMUNICATION

Both theoretical and applied communication researchers have devoted serious and productive effort to the study of innovation. Organizations are quick to support such research efforts given the fundamental nature of innovation as an element of business survival. Innovation is not a Luxury but a requirement:

Innovation enables organizations to improve the quality of their outputs, revitalize mature businesses, enter new markets, react to competitive encroachment, try out new technologies, leverage investment in technologies that are so expensive that no single product can recoup them, and develop alternative applications for existing product categories, to name a few outcomes. For organizations which must adapt to changing competition, markets, and technologies, product innovation is not a fad. It is a necessity.

The emphasis on business innovation is further substantiated by surveys of organizations. CEOs of 669 firms across 10 industries around the world consider technological innovation as being the most critical concern in their competitive advantage. Hogg's 1993 survey of European managerial competencies in telecommunications companies in 6 European countries (Britain, Germany, The Netherlands, France, Italy, and Spain) found that innovation and strategic vision were vital to the effective performance or junior and middle mangers, second only to communication skills. Being an innovator and having vision are included among the top 10 characteristics of successful entrepreneurs in a similar survey by Ernest and Young with Roper Starch Worldwide.

In 1986, Ulijn and Gobits analysed the psycholinguistic aspects of the dissemination of scientific and technical innovation across the main linguistic borders of Europe and concluded that this communication process had a clear cultural embedding. This dissemination process involved the transfer of technology from the national laboratories involved in military research into civilian applications such as environmental protection and energy conservation. Research such as this represents an opportunity for technical communicators to act as bridge builders between different professional sectors.

Other research involving communication and innovation has concentrated on audience analysis. At the core of this research is an application of the reader-writer-text chain-usually at a more refined level than at the broader organizational level. This interactive reader-writer-readability model, including an analysis of the communication process within and between the writer and the reader, developed by Ulijn and Strother, uses psycholinguistics to analyse how international business communicators can format an innovation message on lexical, syntactic, and discourse levels. A systematic evaluation of questionnaires, interviews, and usability testing among the readers of an innovation message creates a feedback loop that can be used to optimize the conceptual and linguistic qualities of the product by increasing its efficiency. Since the classic study by Kaplan on circular (East), linear (Anglo-Germanic), and digressive (Latin) paragraphing in English writing, numerous studies have confirmed culture-related differences in discourse formats between English and other languages and cultures. Recent studies compare the structure of French and Dutch versions of a business letter and a coffeemaker's user manual, and English and Dutch paragraphing in a technical environmental brochure. Readers of Spanish, French, U.S., or Dutch business letters or a French or Dutch user manual have recognized these differences in structure and sometimes prefer their own. The Ulijn and Strother readability system based on their interactive model, which elicits this kind of feedback, might work effectively in professional contexts as business professionals attempt to communicate to an international audience about innovation in an interactive way.

Another body of research involving communication and innovation has concentrated on understanding how organizational members communicate change strategies. Most prominent among this research is that of Everett Rogers. Although Rogers'vast research programme did not always focus on business firms, his model of the diffusion of innovations and subsequent work has served as a touchstone for scholars investigating how innovative products, practices, and even internal dynamics such as organizational reengineering could be accepted more readily by important stakeholders. Highlights from that long-term research programme include how communication networks are used to carry innovation messages and how the acceptance and adoption patterns of individuals can be tracked according to a normal curve distribution of the population.

Rogers identifies five categories of adopters:

- Innovators (those making decisions or even Precipitating innovation).
- Early adopters, C
- Early majority,
- Late majority
- Laggards.

Much of Rogers'work involved communication across organizations, not within an organization. Bach's 1989 study of communication and innovation within a single organization did not find Rogers'categories. Bach has suggested that Rogers'innovation adoption model is less suited for internal organizational communication and more appropriate for innovation adoption contexts among organizations.

Another relevant area of research is implementation strategies. How decisions such as innovation plans are carried out by those responsible for implementation has been examined from multiple perspectives. Two research programmes devoted to implementation are worth noting. First, at a strategic or organization-wide level, Bourgeois and Brodwin identified five strategies that organizations can use when attempting to implement decisions. The commander model is employed when the organization makes a centralized decision, such as adopting a new innovation, and instructs or orders the rank and file to implement it. The change model approaches implementation efforts by using organizational structure and system properties such as incentives and rewards as inducements for acquiescence. When implementation must be negotiated and sold at senior levels, a collaborative model is put into place. The cultural model is employed when the organization attempts to use the corporate or organizational culture as a means of implementation success. Finally, å crescive model attempts to cultivate and nurture implementation among organizational members.

At the individual or interpersonal level, Nutt developed a typology of implementation tactics that managers use with their subordinates that range from coercive moves from upper management where employees are simply told to implement decisions, to persuasive tactics that attempt to sell employees on the decisions made at higher levels. Research suggests that persuasive and participatory strategies have a better success rate in getting decisions implemented at the appropriate levels of the organization.

Other research has focused on interpersonal and network approaches to the strategies used to implement organizational change-a form of innovation adoption. Most studies conclude that information sharing is a powerful tool for desensitizing employees to change, and that information of any type can moderate the anxiety associated with uncertainty that comes with impending change in an organization. Lewis and Seibold conclude that communication is at the heart of change adoption and implementation and those organizations would do well to employ communication strategies that emphasize information sharing, feedback, employee participation and influence, and collaboration.

Attempts to situate the origin and exchange of innovation messages in organizations have led to the study of communication networks. Albrecht and colleagues investigated the extent to which members of various organizations talk about innovation or express innovative ideas to one another. In a series of studies examining various organizations (oncology department of a medical centre, public school systems, human service, and manufacturing) they discovered that innovation talk is quite limited and that employees are rather timid in their expressions of innovative ideas. Innovation talk is usually confined to networks of people who are deemed trusting and accepting. In another study of networks and innovation, Albrecht and Hall attempted to isolate networks where innovation talk and the expression of new ideas were prevalent and rewarded. Such communication patterns were discovered in informal innovation networks composed of"elites"or groups of people who developed strong links to one another through their discussion and interaction about innovation. Elites were considered by other elites to be"idea persons"and competent communicators and were perceived by outsiders (nonelites) to be more influential and credible than nonelites. Through their collective talk about innovation, elite networks were viewed as wielding substantial power within the organizaticn.

The preceding discussion suggests some needed areas of communication research to help organizations that make innovation an important part of their strategy. First, with an increasing emphasis on innovative goals, how will organizations enhance their innovative communication practices through vision and mission statements? Second, with additional stakeholders involved in innovation, how can audience analysis be improved to accommodate a more diverse group of stakeholders? Third, if innovation becomes the norm in an organization with an accompanying lower level of resistance, what type of strategies can be employed to question the utility and integrity of a large number of innovation strategies? Fourth, how will flatter organizational structures affect innovation strategies?

THE CULTURAL CONTEXT

O'Hair, Friedrich, Wiemann, and Wiemann have defined culture as the shared beliefs, values, and practices of a group of people. A group's culture includes the language or languages used by group members as well as the norms and rules about how behaviour can appropriately be displayed and how it should be understood.

A review of the available literature suggests that three different but overlapping contexts of culture have been studied. National culture studies are among the most intensely and widely examined and usually involve an investigation into or speculation about how a country's national culture influences the communication behaviour of domestic and/or foreign members of multinational corporations.

A second prominent area of study has focused on corporate culture, or how members perceive the culture of their organization. Studies of this nature are interested in how the organization regulates, controls, and influence the behaviour of its members through its values, language (jargon), rituals, and customs.

The third cultural dimension, and one less studied by business communication scholars, is professional culture. Issues associated with cultural studies of this type include the extent to which professionals (e.g., scientists, engineers, and managers) identify with their professional discipline rather than with their organization.

NATIONAL CULTURES

Hofstede's work serves as the quintessential representation of how national cultures influence business communication. Hofstede defined culture as the"collective programming of the mind which distinguishes the members of one culture from another".

Based on an extensive research programme involving more than 100,000 employees of IBM in 64 countries, he classified national cultures along five dimensions:

- Power distance.
- Collectivism versus individualism.
- Femininity versus masculinity.
- Uncertainty avoidance.
- Long-term versus short-term orientation.

Hofstede's taxonomy allows us to understand the relative difference in values and structure of organizational members from different cultures, but less so of their communication patterns.

National culture studies have occupied a great deal of journal space in the last two decades. We intend not to review all of the cultural studies that are relevant to business communication but rather to sample that body of work. Several recent studies have focused on Thailand, which has attracted interest from multinational corporations because of its friendly foreign-investment policies. In a study interested in determining the effects of cultural values (high uncertainty, high power distance, low individualism, low masculinity) on the communication practices of Thai business professionals, Sriussadaporn-Charoenngam and Jablin found a coherence between culture and communication.

Thai business professionals reflected their cultural values by communicating in reserved, respectful, deferential, and intimate ways. A study by Gundling determined that Thai business professionals were more favourable toward personal forms of communication and tended not to prefer technological substitutions such as videoconferencing.

The Korean culture has also attracted attention from business communication researchers. Writing styles of Korean and U.S. business managers were compared using letters of complaint. For the comparison, letters for both cultural groups were written in English, although English was the second language for the Korean group. Koreans were found to use a less direct organizational pattern in their letters and tended to delay placement of the main point. The U.S. group, in contrast, employed a direct organizational style and stated very early in the letter the main point of the complaint. In another study, Lee and Jablin conducted a multiple comparison study of organizational employees from Korea, the United States, and Japan.

Contrary to prevailing opinion, their study determined that Korean and Japanese workers do not share wholesale commonalities of business attitudes and communication practices simply because they hail from a similar cultural heritage. In fact, the study discovered that U.S. and Korean workers were more similar than were Japanese and Korean workers. Although some research insists on emphasizing different communication behaviours for Japanese business professionals, Hilton discovered in a survey of Japanese educators and business representatives that the use of English as a business language was perceived to be critically important to professional success and that English training for corporate employees was part of the strategic plan for global competitiveness.

Cultural values were examined in combination with relational, political, and economic variables in a study of Chinese managers'influence tactics with subordinates. Perhaps the most striking finding from this research was that managers used influence tactics that reflected both political and cultural grounding. To a lesser degree, managerial roles also affected which kinds of influence tactics were used. These results suggest that simply knowing the national heritage of organizational members does not guarantee that communication behaviour can be predicted from Hofstedian principles.

Emphasizing receiver perception of messages across national borders was the focus of a study conducted by Ulijn and St. Amant. The study asked 60 students from 5 countries (China, The Netherlands, Germany, France, and Italy) to view a taped Chinese-Dutch negotiation. Results indicated that asking questions and dealing with time were perceived differently depending on the national culture of the respondents.

The final area of research we review in the context of national culture is that of intercultural communication competence. Cooley and Roach offered what has become a well-quoted advisory about intercultural competence:

Communication behaviours that are the reflection of an individual's competence are culturally specific and, hence, bound by the culture in which they are acted out. As a result, behaviours that are understood as a reflection of competence in one culture are not necessarily understood as competent in another.

Beamer postulated a layered or"stacked disk"conceptualization of intercultural competence that included five levels:

- Acknowledging diversity.
- Organizing information according to stereotypes.
- Posing questions to challenge the stereotypes.
- Analyzing communication episodes.
- Generating'other culture'messages".

Sriussadaporn-Charoenngam and Jablin verified their model of communication competence in Thai organizations. Their model proposed three general competence factors composed of several behaviours and skills. Strategic Communication Knowledge included behaviours such as conflict avoidance, showing respect, and using correct language. Tactical Communication Skills included such behaviours as giving instructions/orders, networking, and writing, listening, and persuading. Behavioural Traits/ Cognitive Abilities included three components: empathy, cognition, and complexity. Sriussadaporn-Charoenngam and Jablin ultimately conclude that what is regarded as competence m ay largely depend on the unique characteristics of a national culture, and that certain types of organizations, within the same culture, may require different types of competency.

Numerous other communication scholars have proffered their own conceptualizations of intercultural competence. This review of national culture studies points out the need for additional business communication research. In particular, if the Hofstedian approach to studying business communication is being called into question due to the overgeneralization of cultural effects on communication or because distinct cultural values are converging with other cultural values, where can empirical research productively situate its analysis of cultural influence on business messages? If preference for message style and strategy cannot be completely predicted from previous work, what types of measures and concepts are needed to understand business communication in different cultures?

We also need to understand how media and technology interact with cultural expectations in business contexts. That is, can national culture predict how business professionals use or respond to media and technology? Can definitions of communication competence be determined f or a particular culture, and, if not, can general competency models serve useful purposes? Finally, how can new models of psycholinguistic analysis be used in contexts where cultural congruence is apparent?

NATIONAL AND CORPORATE CULTURES

Since innovation strategy often involves management of change, mergers, strategic alliances, joint ventures, and acquisitions, unexpected culture differences might lead to serious failures as demonstrated by a statistical study of foreign entry and a case study about the decline of the Dutch aerospace industry. Culture was also identified as a factor influencing the behaviour of European multinational corporations. While national culture has received most of the attention of communication researchers, recent work suggests that corporate and organizational culture can affect the content and form of communication.

The broader cultural context of multinational strategy involves an interaction between national culture and corporate culture. On the basis of Hofstede's research, Schneider and Barsoux propose a national culture embedding for a particular corporate culture when innovation is the message. Both the Anglo-Nordic village market culture visible in most North

American and Northwestern European firms from a family or tribe Asian culture share low to moderate on the uncertainty avoidance but have very different power distances.

Some northern European organizations have the more Germanic culture of the well-oiled machine and high uncertainty avoidance but low power distance, while most southern cultures, including Latin America, have the traditional bureaucracy with a pyramid of people, high on both indices. How important are uncertainty avoidance and power distance to the innovative capacity of a firm?

Weggeman and Nonaka and Takeuchi suggest that Japan pursues a different innovation strategy than the West by learning implicitly through oral communication, rather than the more Western explicit learning style by written instructions. In an ultimate effort to bring Northern, Southern, Western, and Eastern leadership roles in innovation together, Kalthof, Nonaka, and Nueno consider the examples of Michelin, Kao, and Sharp to outline the Platonic innovation spheres of the West (with North and South in a nice cooperation) and the Eastern intuition and vision, all of which leads to creation, elaboration, and orientation towards the market. What happens to the corporate culture of a given multinational firm with a rather homogeneous corporate culture when it settles in the United States, Northwestern Europe, Latin Europe or America, or Japan?

When a multinational firm, such as Philips, operates in the United States, it is accepted almost as a U.S. firm since it is loosely related to the individualistic U.S. society where interaction is explicit, low context, and monochronic. On the other hand, to be successful in Japan, Philips should behave as a Japanese firm, where national culture and corporate culture overlap in a tight, collectivistic society where interaction is implicit, high context, and polychronic.

High context cultures use informal implicit ways of communication, while low context cultures need to state messages explicitly in written text. This has implications for the cultural and communication behaviour of Western multinationals that wish to be successful in Asian societies.

Northwest Europe, which is the home region of Philips, and Latin Europe and America are stages between, with the former having a small overlap between corporate culture and national culture and the latter two regions having corporate culture as part of the national culture.

A recent study by Ulijn and Nagel (2000) confirms the different national culture embedding of German and Dutch firms. The Germanic well-oiled machine corporate culture seems to have more problems in changing the technology-push culture of young engineers into a market-pull direction than does the Dutch Anglo-Nordic village market corporate culture. Another study researched the process of getting young Indonesian engineers involved in the innovation process of the information technology products of a Dutch firm.

Both Dutch and Indonesians seemed to gravitate toward the expected ideal innovation culture as a result of low power distance and middle uncertainty avoidance. Other dimensions beyond uncertainty avoidance and power distance, such as loose/tight, individualistic/collectivistic, and implicit and explicit, might affect the innovative capacity of a firm as well, depending on the national culture.

One typical Asian communication pattern within a firm which fits into the high context/implicit/polychronic/circular pattern is the Japanese Ringi system. In this system a document is circulated among managers to gather their sealed agreement. The decision making style is participatory, consensus seeking, and bottom up, but authority is centralized and seniority is respected in a top-down way. As a result, the strategy formulation process in a firm takes much longer than in a Western firm, but once a decision is made, the implementation period is much shorter than in the West.

What impact do communication technologies (especially multimedia, the Internet, and the World Wide Web) have on the interaction among national, corporate, and professional cultures? Do national cultures that prefer an implicit communication style easily accept communiques over the Internet? Some recent studies suggest that this question is still unanswered. If Japanese culture, for instance, silence over speaking and writing because it communicates so well, how would Japanese then deal with the explicit individual means of expression so common with the Internet?

Nishigushi surprisingly demonstrates that at least three distinctive features of Japanese culture explain an Internet boom in Japan. First, the Internet is used as a vehicle for communitarianism. Second, high context allows one to think first before writing or reading, writing being between the silver speaking and the golden silence, an excellent cultural compromise with the no n-Japanese world. Finally, home page creation makes the passive, conflict-avoiding Japanese active in expressing themselves. However, are important strategic documents taken seriously if they are the result of open, explicit consultation involving all employees of a firm?

Other research implications involving the confluence of national and corporate cultures include the following. Can the strength of a corporate culture be measured and compared to the effects of national culture? To what extent does the percentage of indigenous versus expatriate members of the workforce within the organization affect the congruence between corporate and national culture? The clash of corporate cultures of organizations from different national cultures is well documented. What research can communication scholars offer to help move a culturally merged organization toward shared goals? As multinational firms become more technologically affluent and therefore"virtual,"how will these realities influence the sending and receiving of messages in light of the effects of national culture?

PROFESSIONAL CULTURES

A separate issue is determining how the professional cultures of organizational members affect communication and how professional culture is related to the national culture/ corporate culture interaction. How does technical innovation take place within a firm? Obviously an innovation has to be offered from one professional culture to others within an organization. The question then is to what extent the successful innovation is technologically pushed or market pulled. Two important audiences are the R&D department (scientists) and the marketing department. What are their respective professional cultures?

It is a common observation that an emphasis on innovation might precipitate function myopia within a firm. What Marketing wanted, what R&D proposed, what Finance budgeted for, what Design built, what Production manufactured, and what costumers wanted have often led to completely different concepts of a product. It comes, therefore, as no surprise that innovation projects cause conflicts among departments. Biemans lists common mutual misperceptions of engineers and marketers. The latter believe that scientists/engineers have no sense of time, costs, service, or competitive advantage. They hide in the lab and continue developing a product without strategic planning, holding standardization and technology sacrosanct, and expecting the client to adapt. The marketers are, in the eyes of the scientists/engineers, aggressive, demanding, and unrealistic.

They want everything NOW, want to deliver a product before it is ready, are always in a hurry and impatient, or cannot decide what they want. As a result, they promise more than they can guarantee, often change the specifications because they have no sense of technology, have no trust in scientists/engineers, and are not interested in their problems.

Finally, scientists/engineers think that marketers focus on unrealistic targets. Martin proposes different approaches in addressing the disparate functions of engineering, marketing, and production: integration, differentiation, and fragmentation. An integration approach stresses what employees have in common; differentiation emphasizes the deviations and adaptations from the dominant culture; and fragmentation accepts the dynamic, paradoxical, and confusing character of an intercultural process that is seemingly uncontrollable. Gerhard, Amelingmeyer, and Specht present some instruments used in German firms to manage such interfunctional conflicts.

Allen's work shows that scientists and engineers need each other in the R&D department of a technology-intensive company (TIC). Whereas technological innovations will fail without the knowledge provided by the scientists, few scientific insights will lead to innovation unless the engineers intervene. Innovations occur most quickly if the engineer"pulls"the scientist.

Therefore, communication can serve as a cross-pollinator in the innovation process between scientists and engineers in a technology-intensive multinational firm. To what extent can business communication research play a role in this environment?

If science leads to the fastest technical innovation when triggered by engineers (technology pulls science), communication may play a role in this process by formulating and implementing informal procedures in the strategic communication of a multinational firm. While scientists have the production of text as their main target (to be cited or perish) and therefore depend heavily on the written word, engineers prefer to design and make concrete products and therefore prefer oral communication with the lay world of clients and suppliers. Multinational firms may need to pay more attention to the role of oral communication in strategic innovation and to use international business communicators as bridge builders between different professional cultures.

One of the characteristics of a TIC is the fact that the shop floor is crowded by professional knowledge workers, most of whom are engineers. They are highly skilled employees, performing complicated tasks with individual autonomy. The environment is complex but rather stable, enabling standardization of skills as a coordinating mechanism. Mintzberg calls this type of organization a professional bureaucracy.

Examples are software development companies, firms delivering engineering and technical services, machine tool construction firms, and the like. In the case of a complex and dynamic environment, the coordinating mechanism tends to be mutual adjustment, and the organization is characterized by Mintzberg as an adhocracy. In this category we find industrial research departments, firms engaged in one-of-a-kind technology application projects, and most scientific institutions and technical laboratories (space, air, water, ground).

Mintzberg further states that in a professional bureaucracy as well as i n an adhocracy, the operating core exerts the dominant influence in contrast to top-management, line-management, and support-staff departments. Professionals realise that the most expensive and discriminating production factor in TICs is their scarce knowledge, whereas management and supportive capacities are available on a larger scale and, therefore, can be replaced more easily.

This dominant influence of the knowledge workers in the operating core on day-to-day organizational life gives rise to two related questions:

- In a professional bureaucracy or adhocracy, does the professional culture of the knowledge workers in the operating core have a greater impact on daily organizational life than does the corporate culture?
- Is the corporate culture of a professional bureaucracy or adhocracy determined more by the professional culture than by any other organizational subculture? Based on previous work, we suggest that a collective orientation towards corporate goals is difficult to realise because of the knowledge workers'need for their professional autonomy. Some generic characteristics of professional can be offered, however:
- Management rules and procedures to operationalize organizational control have only limited influence (professionals do not believe in standard planning and control mechanisms because of the uniqueness and unpredictability of each project).
- Coordination is realised by mutual adjustment achieved though many informal arrangements and get-together routines.
- The reference framework for the assessment of professional contributions lies outside the organization (with peers and professional societies).

- Allocation of assignments is or should be based on individual learning needs and personal preferences.
- There is a common tendency to form subcultures crystallized around"schools of thought"whose specialized jargon is an additional entry barrier.
- In multidisciplinary cooperation, professionals tend to value their own specialization more highly than that of others. Those who admire the practice or skills of other professional groups often critique their underlying theories or methodologies.
- Honesty, openness, consistency, and historical awareness are considered as essential values. There is little sensitivity to political game-playing, outward presentation, and personal appearance as well as little awareness of financial parametres.
- The professional climate stimulates the inclination to exceed requirements and specifications; the result can always be improved and made more beautiful.

In sum, little respect is reserved for managers functioning above the level of first-line supervisor:

The scientist/engineer sees the manager as a bureaucrat, paper shuffler and parasite, an uncreative and unoriginal hack who serves as an obstacle in the way of creative people trying to do a good job-a person more interested in dollars and power than knowledge and innovation.

Professional autonomy within organizations is likely to increase in the future. As a consequence of rapid developments in communication technologies, the Global Village, predicted by McLuhan in 1964, has been realised. These changes combined with the increase in international trade treaties have raised the mobility of professionals to all-time high. They flow through cross-national networks consisting of high-tech industries, universities, and R&D institutions. As Guehenno argues in"La Fin de la Democratie", the dismantling of the Berlin Wall ended the era in which the national state and the democracy had a major impact. In his view, global networks will be dominant in the near future, networks in which services, information, knowledge, and creative ideas are exchanged and in which contacts and relations are built up and phased out. Multinational companies will take the lead in this process through their professionals and their cultures. It could very well be that national politics be come unimportant, territory conflicts will seem trivial, and common public interest will increase.

These developments may justify the following proposition:

In today's Global Village the professional culture has a higher impact on daily organizational life than does national or corporate culture.

In this section, we will offer additional ideas about how communication research might proceed based on the rapidly changing cultural and global environments discussed previously. It may be an oversimplification to insist that national cultures across the globe are trading values and therefore are converging and becoming more homogenous. Some cultures are more resistant to cultural invasion and integration than others. Still others, upon discerning an unhealthy level of cultural contamination, react with cultural backlash and attempt to eliminate such influences. Examples from Southeast Asia and the Middle East are well known.

We should not assume on face value that cultural convergence is rapidly creating its own place in the status quo. Systematic research efforts offer a way to learn more about the existence of this phenomenon and to discover which value systems are more susceptible to cultural convergence. Conversely, considerable evidence (both anecdotal and scientific) provides us with grounds for speculating that global economics and media are substantially influencing intercultural sensitivity. Regardless of whether such influence leads to widespread cultural convergence is a question for research, but we can safely surmise that exposure to new cultural values will create different cognitive and emotional experiences for both insiders and outsiders of a particular culture. The extent to which these experiences affect communication behaviour requires study.

A separate issue concerns the study of communication in organizations that are becoming increasingly global. As global organizations become structurally flatter, more interactive, increasingly knowledge-based, geographically scattered, and more culturally diverse, traditional methods of communication analysis will miss the mark. How can the study of business communication be approached in ways that adequately capture the multiplicity of relationships within constantly evolving organizational forms? Will corporate or organizational culture cease to exist as a conceptualizing framework? Will structural evolution require different forms of management and leadership? If so, what are the appropriate means of communicating managerial and leadership strategies? Parker may be correct in suggesting that the time has come to reconsider the "organization" as our unit of analysis.

If organizations remain a focus of study for business communication scholars, how do we include in our frameworks the effects of organizational mission and strategy on innovation messages? If organizations construct and adhere to strong institutional missions, their ability to innovate and change during decline will be highly restricted. Alternatively, firms with flexible missions will be able to adapt to shifting economic or market conditions through innovative practices made possible by less rigidity. Message analysis within both types of organizations would reveal differences in how professionals adapt and mobilize for innovation.

The review presented in an earlier section suggests a closer examination of professional culture as a means for understanding communication in organizations that are global in nature and in those that emphasize innovation. Lovitt argues quite adamantly that the emphasis on national culture has distracted scholars from investigating a more appropriate culture-that of professional discourse communities. If organizational members identify more with their professional cultures, how should business communication researchers approach the study of messages?

Are new theories required for understanding various professional cultures, or can existing theories be adapted? Can theoretical frameworks be developed that capture the complex influence of national, corporate, and professional culture on communication practices? What about individuals? Will our quest for the ultimate"cultural analysis"disregard attitudinal to account for personal idiosyncrasies?

APPROACHING RESEARCH FROM NEW THEORETICAL PARADIGMS

Noted scholars have voiced the need for new approaches to the study of globalism, organizations, and communication. Weick, in particular, suggests that theory building could move forward when scholars focus a"reflexive"eye on theoretical development. Maintaining a dialogue among scholars and between scholars and practitioners provides many opportunities to generate and adapt theories in a rapidly changing environment. It serves no one's interest to cling desperately to theories which offer limited relevance or explanatory power.

On the other hand, it is unproductive to ignore theoretical perspectives that have been questioned or poorly tested, or because they do not suit one's worldview. One approach to this tension is employing multiparadigmatic approaches to issues of interest. In essence, multiparadigmatic approaches facilitate the work of scholars who find both value and disappointment in various theoretical perspectives but who understand the need to acknowledge and integrate multiple approaches in an effort to clarify complex and obscure human and organizational phenomena.

By applying multiple and divergent perspectives to the study of business communication in cultural contexts, we may be able to explicate issues that were previously neglected because of unilateral or singular theoretical approaches. Employing a multiparadigmatic approach will likely impose additional complexity on the interpretation process, but the recompense is a richer set of explanations and implications that will pay larger theoretical dividends.

Relatedly, given the shifting nature of the context in which business message analysis is most productively situated, theoretical insights may be more generously delivered through a process of multilevel theorizing. Similar to multiparadigmatic approaches, multilevel theories create a more inclusive environment for research. According to Klein, Tosi, and Cannella,

> Multilevel theories span the levels of organizational behaviour and performance typically describing some combination of individuals, dyads, teams, businesses, corporations, and industries. Multilevel theories, thus, begin to bridge the micro-macro divide, integrating the micro domain's focus on individuals and groups with the macro domain's focus on organizations, environment, and strategy. The result is a deeper, richer portrait of organizational life-one that acknowledges the influence of the organizational context on individuals'actions and perceptions and the influence of individuals'actions and perceptions on the organizational context.

Multilevel theorizing may be especially applicable for research that desires to investigate types of innovation messages among communicators in multinational firms where the influence of national, corporate, and professional cultures is uncertain. It may also offer utility in studies where the organization is experiencing structural or functional change such as in mergers, acquisitions, strategic alliances, or mission or strategy alteration.

Index

I

J

L

M

N

O

P

S

T

V